For Bud: **The Wildcat in WWII**

Many happy landings
Barrett Tillman

To Bud & Jodi,
Christmas 1983
Doug & Chris

Barrett Tillman

THE WILDCAT
IN WWII

The Nautical & Aviation Publishing Company of America
Annapolis, Maryland

ISBN 0-933852-32-0
Printed in the United States of America.

Library of Congress Cataloging in Publication Data

Tillman, Barrett.
  The Wildcat in WWII.

  Bibliography: p.
  Includes index.
  1. Wildcat (Fighter plane) 2. World War, 1939–
1945—Aerial operations. 3. World War, 1939–1945—
Naval operations. I. Title. II. Title: Wildcat in
World War Two.
UG1242.F5T56 1983   358.4'3   82-22563
ISBN 0-933852-32-0

To Rear Admiral William N. Leonard
A professional's professional

CONTENTS

Photograph sections occur on pages 51 to 82, and on pages 179 to 210.

FOREWORD

MY FIRST EXPERIENCE WITH GRUMMAN AIRCRAFT, AND particularly with Grumman fighters, came early in my flying career. I reported to Quantico, Virginia in December 1939 directly from flight training and was assigned to VMF-1, then equipped with F3F-2s. It was the proper place for a young aviator who aspired to be a fighter pilot. At that time the F3F-2 was the hottest airplane in Naval aviation and VMF-1 was loaded with talent.

Two years later I was on Midway Island and stayed there until after the Battle of Midway as a member of VMF-221, which by then was equipped with Brewster Buffalos and a few Grumman Wildcats. Again luck was with me, as I was one of six pilots who flew Wildcats during the battle. It was my first combat experience, and fortunately I was in a sturdy aircraft that could take a lot of punishment.

No aircraft built during World War II could outmaneuver the Japanese Zero at speeds and altitudes normally encountered in combat. However, the Wildcat made up for that deficiency by having superior ruggedness, firepower, and good control at terminal velocity from any altitude. I suspect the F4F was largely responsible for earning Grumman Aircraft and Engineering Corporation the nickname of "Grumman Iron Works."

The combat tour of the Wildcat was relatively short, but it arrived on the scene when badly needed and in sufficient numbers to make a major contribution toward winning the war in the Pacific. Those of us who flew the Wildcat in combat feel nothing but respect and admiration for the people who designed and built the F4F.

I have had the pleasure of knowing Barrett Tillman for several years, and have read his many books and articles on various aspects of Naval aviation. Those who read this book can do so with the assurance that it is written by an historian who is master of his subject.

MARION E. CARL
Major General
U.S. Marine Corps (Retired)

PREFACE

A POPULAR ADAGE IN MILITARY CIRCLES HOLDS THAT IF an airplane has already flown, it is obsolete. The saying, of course, is not entirely true, but neither is it wholly inaccurate. For wars are inevitably fought with yesterday's equipment while trying to catch up with today's technology. The Grumman Wildcat is a case in point. Designed in 1936–37, it had only been in fleet service for twelve months at the time of Pearl Harbor. But the inexorable pace of progress had already passed up the stubby little fighter from Long Island, and F4F pilots found themselves abruptly at war with an enemy who sat closer to the cutting edge of technology than themselves.

For better or worse, the Wildcat was *the* U.S. naval fighter during the year after Pearl Harbor. Faced with opponents in faster, tighter-turning, better-climbing aircraft, the F4F squadrons were forced to devise superior tactics in order to survive. That they not only survived, but prevailed, is testimony to the design and its intelligent use by pilots.

Modern warfare is frequently analyzed in terms of numbers or quality of machines. But the Wildcat is a reminder that the men behind the machines will determine who succeeds and who fails. The F4F squadrons engaged an accomplished, all-conquering enemy who had proven himself and his weapons in far-flung arenas. In the crucial Pacific battles of 1942—Coral Sea, Midway, Guadalcanal— the U.S. naval service was consistently outnumbered and outgunned. On occasion it was outfought. But in the end, Imperial Japan's unbroken string of victories was shattered and the war of attrition was begun—the war in which American production capacity weighed at least as heavily as any other factor.

However, the heart of the Wildcat story is the uncertain period when the U.S. Navy and Marine Corps faced the short end of long odds. The time from initial squadron deliveries until replacement by F4Us and F6Fs was barely two and a half years. The addition of the General Motors FM series still does not quite double the Wildcat's service life. But the F4F's primary contribution was even more compressed, as Navy and Marine squadrons flew the Grumman in combat only from December 1941 to August of 1943.

Those twenty months, of course, represented the first two phases of the Pacific War. In broad terms, the holding phase lasted from Pearl Harbor through Midway. With Guadalcanal and the Solomons campaign, American arms began the long trek across the world's largest ocean. The Central Pacific offensive, with Hellcats in the van, cranked up in the fall of 1943 as the Allied two-pronged strategy unfolded.

What becomes apparent in this context is that the F4F was a good airplane for its purpose, but by no means the best. However, it was all that was available and in that respect was comparable to the Army Air Force's P-40. Neither were war-winning designs, but both held the line when failure to do so could have led to disaster. Therefore, success depended upon the intelligence, skill, and courage of a fraction of the already small number of aviators actually engaged. Intelligent application of tactics, exploiting the F4F's strengths against the enemy's weakness, was the bedrock of that success. Professional leadership helped motivate pilots to tackle superior numbers, and with a reasonable chance of survival. Application of the pertinent skills—air discipline, teamwork and marksmanship—completed the cycle.

Still, it was a close-run thing. Not every flier was aggressive, and not all of the motivated possessed fully developed skill or experience. But there were just enough mature tigers and quick learners among the callow to do the job. Similarly, there were seldom enough dedicated, competent maintenance men to go around, nor were there ever enough aircraft or spare parts to suit everyone. Much credit belongs to the mechanics, armorers, support personnel and to the men and women at Bethpage, Long Island who did more than was expected of them. They made the difference.

If the Wildcat story contains a lesson for today, it may be found under the heading of "double procurement." Criticism is frequently directed at military acquisition policies which seek funding for two or more designs to fill the same requirement. Granting the enormous cost of contemporary military aircraft, a quick game of "what if" can demonstrate the valid reason behind double procurement.

Suppose the F4F had never entered production. Brewster had already won the Navy fighter contract with the F2A-1 and -2, and Vought was working on the next-generation carrier fighter, the XF4U-1 Corsair. Why did the Navy pursue Grumman's interest in an updated version of the XF4F-2, which had proven so troublesome in service tests?

Because military aircraft are unknown quantities until they're proven in combat. And because any such venture is a gamble, BuAer (like any good gambler) rightly hedged its bet by following up the Grumman prospect. In case this seems confusing, just sit back for a moment and imagine the Navy and Marine fighter squadrons forced to rely upon the Brewster Buffalo during the first fifteen months of the Pacific War. The Corsair didn't reach combat until February 1943, and the Hellcat—another shrewd hedge, against the possibility of a failed F4U—didn't shoot for blood until that September. This supposes, of course, that the F2A (which suffered two-thirds losses in its only combat) would have kept us in the war until early 1943. Such a prospect may seem of small concern to those academics pondering the hypothesis today, but to the fighter pilots of 1942, the very notion is enough to induce a cold sweat and chills.

Few naval aircraft of WW II were produced in so many variants as the Wildcat. In all, there were twenty designations exclusive of the original biplane design. Some, such as the Martlet I and II, had no direct American counterparts. Others like the FM-2 and Martlet VI were duplicates. But no fewer than eight fighter variants saw combat, in addition to the F4F-7 photo bird.

Considering the variety of engines, armament and equipment employed in the Wildcat series, it would be easy to become mired in the task of keeping all the models straightened out. I've avoided that trap by largely ignoring the technical differences among all the kittens in the litter, and concentrating on their operational use. The charts and tables customarily included in publications dealing with so varied an aircraft do not appear here for the simple reason they have been widely printed elsewhere. A check of the bibliography will direct the nuts-and-bolts enthusiasts to those sources. Instead, I've included tables dealing with nomenclature and production, most of which is "new."

This operational history completes the series of aircraft "biographies" begun with publication of *The Dauntless Dive Bomber of World War II* in 1976. It follows the same format as most books in the series, making use of contemporary terminology which presumes a certain topical familiarity by the reader. Unlike previous volumes, this one makes use of both nautical and statute miles when discussing distances and airspeeds, the result of discussions with interested readers. Where distances are not specified as to land or sea miles, one may generally assume that nautical measure is intended. All compass bearings are true unless otherwise indicated.

The early chapters contain the anachronism of U.S. code names for Japanese aircraft. Originally adopted by the Army Air Force in July 1942, the popular identification system was absorbed by the Navy and Marines late that year. But four decades of widespread usage has served to institutionalize the Zeke-Betty-Val family, and I use it here for clarity.

Finally, a word about timeliness. The Wildcat manuscript was completed throughout the fortieth anniversary year of Midway and Guadalcanal. As in my previous volumes, I have attempted to draw a few comparisons between similar situations then and now. Some conclusions may or may not be pertinent, but all are offered in the hope that a professional readership will consider them in light of Shakespeare's contention that what is past is prologue.

BARRETT TILLMAN
Athena, Oregon

The Wildcat in WWII

1. SETTING THE STAGE

"New things succeed as former things grow old."
—Robert Herrick

THE BIPLANE ERA WAS END-ing. The fruit of the most productive period in aviation history, and certainly the most colorful, by the late 1930s the military biplane was obsolete for all but training, observation, and reconnaissance purposes. The pre-World War II biplane fighters were faster and stronger than their World War I counterparts, but the differences were more cosmetic than substantive. Enclosed cockpits and, occasionally, retractable landing gear were the major external differences between the fighters of 1917 and 1937. While engines were more powerful, allowing greater speed and reliability, neither armament nor combat tactics had seen much evolution. In short, the air arms committed to biplane fighters in the late Thirties were splendidly prepared to fight the previous war.

When continental powers began equipping themselves with fast, well-armed monoplanes in the late Thirties (notably Britain's Hawker Hurricane and Germany's Messerschmitt 109) the balance rapidly shifted. Qualitative superiority has usually been more important in aerial combat than other forms of warfare, and an air force with a two-to-one advantage in biplanes could not reasonably hope to defeat its outnumbered adversary equipped with state-of-the-art monoplanes. Germany's Condor Legion soundly proved the point in

3

Spain, where the 109 was used against a variety of traditional biplane designs.

The quality-versus-quantity tradeoff was particularly applicable to carrier-borne fighters, which always run the risk of engaging superior land-based opposition. In fact, during the piston-engine monoplane era of naval aviation (roughly 1940–1950) only three carrier-suitable fighters proved in combat their ability to tackle land-based fighters on even terms: the Mitsubishi Zero, the Grumman Hellcat, and Vought Corsair. Britain's Supermarine Seafire—the "hooked Spitfire"—was a tremendous performer but lacked the critical carrier-suitability qualifications. And the greatest prospect of all, the F8F Bearcat, missed combat entirely.

The U.S. Navy's ultimate biplane dogfighter was the Grumman F3F series. An improved design based upon the F2F of 1933, the F3F entered fleet service in early 1936. It was still first-line equipment when the fleet's first monoplanes arrived: the Douglas TBD torpedo plane and Vought SB2U scout-bomber in 1937, and the Brewster F2A in late 1939.

While the F3F compared favorably with contemporary monoplanes in some categories (maneuverability, initial climb rate and low-speed stability) these considerations were insufficient to warrant retaining the twenty-year-old configuration. The worldwide trend was towards faster, higher-flying, well-armed fighters; in all of these factors, the biplane was inherently limited.

In these three areas the popular little F3F was far outclassed. It was a pilot's airplane—light and responsive, a joy to fly—but the numbers dealt it out. At best the F3F managed 260 mph (225 knots) and under optimum conditions it could struggle up to 33,000 feet. Its armanent was a holdover of the rifle-caliber weapons of 1916, with a .30-caliber machine gun reinforced with just one .50-caliber. By comparison, its replacements possessed advantages in speed of some 60 mph (50 knots) and in service ceiling of as much as 4,000 feet. And both the F2A and F4F carried four .50-calibers; light by later standards but sufficient to knock down contemporary bombers.

Ironically, the Wildcat began life on the drawing board as a biplane. Grumman Design 16 owed its impetus to a Bureau of Aeronautics circular published in November 1935, calling for another new fleet fighter. Bigger and beefier than the F3F, the XF4F-1 nonetheless bore a strong family resemblance to its immediate predecessor: an all-metal, closed-cockpit biplane with now-typical manually-retractable landing gear. In early March of 1936, Grumman signed a Navy Bureau of Aeronautics contract for the biplane prototype, but the design never got past the schematic stage.

The reason was the XF2A-1, Brewster's newfangled monoplane entrant. Actually, the progressive Northrop company in California had designed and flown a monoplane carrier fighter a few years before, but in 1933 the XFT-1 was evidently considered too radical, and that contract was won by the F2F. Now in order to remain competitive, Grumman had to abandon the traditional configuration and rapidly adapt Design 16 to match the competition. But there was also pressure from the Navy.

On 30 June 1936, Lieutenant J. B. Pearson of BuAer wrote Roy Grumman with specifications on "your new monoplane." The Bethpage, Long Island firm, in considering the configuration change, gave little thought to including a folding wing. Neither Brewster nor the other entrant, Seversky, had taken that complicated step. But Pearson accurately predicted, "I venture that any monoplane without folding wings will be considered obsolete by the time your design arrives at Anacostia."[1]

The next day Mr. Grumman replied, saying the XF4F-1 had been altered to a mid-wing monoplane with a Pratt and Whitney R-1830-C engine rated at 900 horsepower. Grumman guaranteed a speed of 290 mph (250 knots), a minimum control speed of 65 mph (57 knots) and service ceiling of 27,000 feet. And, as per a previous BuAer request, the factory would consider installation of two 20-mm cannon.[2]

Legend has it that Grumman engineers took the fuselage profile of the dash one, laid a straightedge along the longitudinal axis, and drew a line to indicate the datum of a mid-wing monoplane. In any event, as Grumman's letter proved, that was the result of the redesigning. But the work ahead would be nowhere as easy. The next three years saw numerous setbacks.

In context of the 1980s, the Wildcat seems a marvelously simple airplane. With its hand-cranked landing gear and vacuum-powered flaps, it had no hydraulics and only a simple electrical system. But the transition from biplane to monoplane carrier fighters, with all the design and structural improvements required, made a big step up. In their own way, the F2A and F4F represented as important an advancement in technology as the transition to jet propulsion ten years later.

The XF4F-2 was finally completed with a P-W R-1830-66, a 14-cylinder radial engine rated at 1,050 horsepower on takeoff. Its single-stage, one-speed supercharger afforded 900 horses at 12,000 feet, evidence of the increasing importance the Navy placed on altitude performance. The engine-driven supercharger in effect gave low-altitude power at higher levels by pumping more air into the engine than would normally be possible. The additional air was then compressed before receiving vaporized fuel for better combustion.

The prototype dash two was rolled out at Bethpage in August 1937. The fuselage retained the rounded contours bespeaking the F3F heritage, but with the advantage of 40-year hindsight, the angular silhouette of the production Wildcat is just beneath the surface. Factory test pilot Robert L. Hall, a 32-year-old engineer who preferred flying airplanes to designing them, made the F4F's first flight on 2 September. In early tests the dash two demonstrated 290-mph speed and a service ceiling of 27,000 feet. These met Roy Grumman's guarantees, though the Navy would later require better figures, and the proposed 20-mm armament never came about.

Given BuAer number 0383, the XF4F-2 was slated for three months of factory and Navy tests in Maryland. Hall flew the little fighter to NAS Anacostia, the Navy's aviation test facility, two days before Christmas. Other flights at Dahlgren Proving Ground were interspersed with periodic returns to Bethpage for heavy maintenance and requested modifications. But Bob Hall and other test pilots had some unwanted excitement along the way.

Engine problems caused troublesome delays in the form of crankshaft bearing failures. Pratt and Whitney representatives found that a silver-lead bearing surface was required, and in fact this procedure became standard among powerplant manufacturers. It was just one of the many lessons learned along the way to higher-performance aircraft.

As if that weren't enough, on Valentine's Day 1938, Hall was en route to the home drome when he had a fire at 10,000 feet. Shot bags stowed aft in the fuselage for ballast were ignited after becoming soaked with gasoline or oil, but Hall got down without significant damage.

Back at Dahlgren, things began looking up. Dive and spin tests with representative ordnance loads were passed satisfactorily. Hall flew a series of dives with gradually increasing airframe stress during pullouts. These tests, up to 8.5 Gs in recoveries, were among the first practical indications of the F4F's legendary ruggedness. Spin recoveries were also promising, with control regained in less than one and a half turns, though better recovery would later become possible.

Armament originally amounted to a pair of wing-mounted .50-caliber with two cowl-mounted .30s firing through the prop arc. The wing guns at one time were removable to allow fixture of bomb racks for 100-pounders, but this feature was wisely deleted. Other operational tests that spring included the all-important carrier-suitability trials. In April the XF4F-2 went to Philadelphia for catapult and simulated deck-landing evaluation at the Naval Aircraft Factory. Catapult attachment points were determined, and the appropriate hardware affixed.

Then the engine packed up. And, in accordance with the First Amendment to Murphy's Law, it occurred at just about the worst possible time.

A Navy pilot making landing tests abruptly found himself powerless during an approach on 11 April. He made a forced landing along the Delaware River, coming to grief in a field owned by the Campbell Soup Company. The Grumman nosed over, incurring heavy damage to the right wing, the tail section, landing gear, cowling, and propeller. The pilot was unhurt, but the Bethpage crew lost two weeks making repairs.

About that same time—late April—the Navy was looking at the test results of the fighter competition. The Seversky NF-1 was the first entry eliminated. Speed evaluations showed the Brewster and Grumman entrants 40 to 50 mph faster, respectively. And the NF-1 exhibited marginal deck-landing characteristics, so the choice came down to the XF4F-2 or XF2A-1.

The shoe fell with a dull thud in the halls at Bethpage. Though faster than the Brewster, the Grumman's persistent engine troubles bothered BuAer. Pratt and Whitney had cranked 1,250 horsepower from the R-1830 by 1941, and the attendant problems of powerplant evolution couldn't be ignored. So the Navy ordered a batch of fifty-three production F2A-1s and -2s in June of 1938.

However, all was not yet lost. The Navy was still interested in the F4F's potential, and the Grumman braintrust was ill disposed towards capitulation. Grumman retaliated by installing an R-1830-76 in the prototype. This decision would prove the most significant in the Wildcat's history, after the conversion from biplane to monoplane.

The -76 engine featured a two-stage supercharger which, when operated in "high blower," provided better performance over 11,000 feet. There were tradeoffs, of course, but BuAer was interested enough to investigate. If Grumman and Pratt-Whitney could overcome the inherent cooling problems and increased complexity, the Navy let it be known that a limited-production contract would probably be offered.

At this same time, 100-octane aviation gasoline was becoming generally available. The cooler-burning high-test fuel, in comparison to standard 87-octane avgas, was a significant improvement. Consequently, in October 1938 Grumman and the Navy inked a contract for an XF4F-3.

In retrospect, this almost informal arrangement between the Navy and one of its prime contractors had historic significance. The world was a simpler place in those days, and such things could be done immensely faster and easier than today. But Grumman had a proven track record, and the Allied cause would be fortunate that the two parties operated on such terms. What it meant was simple: the Wildcat, not the Brewster Buffalo, would become the U.S. Navy's standard fighter during the first year of the Pacific War.

BuAer number 0383 made a second debut on 12 February 1939. Bigger, heavier, and more angular, the evolution was nearly complete. A full two years after it had returned from Anacostia as the XF4F-2, Bob Hall flew 0383 for three-quarters of an hour. The much-modified airframe underwent extensive testing of new tail surfaces, cowl and prop, and finally crashed at Norfolk in December of that year. But by then the job had been largely completed. In August the Navy ordered fifty-four production F4F-3s. And just in time. On 1 September the Germans rolled into Poland from the west and barely two weeks later the Soviets attacked from the east. The Second World War had begun.

An undeclared war of sorts was already well underway. In October 1937, one month after the XF4F-2's first flight, the Imperial Japanese Navy issued the design requirements for a new carrier fighter with a maximum speed of 500 kilometers per hour at 4,000 meters (310 mph at 13,100 feet.) Thus was born the F4F's mortal enemy, the Mitsubishi Zero.[3]

The prototype Zero Fighter had rolled out of the Nagoya plant in March 1939. Two weeks later it was taken by oxcart to Kasumigaura naval air station, some twenty-five miles north of the city, and test pilot Katsuzo Shima made the initial flight on 1 April. The thirty-man design team under thirty-five-year-old chief engineer Jiro Horikoshi had produced a worldbeater. As Japan had been fully engaged in China since mid-1937, there was ample data to draw upon for a new naval fighter. Combat experience gained with the A5M, or Type 96 Fighter (Claude to Allied air intelligence in World War II) influenced Mitsubishi's work on the A6M, or Type Zero.

Some confusion arises over Japanese aircraft designations. A6M1, the first Zero design, was designated in a way directly analogous to the U.S. Navy system. The F2A-1, for instance, identified type (fighter), model number by the builder (second) and manufacturer's letter (A for Brewster.) The F2A-1 was therefore the first production model of the Buffalo. Similarly, the Japanese system identified type (A for fighter), model number (sixth) by builder (M for Mitsubishi.) The A6M1, though limited in numbers, was the original.

But each Japanese military aircraft had another designation based upon the traditional calendar. By Japanese reckoning, 1940 was Nippon's year 2600. The last two digits of each year in which the type entered service were assigned as model numbers. The G4M bomber (later called Betty by the Allies) entered service in 1941, hence its designation of Type One Land Attack Plane. Nakajima's B5N (Kate) became operational in 1937 as the Type 97 Attacker, or torpedo bomber. So it was with the A6M series, which became the Type 00 Fighter, or Zero for short. There was also a Type 0 Observation Seaplane (Pete) and Type 0 Reconnaissance Seaplane (Jake.)

Relatively few early problems were encountered, and the only serious setback was loss of the second prototype in a dive test during March of 1940. The elevator mass balance broke, causing elevator flutter which led to airframe disintegration. But otherwise the development phase went smoothly, with particular attention devoted to modifying the propeller (from two to three blades), elevators, and brakes. The first A6M2s were delivered in July, and fifteen pre-production aircraft were immediately sent to China.

From August 1940 to September 1941, the China-based Zeros (eventually thirty in all) flew some 700 sorties, losing only two aircraft to enemy action. None were shot down in aerial combat. The first engagement occurred near Chungking in September 1940, ending in a resounding twenty-seven-to-nothing victory. By the end of the thirteen-month trial period, the Imperial Navy's "sea eagles" had claimed 266 shootdowns.[4] To what extent this figure was exaggerated may never be known (the Japanese overclaimed by orders of magnitude throughout the war), but that was beside the point. The A6M series more than proved itself in China, laying a tactical doctrine which would take Zero pilots to sensational success very soon.

Aside from a good turn of speed (about 320 mph, or 275 knots) and superb maneuverability, the Zero also climbed well and possessed potent armament. In fact, a heated internal battle had boiled within the Imperial Navy's air arm over inclusion of 20-mm cannon in the new fighter. But in the far reaches of the Pacific, the A6M's phenomenal range was to become an equally important factor. A tactical radius of 500 statute miles (430 nautical) was demonstrated in the Philippines and Solomons campaigns—something completely unheard of in western air forces. Crawling through the sky at 115 knots, consuming a mere 18 gallons per hour, the Zero was the world's first long-range fighter.

The U.S. Navy had nothing like it. Nobody did.

Thus, the F4F and A6M underwent nearly parallel design and development. They were started down the road to deployment under vastly differing design philosophies, half a world removed from one another. But almost inevitably their careers would peak in violent confrontation over the beautiful blue waters of the greatest of all Earth's oceans. The one ironically named Pacific.

2. REHEARSAL

"Who should desire peace should be ready for war."
—Vegetius, 375 BC

IN EARLY 1940, WHILE THE "sitzkrieg" dragged on in Europe, the early production F4F-3s were completed and final testing began. The first production bird, BuAer 1844, was flown in February, but the second didn't fly until July. By then the Battle of Britain had begun, and perhaps in view of combat experience gained by the RAF, the U.S. Navy changed its mind about armament. Both early dash threes were equipped with twin .30-calibers in the nose and two .50s in the wings, but all subsequent F4F-3s had four wing-mounted .50-calibers.

About the same time, two other variants were under construction. The most important was the XF4F-4, which would experiment with folding wings. The dash four contract, signed in March 1940, recalled Lieutenant Pearson's letter to Roy Grumman of June 1936, predicting the need of folding-wing fighters. Grumman began work on a hydraulically-folding wing for the F4F, understandably concerned about mechanical complexity and weight. But the Navy was the customer, and the customer—as any businessman knows—is always right. The folding-wing F4F would be a year in the making.

The XF4F-5 showed another glimpse of the future. It was an early -3 with a Wright R-1820-40. Two were delivered in 1940, further modified for supercharger tests of other 1820-series engines, as future

11

Pratt and Whitney supplies looked uncertain in the enormous military buildup of 1940–41. The two -5s were taken to Anacostia in early July by Grumman pilots Connie Converse and Bud Gillies.

Tests continued on production F4Fs at Anacostia and Philadelphia, leading up to squadron deliveries by year-end. Navy pilots were now enthusiastic about the Grumman's future. The F4F-3 was stable in flight along all three axes, and from a fighter pilot's viewpoint, made a good gun platform. Admittedly, the F4F demonstrated some longitudinal instability at top speed (331 mph or 285 knots at 21,300 feet), and there was a noticeable nose-down tendency in a power-on landing. But these quirks were acceptable. Some concern was noted that the -3 fell some 19 mph (17 knots) below the desired Vmax of 350, but the Navy could live with it.

Stall and spin recovery were much improved over the prototype. A ten-turn spin could now be stopped in a quarter to a half a turn, losing some 1,500 feet including recovery. Power-on stalls cost 400 feet; again acceptable.[1]

Two quirks which required adjustment would stick with the F4F series til the very end. The relatively high center of gravity (a mid-wing characteristic) on a narrow landing gear—only six feet, or half that of the F6F and F4U—resulted in a lateral swaying most pronounced during a run-out on a field landing. It was absent from an arrested carrier landing. To the uninitiated, this behavior gave a false signal of an incipient groundloop. Many an F4F pilot instinctively reacted to correct the "problem" and actually induced the evolution he sought to avoid. This behavior also cropped up on full-power takeoff, and was encountered on both field and deck launches.

The other foible was the manually operated landing gear. Most early F4F pilots were familar with the Grumman hand-cranked operation from the F2F and F3F series. But that did nothing to ease the chore of turning that blasted, troublesome handle twenty-six to thirty rotations in order to raise the gear. The handle was located on the right, just behind the pilot's knee. It was rotated forward to lower the wheels, reversed to raise them. And if a pilot's hand slipped during the process, the handle unwound under gravity with ferocious speed if the friction brake were out of adjustment. Some veteran aviators recall that the only way to stop the gear from unwinding completely was to stick one's knee in the whirring handle's path. It was, needless to say, a painful procedure. Broken bones were not entirely unknown. Said one high-time F4F pilot, "The mechanism worked fairly well, but it *lurked.*"[2] Noted another, thinking of manually operated landing gear, gun charging and cowl flaps, it seemed the Wildcat was intent on "making the pilot do all the work except pull the plane through the air."[3]

But these peculiarities were relatively minor, and bore no effect upon the new fighter's operational capacity. Long interested in dive-bombing, the U.S. Navy experimented with its latest addition in that esoteric role. Dives with various ordnance were made at angles up to 80 degrees, which generated airspeeds of 425 mph (nearly 370 knots). F4Fs would seldom indulge in this game for real, but at Wake Island they did so with a vengeance.

However, gunnery remained the Wildcat's meat, and there still existed room for improvement. Because the early -3s were equipped with the telescopic gunsight left over from biplane days, aerial gunnery potential would remain limited for a while. The Bureau of Ordnance reportedly designed the F4F's windscreen because BuOrd's old sight was mounted through the glass. This led to problems galore when the need for an unpierced armor glass center panel was recognized as a combat requirement. These problems were solved by installation changes made as the Pacific War began.

On 26 November 1940, Fighting Squadron Four received the first F4F-3 assigned to the fleet. Based at NAS Norfolk, Virginia, VF-4 had previously flown F3Fs and began transitioning as deliveries allowed. Each pilot got one hop in the XF4F-3 at Norfolk, in addition to delivering a new plane from the factory.

Fighting Four had a lot of talent. Its pilots included future standouts as Dave McCampbell, who became famous in Hellcats, and Roger Hedrick, destined for the Skull and Crossbones Corsairs of VF-17. The skipper was calm, gentlemanly Lieutenant C.T. Booth— Tommy to one and all. The transitions went well, and one of the few items which drew comment was the vacuum-powered flap system, something new to most pilots.

Almost simultaneously a -3 was tested at the Naval Aircraft Factory for arresting gear suitability. Fighting Four was assigned to the *Ranger*, and upon completion of the Philadelphia test, Tommy Booth's pilots made the initial sea trials. They learned that speed management from the downwind leg to the landing signal officer's "cut" was essential to a Roger pass. The F4F, even with hook, wheels, and the flaps down was a relatively clean bird. It was hard to slow down, and whacking back on the throttle late in a pass was no remedy. They found, however, that setting up a steady 80-knot downwind, easing to about 68 on final, seldom drew a waveoff. Said Bill Leonard of VF-42, who earned consistently good LSO grades, "Get your 70 knots on downwind and hold it there with judicious throttle control. Ride this speed all the way to the cut. Art Brassfield was the best in our squadron, and he used this system, too."[4]

Other squadrons began converting the F4Fs on the east coast. Next after VF-4 was VF-72, headed for the new *Wasp*. In July 1940 Bombing Seven became VF-71 and Fighting Seven became VF-72, and the latter received nineteen F4F-3s during January 1941. A similar change occurred in the *Ranger*'s air group, which normally operated two fighter and two scout-bomber squadrons. She had no provision for torpedo storage, hence the unusual air group composition. Scouting 41 was flying SBU-1s when word came through that the unit would trade in its biplanes for Wildcats. Most of the young pilots, eager aviators like Bill Leonard and Dick Crommelin, could hardly believe their good fortune. It was like changing jobs from cabbie to race driver.

Though formally commissioned in February 1941 as VF-42, the squadron was already transitioning to F4F-3s in January. Lieutenant T. B. Williamson's crew had to make personnel adjustments as well as materiel changes, however. Some radiomen-gunners were transferred out, but others were retrained to maintain the unaccustomed .50-calibers with a few new ordnancemen. Tommy Booth's folks provided as much help as possible, but the truth was, nobody yet had much experience in operating high-performance fighters from carriers. Very little was known about fighter direction, interceptions, and the like. However, many of the former scout pilots were hot on gunnery, and for a time VF-42 served as a training squadron for fliers headed to Fighting Four.

From this unheralded beginning was formed the one Navy fighter squadron which might be considered indispensable in the first six months of the war. Fighting 42 remains largely unknown even in naval circles today, but its training under the former exec, Lieutenant Commander Oscar Pederson, paid dividends at Coral Sea and Midway. In fact, VF-42 bcame the Navy's foremost interceptor squadron of that period.

But Pete Pederson's crew saw little of the *Ranger*. There were short neutrality patrols from the *Ranger* and *Wasp* in the North Atlantic that spring, but in May the three-year-old *Yorktown* arrived at Norfolk, fresh from the Pacific. Fighting Five, the *Yorktown*'s regular VF squadron, was the last in the Navy to transition from biplanes. It only turned in its F3F-3s in June, leaving insufficient time to assimilate new equipment, techniques, and doctrine. But VF-42 was on hand, ready to go.

This is not to imply that the Wildcat's early fleet service went unmarred. There were several serious incidents. The first occurred on

16 December 1940 at Norfolk when BuAer 0383, the much-modified original prototype, crashed on takeoff. The fatality was attributed to the pilot's error in switching off the fuel when he intended to raise the flaps. Other early losses resulted from oxygen system failure at high altitude, and unaccountable in-flight inflation of wing-mounted flotation bags. After two of the latter incidents, one fatal, the bags were deleted. They weren't worth the potential buoyancy in event of a water landing.

In the spring of 1941, Congress authorized a series of defense expenditures which eventually brought the Navy's air strength from about 1,800 aircraft to over 15,000. As more F4Fs were delivered that summer and fall, additional experience was gained in the fleet. In September VF-4 went to Beaumont, Texas in preparation for the big army maneuvers at Lake Charles, Louisiana. And most carrier squadrons exercised in the Carribean, flying out of Guantanamo Bay, Cuba. During this period, hard-won knowledge sometimes came harder than anyone liked. The tube sight caused several black eyes or bruised foreheads on catapult launches, since shoulder harnesses weren't used at the time. And the BuOrd-designed windscreen nearly cost a plane and pilot on at least one occasion.

The incident involved Ensign Wally Madden, a puckish VF-4 pilot and drinking buddy of Lieutenant Dave McCampbell. In a dive at about 8,000 feet, the left-hand panel of Madden's windscreen collapsed. The sudden blast of air tore off his goggles and whipped the sunglasses from his face. Madden leveled off and headed back to the *Ranger*, barely able to keep his eyes open in the terrific slipstream. His Wildcat smacked the deck in a skid, collapsing the landing gear.

Badly cut on the face and head, Madden was taken to sick bay for treatment and observation. There, he learned that the landing signal officer had criticized his approach (LSOs are that way) and had given him a low grade. The new squadron CO, Lieutenant Cliff Cooper, investigated and became solicitous of his young aviator's welfare. Ordinarily, pilots were given medicinal brandy if they went in the water, and though Madden kept his feet dry, Cooper approached the flight surgeon on Wally's behalf. Sadly, to no avail.[5]

Shortly before year-end the old tubular sights were replaced with more up-to-date electric reflecting gunsights. There was apparently little standardization from one squadron to the next as to type of sight or reticle image (ranging from circle-and-dot to the "Christmas tree" variety) but at least the F4F squadrons were relieved of a major structural and tactical worry.

Meanwhile, pilots had learned more about operating F4Fs both ashore and "off the boat." Fighting 42 found that a full-power takeoff caused the port oleo strut and tire to flatten owing to the torque of 1,200 horses winding the counter-clockwise propeller. This made the right-hand ground contact light, when more braking control was needed for steering effect. Upon reflection, this was realized to be a factor not of the aircraft itself, but of Chambers Field's short runway at Norfolk, where full power was needed. The handbook power curves showed 1,200 horses with 2,700 rpm at 46.5 inches manifold pressure. But 2,800 revs and 48 inches were permissible, and the higher settings were used when necessary.

Aboard ship, the standard procedure was for each plane to make a prompt right turn after launch to minimize the wait for its slipstream to clear the launch area. But the F4F's behavior at takeoff power made this turn nearly impossible. With controls full right, the stubby little Grumman usually jittered straight ahead. It really wanted to turn left, and full control against this tendency ended in an out-of-control draw. Aboard the *Yorktown*, discussions among the experienced aviators plus encouragement from the captain and his top-notch deck crew led to an effective solution: Wildcats would make a left turn after launch. Captain Buckmaster maneuvered ship to put the wind about ten degrees on the starboard bow. Both these actions made the slipstream clear the deck rapidly and the ten degrees added, in effect, to the F4F's rudder throw—enough to give a good measure of directional control. Successive launches were permitted to proceed at unheard-of short intervals, and there was an end to the out-of-control thrills on deck launches.

Other squadrons experimented with different procedures. One variation called for starting the deck run without flaps, since lowered flaps at the start of a takeoff roll reduced rudder control. But the F4F needed flaps to get off the flight deck safely. So, with no little presumption that the flaps would indeed come down when needed, they were popped in the last few feet of the run. Intervals were not improved by this method, but it removed the rank hazard of poor directional control at the beginning of the takeoff. All pilots were pleased to note they could get off at about 57 knots indicated, and the 30-knot headwind provided by the ship added another layer of comfort.

Combat tactics were also evaluated and tested during this period, with substantial long-range effect. During the summer of 1941, VF-3 at San Diego began experimenting with a four-plane division in place of the standard six-plane formation. The CO, Lieutenant Commander

Jimmy Thach, was already acknowledged to be a gunnery expert. His analytical approach to fighter aviation led to the conclusion that two pairs of fighters were far more flexible than the then-standard organization of two three-plane elements. Furthermore, by flying a fluid formation with proper spacing, a two-plane element attacked by hostile aircraft had only to turn toward the friendly element in order to defeat the threat. Thach was certain this mutual-support weave was the answer to success and survival in combat.

It took a genuine shooting war to prove the validity of Fighting Three's tactics, for some squadrons retained the customary three-plane section into 1942. Others tried the two-fighter element and adjusted formations accordingly. One example was VF-42, which elected to stick with the six-plane division, but employed three pairs instead of two triples.

Though the F4F was now integrated into the fleet, Grumman remained busy as ever. Navy acceptances averaged twenty-seven per month during 1941, with a peak of forty-five in April. That was the month the XF4F-4 first flew, as the folding-wing fighter had been completed. Actually, the first dash four was a conventional -3 decked out with a complex hydraulic wing-fold mechanism. Once again VF-42 entered the picture, conducting carrier suitability tests aboard the *Yorktown*.

The installation worked reasonably well, but the extra plumbing and hydraulic cylinders imposed a considerable weight penalty. Therefore, Grumman devised a manual locking and folding design which proved eminently workable and became the basis for those in the TBF and F6F. This system reduced the F4F's wingspan from 38 feet to barely 14, and the Navy was pleased. The first production -4s were delivered just before year-end.

A look at a shop memo for early October demonstrates the variety of F4F projects facing the Grummanites that fall.[6] Job Number 126 concerned the first ten F4F-4s, but a whole new concept then showed up on the assembly line. Job 129 was the first F4F-7, a gunless, fixed-wing Wildcat solely dedicated to photo reconnaissance. Equipped with two cameras and a staggering amount of fuel, the -7 would see limited operational use. But its incredible range (nearly 3,000 statute miles, or 2,600 nautical) demonstrated what was possible in the state of the art.

With 555 gallons in the wings and 130 in the fuselage, the F4F-7 was literally a flying fuel tank. It was estimated that with proper cruise control the dash seven could remain airborne for 24 hours, and a Sperry Mark IV autopilot was installed. Other modifications included a vertical camera behind the seat, a rounded windscreen distinct from that on the -3 and -4, and fuel dump lines protruding beneath the rudder.

The Navy ordered 100 F4F-7s, but in the end only 21 were produced, since the photo bird had limited application and the need for fighters was acute. The first -7 flew on 30 December 1941, and shortly afterwards its exceptional range capability was proven. Lieutenant Commander Andy Jackson, a BuAer officer at the time, flew cross-country nonstop, from east to west, in eleven hours, averaging about 165 mph. The other twenty airplanes were to be delivered between February and August 1942.

At the same time the -4s and the original -7 went together, another project also occupied the shop at Bethpage. This was Job 127, part of the second British contract involving the last 59 of 100 G-36Bs which the Royal Navy called Martlet IIs. The British F4Fs are dealt with in their own chapter, but it is significant that a U.S. fighter, a special-purpose recon plane, and a version built to British specs were all on the assembly line simultaneously.

Amid the Navy carrier squadrons' operational testing, -7, and British projects, it was possible to forget that the Marine Corps also received F4Fs. In October the Navy adopted a popularized name system for its aircraft, and the Grumman fighter officially became the Wildcat. That same month VMF-211 became the last F3F-2 squadron, joining VMF-111 and 121 as the Marines' Wildcat outfits. By December the Corps had deployed 211 to Hawaii with a total of 22 F4F-3s, while Marine Air Group 11 at Quantico, Virginia numbered 35 dash threes and -3As in 111 and 121.[7]

The F4F-3A (production model of the XF4F-6) was powered by the Twin Wasp engine, and by the end of 1941 the Marines had received sixty-five of the ninety-five ordered to that time. Thirty intended for Greece were taken over by the British as Martlet IIIs. The -3A was lighter than the -3, but owing to the 1830–90's diminished altitude performance with less supercharging, the Navy decided the Marines could make better use of the -3A than carrier squadrons. Consequently, most of them went to VMF squadrons, where presumably their best-speed-at-altitude (312 mph at 16,000 feet) wouldn't be as much of a liability as the straight dash three (331 mph at 21,300 feet). At any rate, by the fall of 1941 three of the Corps' four fighter squadrons were flying Wildcats.

At year-end the U.S. Navy and Marines had accepted some 345 F4Fs. By way of comparison, in Japan the Zero fighter had entered production at Nakajima in addition to Mitsubishi, and at year-end about 520 A6Ms had been delivered.[8] This is a notable statistic. The Zero, which started design work after the F4F, went from first flight to squadron service in sixteen months. The Wildcat's elapsed time for similar milestones was over three years. But the Zero had been in production since May of 1940, with a batch of pre-production aircraft which went directly to combat in China. The first two F4F-3s flew five months apart—February and July 1940—but by December 1941 Grumman, without a subcontractor, had nearly matched the Zero's monthly production rate. American industry was beginning to tell even before the shooting started.

3. TO WAR

"I do not know beneath what sky
Nor on what seas shall be thy fate . . . "
—Richard Hovey, 1898

FIFTY MILES OUT FROM Pearl Harbor, the carrier *Enterprise* was returning from a ferry trip to Wake Island. The Big E had delivered twelve Wildcats of VMF-211 as Wake's garrison air force on 4 December, and now three days later was flying off her squadrons before entering Pearl. The two SBD units had already been launched early this Sunday morning, while the shorter-ranged Wildcats and Devastators were taken closer to shore.

Fighting Six's eighteen F4F-3As were on deck, ready to launch. But air staff officers monitoring radio traffic were first bewildered, then shocked at what they heard. Pilots of the scout-bombers arriving over the fleet base at 0800 were reporting Japanese aircraft. Only later was it learned that seven Dauntlesses and eight aircrew were lost. It was grim irony; many personnel had envied the SBD pilots and gunners, who would arrive hours ahead of the ship. But now, knowing some of their shipmates were dead, Fighting Six pilots wondered about the proper course of action. The first instinct was to launch immediately, jump into the fight, and help protect Pearl.

It would have been easy to do. The squadron skipper was Lieutenant Commander Wade McClusky, a stocky trade-school professional from the Annapolis Class of '26. His squadron was ready and willing, and McClusky literally begged the task force commander, Vice Admi-

20

ral William F. Halsey, for permission to launch. But Halsey recognized the potential danger to the invaluable ship. If enemy carriers were about—and they obviously were—every F4F was needed to defend the Big E. The Wildcats were kept with the task force, on combat air patrol.

Then, at 1645, Halsey ordered a search-strike by the TBDs of Torpedo Six, with a half-dozen F4Fs as escort. They found nothing— the Japanese force withdrew well to the northwest—and by the time the flight returned, darkness was setting in. Recovery was unusually slow because each TBD kept its torpedo, something not previously attempted. Due to the delay and late hour, the airborne fighters were ordered to land at Ford Island, Pearl Harbor.

Over a week passed before VF-6 learned what happened to all six pilots.

The division approached Ford Island in column, preparing to land with running lights switched on. Then, recalled a veteran of the squadron, "our own trigger-happy, shell-shocked gunners" opened fire.[1] Two Wildcats were shot down immediately, scattering the others in all directions as the survivors doused their lights, added power and cranked up their wheels. Two pilots, running extremely low on fuel, bailed out rather than try to land amid the lethal confusion below. Another pair somehow got down. Both landed at Ford Island, where Ensign Gale Hermann found that not even a "safe" landing was a guarantee of safety. Jittery machine-gunners continued shooting at him as he taxied in. When the young pilot climbed out, he counted 18 holes in his plane.

At that, Hermann was luckier than three of his friends. One was killed immediately and two others died of wounds. Fighting Six's first day at war had cost the squadron four aircraft and one badly damaged, at no expense to the Japanese.

The Marines were also hard-hit. Marine Air Group 21 counted forty-eight aircraft at MCAS Ewa that morning. Besides SB2Us, SBDs and assorted utility planes, Ewa based the ten rear-echelon Wildcats of VMF-211. By mid-morning, when the last Japanese bombers flew back to their six carriers, MAG-21 had exactly one operational airplane. The others were all destroyed or badly damaged on the ground.[2]

At the start of the Pacific War, Wildcats equipped seven of the eight Navy fighter squadrons and three of the Marines' four. Only the *Lexington*'s VF-2 and Midway-bound VMF-221 still flew Buffalos, but the F4F squadrons of the Pacific Fleet were scattered and, as of 8 December, badly under strength. The *Saratoga* was in San Diego embarking the Marine Brewsters, but her Fighting Three possessed only ten Wildcats: seven -3s, two -3As, and the XF4F-4.

Curiously, in light of the Navy and Marine Corps' main arena, two-thirds of all available F4Fs were on the east coast. Excluding recently accepted aircraft from Grumman, the combined number of operational Wildcats was some 225, of which about 155 were nominally assigned to Atlantic operations. The large majority of these were based at Norfolk and Quantico. Obviously, a rapid redistribution was required.

MAG-11's two fighter squadrons were VMF-111 (fifteen F4F-3As) and VMF-121 (twenty F4F-3s.) On Pearl Harbor Day the latter was at New Bern, North Carolina, upstream from the future air station at Cherry Point on the Neuse River. One-Twenty-One had been operating from what one pilot described as "a huge sandlot" in recent months, conducting gunnery training.[3] Upon word of events in Hawaii, the squadron's aircraft were dispersed in revetments as a precaution against possible attack.

Two days later the colorful CO, Major Sam Jack, led 121 home to Quantico. Alerted for transfer to the Pacific coast, the Marines indulged in a whirlwind of activity, packing equipment and readying aircraft. But there was too little time to do much more than install armor plate. Self-sealing tanks and the new YE homers would have to wait until later. On 11 December (the day Germany declared war on the U.S.) VMF-121, reinforced to twenty-eight Wildcats, headed west.

Or, at least most of them did.

Second Lieutenant Bruce Porter, in the division of Staff Sergeant Ken Walsh, lost directional control on takeoff. By the time Porter got things straightened out, he was speeding down two rows of SB2Us, with mere feet to spare on either wingtip. He gratefully noted that the end of the line was clear, when an SNJ trainer taxied into his path. Porter prepared for a collision and hoped he wouldn't be killed before he got to shoot at something in this war.

Miraculously—Porter still doesn't know how—the "J-Bird" avoided the onrushing Wildcat. Just when it appeared Porter could bring the runaway F4F to a stop, it ran headlong into a ditch and pitched up sharply. Porter was thrown forward into the gunsight, hitting his head.

One-Twenty-One had suffered its first casualty of the war—5,000 miles from Pearl Harbor. But Bruce Porter more than redeemed himself during two Solomons tours, and finished the war as a squadron commander on Okinawa.

It took five days for the squadron to reach San Diego. But deployment was postponed indefinitely when 121's precious combat-ready Wildcats were transferred out, and squadron personnel were unceremoniously deposited at Camp Kearney (now Miramar Naval Air Station) on Christmas Eve. In the tremendous expansion necessary with the onset of hostilities, VMF-121 became an incubator of sorts. It provided the nucleus of MAG-12, which in turn spawned three new squadrons: VMF-122, 123, and 124.

Meanwhile, the war progressed with increasing violence and misfortune in the Pacific. The Japanese, in a stunning display of power and audacity, swept to undreamed-of success from Hawaii to the Philippines to the oil-rich Dutch East Indies.

Some 2,300 statute miles west of Pearl Harbor waited a pitifully small group of Wildcat pilots who would bleed the Japanese considerably. In fact, by orders of magnitude beyond what could reasonably have been expected.

Major Paul Putnam's dozen F4F-3s had only been on Wake Island four days when the war began. Flown in from the *Enterprise*, the forward echelon of VMF-211 found the island garrison barely ready to receive the newcomers. The squadron had forty-seven enlisted men—mostly ordnance specalists—but few facilities. The longest runway was a narrow strip about 5,700 feet long, but there were no revetments, no early-warning radar, and inadequate parking ramps. Refueling was accomplished by hand pumps.

Two-Eleven had been redesignated from VMF-2 at Ewa in July. Putnam had been CO only since November, and the squadron was among the last to transition from F3Fs. Therefore, though the experience level of pilots was generally high—most had 800 hours or more of flight time—the squadron was still learning about the F4F. On the average, each pilot had logged only about thirty hours in type, and there had been no gunnery or bombing practice in the new Grummans.[4]

Under such conditions, Putnam realized his half-squadron couldn't hope to manage a set-piece interception. The alternative was to maintain a four-plane CAP at the most likely hours. And a glance at the map showed the obvious threat: the Imperial Navy's 24th Air Flotilla, based at Kwajalein Atoll in the Marshall Islands, 600 nautical miles to the south.

Mitsubishi G3Ms raided the Marines for the first time shortly before noon on 8 December, local time. (Wake, being across the Date Line, was 22 hours ahead of Hawaii.) A CAP earlier that morning had been uneventful, but when the bombers finally attacked, Captain

Henry Elrod's four Wildcats were at 12,000 feet to the north of the island. Concealed by a rain squall, some three dozen of the twin-engine bombers came in at low level and played merry hell. Before launch from the *Enterprise*, VMF-211 had received an intelligence briefing on Japanese aircraft but these twin-tailed raiders (later called Nells by Allied airmen) remained unknown until they appeared over Wake. Bombing and strafing, they destroyed seven of the eight parked F4Fs. Personnel casualties were also heavy: twenty men killed and eleven wounded. It amounted to half the squadron roster, including three pilots dead and one injured, and all the mechanics killed or wounded. In ten minutes, Wake's effective air force was reduced to five aircraft and eight pilots.

Nor was that all. The runways were holed, though easily repaired, but 211 lost irreplaceable materiel in the form of over 12,000 gallons of fuel, plus oxygen bottles, tools, spare parts, and maintenance manuals. Putnam's men were short of everything but guts and initiative, as they proved the next day.

Lieutenant Dave Kliewer and Sergeant W. J. Hamilton were upstairs at 1145 when the bombers returned. The two Marines attacked and their .50-calibers scored; they knocked down one bomber while AA gunners destroyed another. But the F4F's first success went almost unnoticed as the Japanese knocked out Wake's radio station and hit the hospital. Another twenty-six Nells returned at 1045 on the tenth, and Captain Henry Elrod hacked down two, but the others blew up most of Wake's remaining major-caliber ammunition.

There was little doubt the Japanese would attempt to recapture Wake, and the five remaining F4Fs were crucial to the defense. By swapping and cannibalizing, four could be maintained airworthy, and this job fell to Lieutenant John Kinney. With no mechanics available, Kinney and his assistant, Sergeant Hamilton, had to oversee all maintenance and perform most of it. After a few days they discovered a Navy chief named Hesson who had no experience with F4Fs, but knew his trade. Kinney had nearly completed his commercial airframe and engine license while working at Pan American Airways before starting flight training, so he was just the man for the job.

Scrounging tools was the first order of business. Kinney and company borrowed tractor tools from the civilian construction contractor, and "gundecked" most everything else. "We had to improvise a gauge, for instance, to measure the pitch of the electric propeller when we changed an engine," he recalls. "We would measure the setting from an operating F4F and use it for the new installation."[5]

Engine changes were accomplished with the aid of a hoist on a farmall tractor, but for counter-balance the Marines employed four men standing on the rear of the tractor. In at least one instance an invaluable engine was removed from a burning Wildcat after an air raid. Fortunately, Grumman had designed one of the first quick-exchange components in the Wildcat, allowing the entire engine assembly (firewall forward) to be removed or installed easily. Two bolts were withdrawn, enabling all fluid lines between engine and cockpit to be disengaged. This amounted to a time-saving of several hours, and Kinney's crew changed a number of engines with the QEC setup overnight, with inexperienced men.

Running out of shotgun-style starter cartridges, the innovative Marines devised a manual method of starting the Pratt and Whitneys. A slingshot of sorts was made of truck inner-tube tires, with a boot which fitted over the end of one propeller blade. One man held the prop stationary against the tension of several others pulling on the inner tubes. When the "slingshot crew" exerted tension, the individual holding the prop blade let go and the inner-tube shot out between the two lines of men. This method was crude, time-consuming, and unreliable. It was also ingenious, for it insured the Wildcats kept flying. Mused Kinney, "It seemed to me that if we could have had a couple more revolutions per start attempt, we could have always obtained a start."[6]

Improvisation was mandatory. Captain Herb Frueler conjured up a plumbing equalizer system to transfer welding oxygen from the civilians' large bottles to the much smaller aircraft bottles for high-altitude flight. And he took the mounting bands from Navy water-fillable practice bombs, adapted them to Army high-explosive, and thereby enabled the F4Fs to carry 100-pounders. Otherwise, the Navy bomb racks wouldn't have accepted Army ordnance.

He was just in time. The Japanese made their first landing attempt early in the morning of the eleventh, with three light cruisers, six destroyers, two destroyer-transports and two Marus. Approaching from the south at 0520, the would-be conquerors ran up against Marine Corps marksmanship. At an initial range of 6,000 yards the gunners of the First Defense Battalion picked their targets and allowed the ships to close in. At 0610 the 5-inchers began to hammer round after round into the X-rings of two destroyers. One was shot to pieces, eventually drifting ashore as a perforated hulk. The other was literally blown out of the water, and two more received hits.

An hour and a quarter after the commence-fire order, four Wildcats attacked with .50-calibers and 100-pound bombs. They dived on the light cruiser *Tenryu* from her starboard bow, shooting the aging CL full of half-inch holes. Making smoke, the Japanese pulled off to the southwest but the Wildcats had their teeth into their prey and wouldn't turn loose. Thirty miles out they worked over the destroyer *Kisaragi*, with gratifying results. Somebody's bomb or .50-calibers— not even the Japanese were sure—found her depth charges. There was "a huge explosion" and the DD sank with all 150 crewmen.[7] Later that day, Dave Kliewer dropped two 100-pounders on a submarine ten miles south of the island, with undetermined results. But the occupation force was by then en route back to Kwajalein to rethink its plan.

Kawanishi flying boats pestered Wake early on the twelfth, and Captain Frank Tharin spared one the tedium of a return trip. There were no raids on the thirteenth, but the wear and tear plus one takeoff accident had now reduced VMF-211 to just two flyable Wildcats.

During the next eleven days more air attacks were flown from Kwajalein. And beginning the 21st, the carriers *Soryu* and *Hiryu*, diverted from the returning Pearl Harbor strike force, pitched in with their 100 aircraft. All told, the final assault against Wake was mounted by twenty-two ships of the Imperial Navy against the grimy, exhausted surviving Marines.

The penultimate day was 22 December. Herb Frueler and Lieutenant C. R. Davidson were aloft in the last Wildcats to intercept a thirty-nine-plane raid from the *Soryu* and *Hiryu*. At 20-to-1 odds the F4Fs attacked. Davidson disappeared in the tussle with six escorting Zeros, though Frueler got through to the bombers and shot down two Nakajima 97s. The second one blew up in his face, crippling his Wildcat. Somehow he evaded a vengeful Zero which put a bullet through his shoulder, and crash-landed Wake's last airplane. Years later Americans learned that Frueler had exacted a measure of revenge for Pearl Harbor. One of the bomber crews he killed had been credited with sinking the *Arizona* on 7 December.

The airmen who could raise a rifle or pistol waited for the climax, and it came early the next morning. In the wee hours of the 23rd, Japanese marines came ashore from two converted destroyers and two barges. In scattered groups the fighting continued from before dawn until after mid-day. At the end, Putnam had merely six men from his original sixty-one available for ground defense. Hank Elrod was killed when 211's position was overrun. Nobody in the States knew what happened for three and a half years; after the story was pieced together, in 1946 Elrod retroactively became the first F4F pilot awarded the Medal of Honor.[8]

The Wake Wildcats were the first Navy or Marine fighters to engage the Japanese. They claimed eight enemy planes shot down in exchange for two F4Fs actually lost in aerial combat, and the Japanese admitted the loss of ten, including one to AA fire. Two-Eleven's record is all the more impressive when one remembers that none of the pilots had flown a gunnery mission in F4Fs before arrival at Wake. In the air and on the ground—particularly from the maintenance aspect—Putnam's men worked minor miracles. It was not the sort of dedication the Japanese had expected from presumably pampered, comfort-loving Americans.

Yet Americans are capable of such things, whether the siege has been the Alamo or Wake Island. And if praise from the enemy is the highest possible in military circles, VMF-211 received high praise indeed. Interrogated after the war, a Japanese naval officer who was present at Wake said, "The American fighter pilots were admired for their skill and bravery."[9]

Retaliation for Pearl and Wake was quick in coming, if not up to scale. Through February and into early March the three active Pacific Fleet carriers conducted six raids against Japanese-held islands. The *Saratoga* had been torpedoed by a submarine in mid-January and was out of commission for five months. But the *Yorktown* was quickly dispatched from Norfolk, arriving in time for the first operation. She re-embarked VF-42, which had been operating with her through much of 1941. When Fighting Five was at sea on neutrality patrol, Captain Elliot Buckmaster insisted on Fighting 42, and he got his way.

But there were last-minute problems. Though VF-42's Wildcats had been fitted with self-sealing fuel tanks and armor plate at Norfolk, the old-style tubular gunsights were still retained upon departure. Only during a short stay at San Diego were reflecting sights obtained, featuring a 35-mil reticle (i.e., the reflected image subtended 35 feet at 1,000 feet.) The electric sights were jury-rigged en route west. But other problems plagued the squadron along the way, with rubber fuel cells featuring prominently. At least two planes were lost at sea during the *Yorktown's* transit, as bits of rubber flaked off and clogged fuel lines, leading to engine failure. It would prove a nagging problem for quite some time.

The initial carrier raid was a double-header against the Marshalls and Gilberts on 1 February. The *Enterprise* set her sights on Kwajalein, launching a full deck-load into the predawn darkness, 150 miles out. When the torpedo planes and dive-bombers had set course for their targets, six Wildcats of VF-6 climbed into their perch, orbiting and waiting for something to happen. Then big Lieutenant Jim Gray, a six-and-a-half foot Wisconsin pilot, led another half-dozen F4Fs toward Maloelap Island. But it was still nearly an hour to sunrise, and in the tropical blackness a young ensign apparently succumbed to vertigo during launch. His Wildcat stalled, spun, and splashed. Gray set course with five fighters.

Owing to darkness and sketchy charts, the VF-6 formation attacked the wrong target before discovering its real objective nearby. This was Taroa, a modern, well-equipped naval air station with two 5,000-foot runways, a pair of hangars, an administration building, and assorted amenities. Not to mention a well-stocked parking ramp with an estimated thirty-five to forty fighters and twin-engine bombers.

Gray's pilots dropped the rest of their light bombs, then made repeated strafing passes against the bombers. Then the Wildcats' guns began malfunctioning. It was by now a painfully familiar hex: ammo belts snarled at the top of the cans in negative-G maneuvers, or failed to feed on aluminum trays.

Then Japanese fighters hit the F4Fs from above. The *Enterprise* pilots reported "Type 96 and 97 plus one Zero."[10] Actually there were eleven A5Ms, the Type 96 carrier fighter later code-named Claude. It bore a resemblance to Nakajima's Type 97 Army fighter (Nate) but there were no Zeros. And a good thing, for the Wildcats' speed advantage was mainly what saved them.

Lieutenant (junior grade) W. E. Rawie, pulling out of his second pass, found two fixed-gear fighters approaching head-on. He bored in at the leader, narrowly avoided a collision, and triggered a quick burst as the Japanese pulled up. Then Rawie's last gun jammed and, like his three partners, he had no choice but to head for home. But his snap-shooting was good. The Claude went down, the first victim of a carrier-based F4F.

This left Jim Gray alone in an uneviable position. Caught at low level with one gun working, he never saw the Claudes until his third pass. He shot at two of them, claiming kills, but was immediately more concerned with mere survival.

Gray had been the youngest licensed pilot in the United States twelve years before. Now, however, any fledgling could have told him he was in deep trouble. With his rudder shot out, low on fuel, he plunged into a convenient cloud and tiptoed back home. When he plunked onto the Big E's deck he was unable to taxi out of the wire; he'd run out of gas. It was that close. His battered Wildcat had taken over thirty hits, including about fifteen dents in the improvised armor plate behind the seat. That 135 pounds of armor in the F4F-3 cut into performance—but sometimes it paid its own freight.

Wade McClusky had meanwhile led three two-plane sections to Wotje, a hop so short that "he barely had time to crank up the wheels of his Wildcat before he was over his target."[11] Sailors aboard the *Enterprise* watched the F4Fs make repeated gunnery runs at the airfield and harbor. But the largely unmolested bombers at Taroa were a major source of worry, and after nine intense hours of flight ops, Halsey hauled out.

Between 1530 and 1600 hours the retiring task force was pestered by Japanese aircraft. Lieutenant Roger Mehle, an Annapolis grad from Ohio, shot down a snooping floatplane and half an hour later joined McClusky and Lieutenant (junior grade) Jim Daniels in helping break up an attack by two Nells. The VF-6 trio, caught at an altitude disadvantage, had to watch AA gunners engage the bombers at 14,000 feet but caught one Mitsubishi following an ineffective bombing run. It splashed within sight of the task force. Halsey had been lucky.

That same day the *Yorktown* launched strikes against three island bases in the Gilberts. Fighting 42's Wildcats remained with the ship, and though the air group lost seven planes operationally in terrible weather, the Japanese remained curiously inattentive.

But about 1300 a two-plane section was scrambled in response to a radar plot 34 miles ahead of the ship. Ensigns E. S. McCuskey and John P. Adams glimpsed the intruder, a Kawanishi H6K flying boat. But the snooper ducked into the clouds, beginning a lethal game of hide-and-seek. Sailors listening to the fighter-direction channel heard the excited aviators whooping it up as they finally cornered the Mavis. Moments later burning fragments fell out of the clouds, spattering into the sea. "Doc" McCuskey, always ebullient, radioed that he and Adams had just shot off the Kawanishi's tail. Only he didn't say "tail."[12] Awhile later, after his colorful description appeared in print, a bemused McCuskey began receiving chastening letters from teachers and other citizens concerned that he'd corrupt the nation's youth.

The next operation came on 20 February when Lexington prepared to launch a strike against the naval-air complex at Rabaul, New Britain. The Bismarck Archipelago, situated northwest of the Solomons and directly east of New Guinea, was the major funnel through which Imperial Japan poured troops and materiel into both these important arenas. Therefore it offered a lucrative target.

But the *Lexington* never launched her intended strike. Instead, she would become the first carrier on either side in the Pacific to absorb a major land-based air attack. That she survived was due almost wholly to her fighter squadron, VF-3.

Lieutenant Commander John S. Thach hailed from Fordyce, Arkansas and the Academy Class of '27. He was widely known as Jimmy, owing to his resemblance to an older brother of that name who preceeded him at Annapolis. By early 1942 Thach was a highly experienced aviator with some 3,500 hours flight time and definite ideas on fighter tactics. He had grown up hunting pheasant, and believed that any pilot with a similar background was potentially good VF material. Therefore, he stressed gunnery and teamwork.

It was a philosophy shared by one of his division leaders; dark, husky Lieutenant Edward H. O'Hare from St. Louis and Chicago. Not quite twenty-eight, Butch O'Hare (Class of '37) had been with Thach since joining Fighting Three in 1940. They'd been on the squadron gunnery team which captured the fleet trophy flying F3Fs. By the end of 1940, Jimmy Thach was CO and his intense training had produced a passel of sharpshooters. Over half his pilots had earned the coveted Gunnery E, painted in traditional white with black shadowing on peacetime aircraft. But the days of making textbook passes on a towed banner target were behind them. From now on, Fighting Three would shoot for blood.

Nearly 400 nautical miles out of Rabaul that Tuesday, the Lex's radar developed a contact 35 miles to the south. Thach led his first division off the big carrier at 1015, leaving four Wildcats to orbit the ship while he investigated with his wingman, Ensign Ed Sellstrom. Expert fighter direction put the two F4Fs in visual contact of the snooper, a Mavis hiding in a rain squall. It was one of four which had left Rabaul early that morning on a sector search.

After a chase in and out of clouds and squall lines, the Wildcats gained a favorable position and attacked from overhead. It was the moment towards which Jimmy Thach's twelve years as a naval aviator had been directed. Bracketing the Kawanishi from port and starboard, the F4Fs' gunfire ruptured the fuel tanks and the giant seaplane careened burning into the ocean. Less than an hour later another Mavis was splashed by two more VF-3 pilots, but the search planes had notified their base of the Americans' presence.

The attack developed at 1630 as seventeen fat, round-bodied G4Ms of the Imperial Navy's Fourth Air Group approached. These were the first Bettys encountered by U.S. carrier pilots, and the *Lexington* folks were impressed. Fast, slick and dangerous, the new Mitsubishi "looked like a B-26 but acted like a wild Asiatic."[13]

Flying in two waves of eight and nine planes, the G4Ms were each armed with two 550-pound bombs, and they got within 25 miles before radar detected the first group at 11,000 feet. To complicate things, Lieutenant Commander Don Lovelace, VF-3's executive officer, was just leading his division into the landing pattern. The relief CAP flight of six planes under Lieutenant Noel Gayler never had time to form up. Vectored out by two-plane sections, Gayler's division arrived with a 2,000-foot altitude advantage. Lovelace and company barely had time to crank up its wheels, add power, and turn west toward the threat.

The Bettys, dark-green oblong shapes making 170 knots, were dangerously close before the first shots were fired. Gayler's pilots knocked down three and cut another out of formation before the G4Ms actually arrived over the *Lexington*, and precious moments were gained when the bombers turned in their approach to attack from astern. This allowed Don Lovelace's division to pile in at the last minute, and evidently the concentrated fighter attack disrupted Japanese accuracy. The nearest bombs fell some 3,000 yards from the carrier.

Meanwhile, Lex's deck crew worked like slaves, respotting F4Fs and SBDs. Jimmy Thach led three of his pilots in a hasty scramble, and personally caught two of the fleeting Bettys. He splashed one himself and shared the second, much as Gayler and Lovelace's people were doing. But as a reserve, Butch O'Hare and Lieutenant (junior grade) Marion Dufilho were kept near the ship. And a reserve was definitely needed. Fourteen of VF-3's 16 operational fighters were now committed, and two of those had been shot down. Some of the Japanese gunners were marksmen; Thach saw a direct hit on one F4F's canopy and watched the Grumman dive into the water. The other pilot was rescued, wounded, but both had fallen prey to the inherent danger of a stern attack. And Noel Gayler narrowly escaped when a 7.7-mm bullet starred the thick armor glass directly ahead of his face.

At 1700, just a half-hour after the first radar plot, another threat appeared on the *Lexington*'s CXAM set. But this time it was much closer and on the disengaged side of the task force. Nine miles to the east, eight more Bettys bored in—the second wave from Rabaul, completely unopposed. Five Wildcats were ready to come aboard, sucking the last gallons from their fuel tanks, and the remainder were too far out of position to intercept. It fell to O'Hare and Dufilho, who flew out on 080 degrees and rolled in from starboard on a high-side run as the Bettys descended in a fast, shallow dive towards the carrier.

Butch O'Hare was cool and professional. He made only beam or quartering runs, denying the deadly tail gunners a clear shot at him. He held his fire until about 100 yards out, then triggered his four .50-calibers in short, precise bursts against the nearest bomber in the V-of-V formation. The starboard engine gushed smoke which turned to flame, and O'Hare shifted targets. He continued his run, slanting down into the formation, and in the same pass engaged the next bomber in line. It lurched and banked into him as the Wildcat marked F-15 passed below the bombers and pulled up to port.

Only then did O'Hare realize he was alone. Dufilho's guns had jammed from the same damnable feed problem which had vexed F4F squadrons for months. O'Hare was on his own against six bombers.

It is said that twentieth-century wars are decided by weight of numbers and what strategists like to call fire superiority. The lone man, the solitary marksman, is considered a relic of the past, for presumably he can make no difference in modern warfare. But the fate of one-third of the Pacific Fleet's carrier strength now depended solely upon just such a man. Fortunately, Butch O'Hare in his own way was as much a marksman as Davy Crockett or Alvin York, and he acted accordingly.

On his next pass O'Hare concentrated on the two bombers trailing on the left side of the formation. Again closing the range to make sure, he flamed one G4M which dropped out, and pressed his run on the next in line. This bomber exploded as O'Hare's bullets found the engine and fuel tank.

By now the surviving five Bettys were within gun range of the task force. Despite flak bursts snapping around the formation and tracers from every bomber which could line up a gun, O'Hare dived in for a third pass, again from portside. He blew up the leader, and then there was nothing more he could do. Four Bettys pressed their attack, dropping bombs within 100 yards of the Lexington's stern even as Lovelace's fuel-starved Wildcats were catching the arresting wires and taxiing up the deck.

O'Hare, still hungry, fired nearly all his remaining ammo at one of the retreating survivors. Then he reined in and headed for the barn. His first request upon landing was for a glass of water, and small wonder. In a sizzling four minutes he made three gunnery passes, shooting five Bettys out of formation. Thach always said O'Hare had bagged six, but one which had been set afire somehow saved itself and limped back to Rabaul, though another ditched en route. Credited with five victories in his first combat, O'Hare became an instant celebrity. The fact that "only" four Bettys actually went down does nothing to diminish his feat of arms, for he had personally saved his ship from possible destruction or damage. It is uncertain whether the *Lexington*'s luck would have held out against the extra bombs of five more Bettys.

Against the loss of two F4Fs and one pilot, Fighting Three claimed fifteen of an estimated eighteen bombers. It was an unusually precise report, as the actual score was fifteen of seventeen, including the two which ditched on the way home. Seven Wildcats were damaged, including O'Hare's, which sustained one 7.7-mm bullet in the fuselage and two shrapnel hits in the wings.[14]

Originally recommended for a Navy cross, O'Hare received the Medal of Honor from President Roosevelt—the only carrier-based aviator among the eight F4F pilots eventually awarded that distinction. When the folks at Bethpage heard about his feat, they sent him the most precious gift they could imagine. Somehow, in ration-shortage wartime, they collected 5,000 cigarettes.

Four days later the *Enterprise* struck Wake—an ironic twist, since the Big E had delivered VMF-211 to that unhappy isle only eighty-three days before. The 24 February raid saw little aerial activity among the Japanese, though the McClusky-Mehle team splashed another Kawanishi. Then on 4 March the *Enterprise* hit Marcus Island, less 1,000 miles from Japan, but remarkably little resistance was stirred up.

However, on 10 March another joint venture was launched as the *Lexington* and *Yorktown* attacked Lae and Salamua in southeastern New Guinea. Both positions had recently fallen to the Japanese, and U.S. planners reckoned the harbor and port facilities would yield worthwhile targets. In the largest American carrier strike to date, 103 aircraft set course at 0840, flying north from the Papuan Gulf. Heading across the rugged, beautiful Owen–Stanley Mountains, the two air groups achieved complete surprise. The SBDs and TBDs sank three auxiliary vessels, but the only airborne targets were a pair of float biplanes, one of which Noel Gayler dropped into VF-3's growing bag. One Dauntless failed to return.

Thus ended the hit-and-run phase of the carrier war. Valuable lessons had been learned, and some of the materiel problems were addressed. The F4F's limitations were now known in relation to the opposition. Despite their weight penalty, armor plate and self-sealing tanks were retained for obvious reasons; but this did little to alleviate concern in the squadrons about the F4F-3's reduced performance. Speed was considered adequate, but maneuverability, climb, and range were all matters of concern.

However, some improvements were made. The easiest fix was shoulder harnesses, installed by the factory early in the war after a fatal flat-spin incident at Norfolk. Even so, they weren't generally retro-fitted until mid-1942, and didn't become standard until late that year. Some pilots balked, concerned about lost time in emergencies, but the straps proved life-savers and became universally accepted.

Realistically, however, the rate of attrition continued to tell in many squadrons. The war was still young, and VF-3 provides a grim reminder of how rapidly the percentages diminished with prolonged exposure. By year-end, five more Fighting Three veterans were dead, and only six of the nineteen who fought the battle off Rabaul would live to see V-J Day.

As an anonymous aviator later remarked, "The trouble with war is, the price is usually too high to enjoy it."

4. CORAL SEA AND MIDWAY

"... quenched the violence of fire, escaped the edge of the sword, out of weakness were made strong, waxed valiant in fight, turned to flight the armies of the aliens."

Hebrews 11:34

THE TROUBLED SPRING OF 1942 brought changes and combat to the carrier-borne Wildcat squadrons. By depriving the west-coast Marine fighter units of their newly-modified F4F-3s and -3As, Navy squadrons could be maintained for the time being. Fighting 2 in the *Lexington* proved the main beneficiary of this move, putting its F2A-3s ashore in favor of F4F-3s.

But there were other changes afoot for the "Flying Chiefs." Famous in prewar years as an elite squadron, VF-2 had been staffed almost entirely with enlisted pilots. This was due in large part to a 1932 law enacted by Congress which required that noncommissioned fliers compose one-fifth of the total naval aviator pool. The intent was presumably financial, as chief petty officers were paid less than ensigns, though anybody who'd ever set foot on a quarterdeck knew that good CPOs were worth about four times most fresh-caught ensigns.

These enlisted fliers were officially termed Naval Aviation Pilots. By 1941 the Navy had 850 of them, the Marines 45. As a group they performed magnificently throughout the war. Most NAPs were electronics, machinist, or ordnance specialists in their late twenties to early thirties, with a substantial amount of flight time. As such, they brought with them a degree of experience and professionalism which their newly-commissioned counterparts often couldn't match.

35

Fighting 2, with a solid background of NAP experience and tradition, made excellent use of its non-com pilots. Other squadrons regrettably didn't always follow suit. The Navy has been called the most rank-conscious of American armed forces, and a good many officers wearing Annapolis rings openly discriminated against NAPs. In some extreme cases, experienced chiefs weren't even assigned flying duties. To a lesser extent, this attitude became institutionalized after the war when former NAPs who gained commissions were labled "limited duty officers." They could achieve squadron command, but little more since their careers usually peaked at commander or lieutenant colonel.

Still, some squadron commanders were ruled by pragmatism rather than pride. In division organization the most experienced airman, regardless of rank, was made leader. It's interesting to note that in such a non-democratic force as the Luftwaffe this practice was widespread (unlike the Royal Air Force), while most of the Imperial Navy's pilots were non-commissioned.

Fighting 2's skipper was among the more enlightened fighter squadron commanders in the United States Navy. Enormously respected as a pilot's pilot and a leader's leader, the hard-charging, flamboyant Lieutenant Commander Paul Ramsey from the Class of '27 was already on his way to an outstanding career. An extremely enthusiastic aviator, he recognized his NAPs for the experienced professionals they were. But he lost ten of them during April in a transfer to the more traditional VF-6 in the *Enterprise*. Filled out with replacement pilots—mostly ensigns and jaygees from VF-3—Fighting 2 rode the *Lexington* to the Southwest Pacific, where something big was brewing.

The *Yorktown* was already there. On 4 May she launched strikes against Tulagi, a new Japanese base in the southern Solomons. Bombing, Scouting, and Torpedo 5 all pitched in while Rear Admiral Fletcher kept Charlie Fenton's VF-42 with the task force. There seemed little chance of serious airborne opposition to the bombers, since Tulagi was known to harbor only seaplanes.

That was true enough, and SBDs shot down the first "meatball" which bothered them; a Nakajima 95 Dave. But shortly after 1300 the *Yorktown* heard Torpedo 5 report more interceptors. Unsure of the exact situation, a division of Wildcats was scrambled to lend a hand from 100 nautical miles south.

Lieutenant (jg) Bill Leonard's pilots had expected only to taxi their planes for respotting. His section leader, Doc McCuskey, hadn't even bothered to take a plotting board. So the four Wildcats departed hastily, penetrating a cold front in a fast cruise. Emerging into the clear, Leonard took his division over the high central mountains of the big island called Guadalcanal, then dropped down, hunting the reported bandits.

By this time the TBDs had shot down another floatplane and driven off the others, so Leonard elected to escort the bombers back along the Florida coast. But he was in luck. Three float biplanes appeared in line astern formation. Leonard rocked his wings, alerting his wingman Ed Bassett, and the lead section split for opposite-side gunnery runs on the newcomers.

Leonard drew a bead on the second plane in line as Bassett took the third. The floatplane pulled up in a climbing turn to meet the overhead threat, shooting as it came. But Leonard connected and his target dropped flaming into the water. Recovering low, he craned his neck, looking for the enemy leader. When Leonard found him, it was where he least expected—on his tail. Marveling at the Jap's maneuverability, Leonard cooly accepted the possibility of a full-deflection shot by the floatplane, and pushed his throttle, mixture, and prop controls to the firewall, pulling into a climbing turn. Safely overhead again, he nosed down and dumped the bandit in a head-on run. It made two sure kills in his first combat, lasting under three minutes.

Bassett had chased his victim back toward Tulagi, reeled him in and splashed him. Fighting 42 had destroyed the first Mitsubishi F1Ms encountered by the U.S. Navy. These Type O observation planes had come from the Shortlands, up near Bougainville, and Bill Leonard sketched remarkably accurate profiles of them, right down to the tapered wings. Thus did Pete enter the lexicon of Allied airmen. But Pete would require some careful handling; his maneuverability was astonishing.[1]

Heading home, the four Wildcats found a lone TBD and Leonard split the division, putting two fighters on either side of the torpedo plane. Entering the cold front again, this would give better prospects for sighting the *Yorktown*. But the torpedo pilot was so low on fuel that he turned back, preferring to ditch near Guadalcanal. Leonard was then free to climb through the clouds to home in with the YE-ZB equipment, but Doc McCuskey, with radio trouble, missed the signal. He and Ensign John Adams also landed on Guadalcanal, setting their Wildcats down on the beach with wheels half extended. They radioed *Yorktown* of their intention to indulge in "a stretch of beach combing," but it was no laughing matter. Johnny Adams had been in radio contact with the ship throughout this escapade but felt bound to

remain with his leader. The destroyer *Hammann* retrieved them,
though Charlie Fenton was vocal in his displeasure over McCuskey's
loss of two fighters.[2]

The Tulagi raid was hailed as a tremendous victory since the
Yorktown squadrons were credited with sinking fourteen enemy
warships. In reality, they wrecked a destroyer, three minesweepers
and damaged two other DDs. But his otherwise obscure action served
as curtain-raiser to a much larger and far-reaching event.

Both sides now possessed information on the approximate location
and composition of the opposition: the Americans through cryptanal-
ysis, the Japanese through maritime reconnaissance. The *Yorktown*
was snooped by a Mavis before 0800 on the fifth, and VF-42 launched
a division to handle it. Lieutenant Vince McCormack, the flight
officer, led his pilots on a 30-mile vector to the southwest where he
found the now-familiar Kawanishi silhouette below 1,000 feet. The
Yorktowners made four or five separate gunnery runs, burning the
big seaplane with an economical 260 rounds.

Next day the *Yorktown* task force joined the *Lexington*'s, under
tactical command of Rear Admiral Aubrey Fitch in the Lex. The
code-breakers knew of Japan's ambitious plan to occupy Port
Morseby on New Guinea's southeast coast as prelude to an invasion of
northern Australia. The enemy fleet was composed of a transport
group, covering group, and the Fifth Carrier Division with the *Shokaku* and *Zuikaku*. Fitch's task force was to intercept and disrupt the
Port Morseby occupation force.

The world's first aircraft carrier battle was 24 hours away. Viewed
solely from the flattop viewpoint, it shaped up as an approximately
equal contest. Both sides possessed two fleet carriers with some 120
aircraft. Rear Admiral Goto's covering group with the CVL *Shoho*
had another eighteen planes, including a mixture of fighters; eight
Zeros and four Type 96 Claudes. Rear Admiral Hara's CarDivFive
had 100 percent availability among its thirty-six Zeros. On the American side, Paul Ramsey's maintenance crew promised him nineteen
operational Wildcats of the twenty-one embarked in Lex while Fighting 42 gave up-checks to all seventeen of Fenton's dash threes.

The sun rose on the eastern rim of the Coral Sea on 7 May to reveal
good flying weather, and the Japanese spread their search net over a
goodly portion of that well-named body of water. Twelve Kates and
four cruiser floatplanes fanned out, probing for the American carriers
while Bettys from Rabaul and Mavises from the lately disturbed nest
at Tulagi joined in. Almost simultaneously Dauntlesses from Task

Force 17 began their wedge-shaped scouting patterns, aided by land-based bombers from Australia.

Both sides found elements of the opposing fleet and both acted upon the information. And, as if the fates were determined to withhold their favors for the moment, both sides launched air strikes at the wrong targets.

One of Hara's Nakajimas discovered a small force some 150 miles south of CarDiv Five, reporting a carrier. Hara hastened to fling a seventy-eight-plane attack at this "priority" target at 0800. But there was no carrier—only the oiler *Neosho* and destroyer *Sims*. The U.S. flattops were 300 nautical miles to the west. The *Neosho* had narrowly avoided destruction at Pearl Harbor exactly five months before—but not today. Both ships were overwhelmed in the attack, depriving Fletcher and Fitch of half their refueling group.

Meanwhile, a *Yorktown* SBD came across part of the Morseby-bound transports' support group of light cruisers, 220 miles northwest of Task Force 17. The scout's message specified two carriers and four cruisers; it had to be Vice Admiral Takagi's striking force with the *Shokaku* and *Zuikaku* under Hara. The Lex and *Yorktown* prepared to launch.

The *Lexington*'s forty-plane launch commenced at 0920 and continued for 30 minutes. Ramsey led ten Fighting 2 Wildcats off her deck, followed by twenty-eight Dauntlesses and twelve Devastators. The SBDs climbed to about 16,000 feet escorted by a division under Lieutenant Fred Borries—better known to football fans as "Buzz," who'd scored some of Navy's biggest touchdowns against Army in a bygone era. A section of F4Fs stuck with the CAG, Commander Bill Ault, at 10,000 and Paul Ramsey's division provided escort to the TBDs down low.

There was little standardization in U.S. carrier doctrine at this time. After all, nobody had ever fought a flattop battle before. But *Lexington* Air Group preferred to form up near the task force, assembling into an organized unit before heading out. Therefore, Lex's strike didn't set course until 0947.

The *Yorktown* worked differently. The dive-bombers launched first, climbing to 18,000 feet over the task force while the TBDs went directly ahead at 500 feet, indicating a mere 100 knots with their heavy Mark 13 torpedoes. Finally came two divisions of VF-42. Vince McCormack, who'd splashed a Mavis two days before, was assigned to cover the Dauntlesses. The second division was led by Lieutenant Commander James Flatley, who by rights shouldn't have been there at all. He had orders to return to San Diego and form VF-10, as he was in line for a command of his own. But with a chance to tangle with Japanese carriers only days away, he wouldn't hear of it. Friendly but intense, he'd talked his way into this battle, and now he was escorting Torpedo 5. Charlie Fenton stayed home to run the CAP while Oscar Pederson as CAG handled fighter direction.

In aviator's parlance, the *Yorktown* Air Group made a running rendezvous. The SBDs and F4Fs had a 30-knot edge on the torpeckers and caught up with them en route. Both systems had advantages; the "deferred departure" of Lex's squadrons insured tactical cohesiveness on the way out but ate into fuel reserves. The Yorktowners got best mileage but ran the risk of losing contact along the way. The one common feature was ratio of fighters in each formation: one Wildcat for every five bombers.

Ninety-three TF-17 planes were on course by 1015, the largest carrier-launched air strike the U.S. Navy would put up until nearly the end of 1943. But barely had the two air groups disappeared to the north when the *Yorktown*'s scout landed aboard with disturbing news. He'd mismatched the grid on his code pad. Instead of reporting the light cruisers he'd actually found, he'd sent a contact report of two flattops. Radio failure on the return leg imposed the delay.

A correction was radioed to the strike groups, but by then events had taken charge. Another Mavis appeared, getting within a mere ten miles of the task force before Dick Crommelin and his wingman shot it down at 1100. By now there was no doubt in anyone's mind that the Japanese knew where to find TF-17.

But the U.S. fliers had a hostile flight deck in sight. The *Lexington*'s strike found Rear Admiral Goto's covering force at 1045, with the *Shoho* and escorts heading northwest off Misima Island. Fighting 2 got in the first shooting. Near the island, Paul Ramsey noted a twin-float biplane on a reciprocal heading, low on the water. He detached his second section to handle the nuisance, remaining with his own wingman at 5,000 feet to cover the TBDs. Lieutenant (jg) Paul Baker, an ex-NAP, jumped the Kawanishi 94 (later code-named Alf) at about 500 feet and got in some accurate shooting. The float-plane alit on the water, apparently damaged, but Baker didn't want to stick around. He led his wingman back to the northwest, hoping to rejoin Ramsey before the main event began.

The *Shoho* was taken by surprise. She'd just recovered a Zero CAP and only launched one Zero and two Claudes before the *Lexington*'s attack began. As VB-2 deployed, Buzz Borries kept his division on the perch, watching the torpedo planes swing wide for an anvil attack. At

1118, as a combined dive-bombing and torpedo attack developed, the *Shoho* had her bows into the wind and launched three Zeros.

Two Claudes met Torpedo 2 as the TBDs split for their opposite-bow approaches. But at this moment Paul Baker's section arrived and intercepted before the Japanese could interfere. The Claudes indulged in some nifty aerobatics, evidently hoping to lure the Wildcats into a dogfight, but Baker wasn't buying it. He kept up his speed, retained his height advantage, and controlled the combat nicely. It was mainly snap-shooting, his bullets kicking up big plumes of spray in the water, as hasty setups presented themselves. Perhaps feeling good about starting the day by downing a floatplane, he claimed both Claudes as well, but apparently they survived this encounter.

That aggressive aviator, Paul Ramsey, saw no hostile fighters. But he professionally set about noting the *Lexington* squadrons' attacks, compiling information for the debriefing. Torpedo 2 was also professional. Its anvil attack netted five hits on the light carrier.

The *Yorktown* Air Group was fifteen minute behind. Scouting 5 attacked at 1125, contested by three Zeros. But the Mitsubishis couldn't easily stay with the SBDs in a dive, and they did little harm. Lieutenant Wally Short's Bombing 5 pushed over moments later, and the *Shoho* coasted to a stop, burning. The engagement was by now, for practical purposes, over. But these things have a momentum of their own, and the action continued.

Jim Flatley, leading his division at 10,000 feet, had a better view of the *Shoho* than Torpedo 5. Therefore, he radioed instructions to the TBDs and helped them set up the most efficient approach. As professional as Ramsey, he quickly concluded that VT-5's attack was probably unnecessary, as the carrier was done for. He made a mental note to recommend a strike co-ordinator from now on, to assign unused ordnance to more lucrative targets.

He also saw something else: two Claudes stalking some SBDs. Since the *Shoho* only launched two Type 96s and four Zeros during this action, Flatley's pigeons were surely the same ones Baker of VF-2 had jumped. Flately nosed into a steep spiral to keep the Claudes in view, followed by his division. It was a neat setup. The Claude he chose as his victim was caught at low level with little maneuvering room. Though it indulged in some spectacular evolutions, Flatley had only to press the trigger and walk his bullets on target by reference to splashes in the water. When the lead Wildcat pulled out at 500 feet, the little fixed-gear fighter smashed into the sea.

Flatley wisely pulled up, grabbing back the altitude he'd used in his attack, and a good thing, too. A Zero happened along just then, and though Flatley tried to catch up, the A6M climbed out of danger. Other F4F pilots fought inconclusive engagements with Zeros, quickly gaining an unpleasant knowledge of the remarkable little fighter's capability.

Ensign Walt Haas fared better. He'd regained some altitude after the initial tussle and noticed a fleeting Japanese plane outpacing a pursuing F4F. With good position and height, Haas hauled into gun range and fired from six o'clock. The Jap foolishly slow-rolled, losing airspeed, and climbed to starboard. Haas pulled deflection and hit him again. The Japanese stood up as if ready to bail out of his burning plane, but it went into the water before he jumped.

Identified as a Type 96 at the time, this was nevertheless the first Zero shot down by any F4F. All credit to Haas and Fighting 42, though the error seems peculiar since Claudes had fixed landing gear. But moments later Haas did bag a 96. He saw a nearby scrap in which the enemy pilot skillfully feigned destruction, falling away from another Wildcat in a dive toward the water. Abruptly the Mitsubishi pulled out and ran for it, with enough head-start to escape. But as before, Haas was positioned for a stern chase and overtook the bandit from a dive. He placed his gunsight reticle squarely on the Claude's fuselage and fired from close range. The plane exploded, scattering debris into the water.

The main phase of the battle was now over. The *Shoho* was sinking and the U.S. strike groups had turned for home. Wildcats claimed five shootdowns over the Japanese ships; three by VF-42 and Baker's pair for Fighting 2. While Baker apparently did destroy the floatplane before engaging in the carrier attack, only the *Yorktown* F4Fs actually scored against the *Shoho*'s fighters. The SBD squadrons reported six hostiles splashed, but in reality got none. It didn't much matter— they'd helped sink the first Japanese ship of the war bigger than a destroyer.

But the Emperor's "sea eagles" weren't about to let that situation go unavenged. That afternoon Rear Admiral Hara launched twelve Vals and fifteen Kates under the tactical leadership of the *Zuikaku*'s air group commander. Armed with accurate information of the Americans' position, Lieutenant Commander Takahashi led his twenty-seven planes into one of the most bizarre episodes in the history of carrier warfare.

Task Force 17 had launched three fighter divisions at 1520, an hour before the Japanese strike went winging southward. Japanese snoopers were almost certainly following the Americans, but the CAP found nothing during two vectors. Then radar plotted a major inbound contact. It was an inopportune time for an air raid. The dozen airborne F4Fs had been up nearly two ours, darkness was fast setting in, and heavy clouds further reduced visibility. The force fighter director, Lieutenant F. F. "Red" Gill in the *Lexington*, determined that conditions were unfavorable for a forward interception. So he sent Paul Ramsey's division outbound because it had IFF, and kept the VF-42 and second VF-2 flights near the force.

Then he scrambled seventeen more Wildcats. The *Yorktown* put up twelve and the *Lexington* another half-dozen. Thus, in gathering darkness thirty fighters prepared to defend Task Force 17 against the first carrier-launched strike ever flung at American flattops.

Gill worked Ramsey's four planes 30 miles to the southeast. Flying at 5,000 feet the mustached CO looked down and saw a V formation of strange aircraft. They were nine Nakajima 97s, and the FDO had positioned the Wildcats for a beautiful bounce. Ramsey took one side of the Kate formation with his wingman, assigning his experienced section leader, Paul Baker, to the other side. Then, in a gorgeous display of aerial gunnery, Paul Ramsey initiated a high-side pass from extreme range, placing his first tracers smack on target at 700 yards. The Nakajima exploded as the CO pressed his run on a second Kate, which also flamed and dropped into the murk. Another clean kill.

On the opposite side of the formation, Baker and his wingman destroyed a third Kate and damaged a fourth. Then Baker pursued another of the harried torpedo planes, but was lost from view in the darkening sky. He was never seen again. His wingman eventually reported an explosion in the clouds, and some theorized that the former NAP had collided with his intended victim.

Fighting 2's first division had completely broken up the Japanese torpedo attack before it even developed. Ramsey and his team had shot down five Kates (he radioed Lex he'd bagged four fighters) and scattered the others all over the evening sky. But now his Wildcats were low on fuel and returned to the task force, awaiting events.

But events took care of themselves. In about twelve minutes, amid a scattered series of running battles, the CAP knocked down a total of seven Kates and a Val. Another Nakajima ditched with battle damage while headed home. Jim Flatley's *Yorktown* division got in most of the additional shooting as his F4Fs pounced on a group of bogies emerging from a cloud bank. The Fighting 42 pilots knocked down two more torpedo planes and a dive bomber, as the night sky was full of milling, confused airmen in Grummans, Aichis, and Nakajimas.

The *Yorktown*'s LSO, Lieutenant Norwood Campbell, nearly brought aboard the first of three Vals on a long final. Other hostiles flew close aboard the *Lexington*, and nervous AA gunners shot at anything. Things got so tense that somebody in the *Yorktown* announced "Stand by to repel boarders."[3]

Finally things settled down. Though few American carrier pilots were qualified for night landings, they all got aboard. All, that is, but one. Somewhere amid the melee with red tracers, looming dark clouds, and blacked-out ships, a *Yorktown* F4F disappeared. And the surviving Japanese expertly navigated back to their force, though only eighteen of the twenty-seven returned.

Thus ended the first day of the world's first carrier duel. Round two started next morning at 0600.

At dawn on 8 May the balance was little changed. Despite the loss of the *Shoho* and her planes, relative air strengths were roughly equal: 117 TF-17 planes operational to 95 in *Shokaku* and *Zuikaku*. The Americans had a big advantage in dive-bombers but Hara had slightly more fighters and torpedo planes. The fighter situation stacked up to thirty-seven Zeros against thirty-one Wildcats.

But that wasn't as important as the weather. Heavy clouds blanketed Hara's operating area while TF-17 steamed in the clear, open to easy sighting to the south. Both sides put up their CAPs and sent their scouts sniffing the night's cold trail, trying to pick up the scent. As before, both teams found the opposition and flung nearly simultaneous strikes.

A Scouting 2 SBD found Hara 200 miles northeast of TF-17, course due north. The *Lexington* launched fifteen Dauntlesses and twelve TBDs escorted by nine F4Fs under the nominal control of Lieutenant Noel Gayler, on loan from VF-3. The *Yorktown* Air Group put up twenty-four SBDs, nine TBDs and six Wildcats, all on course by 0930.

This time the Yorktowners were first in line. Fighting 42 skipper Charlie Fenton and his wingman stayed with the Dauntlesses while Bill Leonard's division escorted VT-5, flying at 2,000 feet. Leonard and company maintained a weave above the TBDs, keeping a 130-knot airspeed for maneuvering should it prove necessary. This differed from Fighting 2's practice, as Noel Gayler's division made only 105 knots at 6,000 feet covering Torpedo 2.

The two strikes amounted to sixty bombers and fifteen fighters, but direct fighter support wasn't possible over the target. Fenton's section lost contact with its Dauntlesses as the SBDs actually outpaced the F4Fs in a shallow climb. It wasn't a good omen, particularly when the American aviators noticed a large formation on a reciprocal heading.

It was the Japanese strike, headed for Task Force 17. Neither side had enough fuel to engage. All anyone could do was press on and hope his flight deck was still there when he returned.

When the *Yorktown*'s air group arrived over CarDiv Five, Hara had six Zeros up on CAP. Seven more would be launched during the attack, nearly equalling the total Wildcat escort. Fenton, trailing the Dauntlesses, would remain high during the strike, intending to mix it up with any Japanese interceptors after the SBDs. As it turned out, he saw none.

Leonard saw plenty. Following the dive-bombing attack which damaged the *Shokaku*, VT-5 went in. Flying at wavetop height the two Wildcat sections were covering Lieutenant Commander Joe Taylor's TBDs when Doc McCuskey on Leonard's starboard wing saw three Zeros approaching from ten o'clock high. McCuskey hauled up and over Leonard, spoiling the Japanese leader's tracking. The other two Zeros jumped Leonard, who avoided them with some hard turns and popped into a cloud. Meanwhile, McCuskey saw a shot developing as a Zero chandelled. He nosed up, cranked in deflection as the Zero slowed, and fired. His aim was good. The A6M went right into the water, guns firing as it splashed.

The second section of Ensigns Bill Woollen and Johnny Adams had stayed with the TBDs which were nearing their drop point on the *Shokaku*. The two Wildcats bounced a pair of Zeros harassing the torpedo planes, and Woollen hit one solidly enough to claim its destruction. At any rate, Torpedo 5 continued its run without serious interference. Following the torpedo attack (which gained no hits) Leonard regrouped his troops, but McCuskey was missing. He'd found some enthusiastic playmates who chased him in and out of the clouds before escaping their unwanted attention, and set sail for home by himself. Fenton's section was also headed back as the *Yorktown*'s strike had badly damaged the *Shokaku*, at a cost of two SBDs.

The veteran enemy flattop probably wouldn't have survived if the *Lexington*'s air group had arrived intact. But the heavy clouds broke up the Minutemen en route. Bombing 2 never made contact, and a three-plane fighter division under Lieutenant Albert O. Vorse had to abort when it became separated from the formation. That left the CAG division of four SBDs, Torpedo 2 with eleven TBDs and six Wildcats.

There were now a dozen Zekes up and alerted. Three spotted the CAG flight with two F4Fs between 5,000 and 6,000 feet, and they attacked with superior position and speed but did no damage. And a good thing, as the *Lexington* formation had been low and slow. Lieutenant Richard Bull and Ensign John Bain, the F4F pilots, went down with the SBDs to cover Commander Ault, recovered lower yet, and were jumped from astern by two more Zeros. Bain turned the tables on one and probably bagged him as he overshot. But Dick Bull disappeared and wasn't seen again.

Things went no better for Noel Gayler's division escorting Torpedo 2. With only 105 knots on the dial, necessarily flying low to stay with the TBDs, the Wildcats were taken apart by four Zeros. Gayler's wingman disappeared after the first pass, and the second section was chased into some clouds, thereby dispersing the F4F escort. One of these pilots also failed to return and Gayler—"a bold, accomplished aviator," in the words of a contemproary—had all he could do to stay alive. He finally dodged his two assailants by the well-tested expedient of ducking into a handy cumulus.

John Bain provided the only direct support to VT-2, which he found retreating under Zero attack. He found one A6M crawling all over a TBD, and drove it off by expending his remaining ammo. Fighting 2 claimed three victories in the fracas over the Japanese carriers, though Bain's probable was evidently the only real kill. In exchange, three F4Fs had fallen to Zeros—an early lesson about keeping one's airspeed up to maneuvering momentum. Fighting 42 had done so and got away without loss.

Still, the Minutemen made an impression on the Japanese. Gayler's four Wildcats escorting eleven Devastators were reported by Zero pilots as twelve Grummans and thirty-two torpedo planes. Total Japanese fighter claims amounted to thirty-nine. In fact, one *Shokaku* pilot was credited with six confirmed and two probables—more than the actual total of two SBDs and VF-2's three Wildcats known or presumed lost in air combat.

But several homing Wildcat pilots helped redress the imbalance. Residue of the now-completed Japanese strike on the U.S. carriers ran afoul of returning F4Fs, and VF-42 benefitted the most. The *Yorktown* pilots splashed a returning Kate for sure and probably two Vals. Bill Leonard, shepherding a lone Dauntless, almost certainly shot down the *Shokaku* Air group commander, who had directed the strike on TF-17. But like the others, Leonard was too low on fuel to confirm the kill. Likewise, Noel Gayler probably destroyed one or two Aichis for VF-2.

Despite these successes after the fact, Japanese squadrons had swarmed over an inadequate defense. Well-informed of Fletcher's position, Hara's fliers had little difficulty finding their target. For unlike the Japanese ships, the *Lexington* and *Yorktown* were exposed under generally clear skies.

Things were complicated by lack of IFF in all U.S. planes, and time and effort were wasted by checking out radar blips which proved to be friendlies. False alarms heightened tension in the task force up to the genuine contact at 1055 when the *Yorktown*'s radar watch exclaimed, "Hey, look at that!" It covered about an inch of the five-inch scope, and the radar expert knew trouble was on the way.[4]

Indeed it was. The Americans thought there were 103 hostiles at the time, but actually there were 69 planes from the *Shokaku* and *Zuikaku*, including 33 Vals and 18 Kates.[5] The bearing was north-northeast, distance 68 miles and closing. With part of each fighter squadron escorting the strikes, only seventeen Wildcats were left to defend the task force—nine VF-2 planes of "Doris" and "Agnes" divisions and eight *Yorktown* fighters, call sign "Wildcat." They were augmented by twenty-three Dauntlesses flying inner air patrol as a low-level barrier aginst torpedo planes. The fighter directors ordered airborne planes to intercept or hold, depending upon the need, while scrambling the rest.

Paul Ramsey's three-plane Agnes Red section was directed out on the 020 radial with the contact down to 38 miles. Climbing to 10,000 feet, he was given a "Buster" which in fighter direction lingo meant "Step on it." Jim Flatley's VF-42 division was sent hunting inbound torpedo planes beyond the low-level SBD screen which remained about three miles from the carriers. Ordered down to 1,000 feet, Flatley kept at about 2,500 for better visibility.

Thus, nine Wildcats were intended to intercept the Japanese at 15 to 20 miles with the remaining eight directly over the task force. But too many F4Fs were kept low, and the versatile Japanese torpedo planes got in above them. Lacking prior experience with the Naka-jima 97, the Americans would learn the hard way that the Imperial Navy operated under few of the restrictions afflicting their own VT squadrons.

Fighting 2's lead division made first contact. Ensign Ed Sellstrom in Ramsey's section spotted many bogies overhead while still climb-ing 20 miles from the *Lexington*. He quickly estimated them as fifty to sixty hostiles, layered from ten to twelve grand as VT, VF, VB, and more VF on top. It was a good assessment, but a dangerous situation. The F4Fs had no chance of working up to proper altitude in time to intercept, and doing so under a Zero umbrella was hazardous at best. The other forward sections missed the bandits completely in clouds.

As the Kates split for their attack (twelve on the *Lexington*, four on the *Yorktown*) Sellstrom saw the situation developing but couldn't get Ramsey's attention. So he went freelancing. Diving on the Nakajimas with tremendous speed generated in a descent from 12,000 feet, he overhauled and splashed one less than five miles from the task force. This action drew a sharp response from three Zeros, and in the ensuing combat Sellstrom thought he knocked down two. In reality, no Japanese fighters were lost over TF-17, but Sellstrom had done just about all anyone could expect of a lone F4F.

The Kates had a little difficulty getting by the inner air patrol. Scouting 2 managed to dump a pair of B5Ns but then the Zeros came down and splashed four SBDs. The other Nakajimas pressed their attack, losing a couple to flak, but put two torpedoes into the *Lexington*. No more than five minutes later the Vals pushed over, unimpeded. Fourteen went for the *Yorktown* and nineteen for the *Lexington*, maneuvering to the north.

Only four VF-2 Wildcats, under Buzz Borries, stood a chance of intercepting the dive-bombing attack on the *Lexington*. These two sections—Doris Red and White—were over the Lex when six Zeros hit them at 12,000 feet. The engagement became a tailchase, interrupted momentarily by the arrival of Lieutenant (jg) Art Brassfield's *Yorktown* section. But both VF-42 pilots were swarmed by Mitsubishis and had to dive away to save themselves, one escaping in a shot-up Wildcat. Then Brassfield, having shaken his pursuers in a 6,000-foot dive, came across a Val near the *Lexington* and opened fire. But the Aichi exploded simultaneously with an AA burst, so credit was uncertain.

Only the Wildcat Brown section now remained topside. Orbiting the *Yorktown*, Vince McCormack and Walt Haas sighted Vals while climbing to 13,000 feet, and rolled into overhead runs, pressing through the thickening AA bursts. Spiralling steeply, trying to draw a bead on the surprisingly agile Aichis, the *Yorktown* pilots only got in some snap-shooting. But they may have helped disrupt the ordinarily excellent Japanese accuracy, as the *Yorktown* escaped with only one direct hit. But several near-misses compounded the damage.

Probably about this same time, unintended reinforcements arrived. Albert Vorse's bob-tailed VF-2 division returned after losing contact with the *Lexington*'s strike group. The three F4Fs found Vals diving on the *Yorktown*'s starboard quarter, and "Scoop" Vorse latched on to one and shot off its port wing.

The Japanese had now completed their attack, torpedoing the *Lexington* (mistaken as the *Saratoga*) and damaging the *Yorktown*.

But they had to fight their way out. Several bandits tangled with the low-level SBDs north of the task force, plus Vorse's three Wildcats and two more from VF-42. Vorse's wingman, Ensign Leon Haynes, claimed a probable Kate but Walt Haas, McCormack's number two, was shot at by his own *Yorktown* gunners. Then he was chased into some clouds by Zeros and emerged to find a convenient Val which he splashed from low level. In a short fight with another Zero he claimed hits and a kill, then called it a day.

Buzz Borries' scrap had now evolved into a good-sized tussle as ten F4Fs (including the two from VF-42) shot it out with five or six Zeros. The *Lexington* pilots claimed two shootdowns—erroneously, it turned out—but lost a pair themselves.

Jim Flatley's *Yorktown* division fought nine A6Ms but fared much better. That is, the Wildcat pilots survived. Seeing the SBDs were hard-pressed, Flatley dived to help and chased one Zero off a Dauntless. The Mitsubishi wasn't bagged as Flatley claimed, but score-keeping immediately lost its appeal; things fell apart when the F4Fs became dispersed and fought individually. Flatley himself narrowly escaped destruction, and if any of his pilots had a good time of it, that must have been Dick Crommelin.

Crommelin engaged four Zeros and was confident he'd knocked down two. But after two or three more encounters he realized he hadn't gotten away clean. Losing oil, he nursed a failing engine until the Pratt-Whitney quit and he ditched near the *Lexington*. He was rescued by a destroyer.

Nobody knew it yet, but the Lex was doomed. The torpedo hits damaged gasoline lines, and vapors ignited at 1530 which sealed her fate. She sank toward evening, taking thirty-three aircraft, including nine Wildcats, to the bottom. That left thirteen F4Fs operational in the *Yorktown*, including six from VF-2.

In the Japanese attack on Task Force 17, exorbitant claims were made on both sides. The two Wildcat squadrons thought they'd knocked down fifteen planes, when they'd accounted for three Vals and a Kate, losing four of their own number. The roughly-handled SBDs claimed seventeen shootdowns, losing five, but they did splash four raiders. Another seven Japanese planes, including one Zero, ditched en route home. For their part, the Imperial Navy pilots boasted of fifty-six American planes destroyed. This magnification by a factor of seven over actual results was nearly twice the U.S. error.

Coral Sea is best-remembered as the first carrier battle in history. Its broad lessons included the need for additional fighters, for forward interception and better electronic identification and communication.

For the Wildcat squadrons, the lessons were equally important. Better climb and careful positioning were essential for adequate task force defense. And the absolutely crucial aspects of fighting the Zero were painfully evident: maintain airspeed, keep an altitude advantage, and stick together. Despite the claims of the moment, F4Fs hadn't fared well against Zeros at Coral Sea; the final count in fighter combat is reckoned at six to three in favor of the Mitsubishi.

But the next chance to even the score was only four weeks off.

The *Yorktown* beat a hasty path back to Pearl, arriving on 27 May. But instead of the rest which many expected, they found frantic activity. Incredibly, the bomb-damaged flattop was to sortie again in three days. A huge Japanese armada, bent upon capturing Midway and thereby forcing the remaining Pacific Fleet carriers into combat, had to be stopped.

The *Yorktown* would be operating by herself, still designated Task Force 17, while the *Enterprise* and *Hornet* comprised Task Force 16. But the latter pair were fresh—the *Hornet*, in fact, was green. The *Yorktown* Air Group was rapidly reshuffled and turned around.

It was a complicated situation. Scouting 5, badly knocked around at Coral Sea, left the ship and was replaced by a *Saratoga* squadron, Bombing 3. Wally Short's Bombing 5 stayed aboard but because of several replacement crews was temporarily redesignated VS-5. The *Yorktown*'s TBD squadron was also replaced by another *Saratoga* outfit, Torpedo 3.

That left Fighting 42. Charlie Fenton and Vince McCormack would remain in Hawaii to receive new pilots while Jimmy Thach moved in with ten of his VF-3 fliers. They were familiar with the F4F-4; that was another consideration. There was also Don Lovelace, headed for command of VF-2. He learned of the aviator shortage and volunteered as Thach's exec for the upcoming deployment. It was a gallant, unselfish gesture which would cost Lovelace his life.

Though designated VF-3, *Yorktown*'s fighter squadron was 55 percent VF-42. Bill Leonard was flight officer; the former Arkansas art teacher, Art Brassfield, ran engineering; and Doc McCuskey had the gunnery department. Fenton's old maintenance crew remained intact. Captain Buckmaster insisted upon it, as he was convinced they were the best F4F people in the Pacific.

And their talent was badly needed. The new Wildcat was now in service, but nobody really knew much about the F4F-4. Chief Milton Wester, leading the mechanics of VF-3 (formerly VF-42), wasn't even

(*Text continues on page 83.*)

Forerunner of the Wildcat was the F3F, Grumman's last biplane fighter. The F3F-1 was assigned to VF-7 in 1940. (National Archives)

The XF4F-2 was the first step up from the original biplane design, but the final Wildcat silhouette was yet to emerge. (D.A. Anderton)

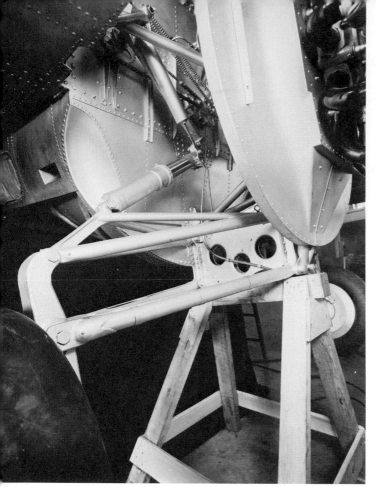

A superb shot of the XF4F-2 landing gear. Unchanged throughout the Wildcat line, it was manually operated, employing the bicycle chain and sprocket system, clearly visible. About twenty-eight turns of the handle raised the wheels. (D.A. Anderton)

Cockpit mockup of the XF4F-2. (Grumman)

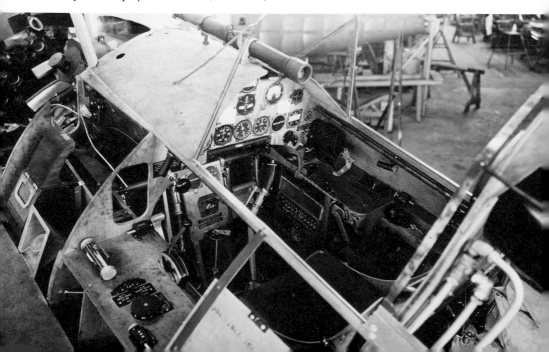

The Wildcat followed a troubled road to production. Here the modified prototype has suffered a landing gear failure during trials at NAS Anacostia in March 1939. (Grumman)

In semi-final form, the prototype F4F had evolved from its original rounded lines to a more angular tail configuration by May 1939. (Grumman)

The XF4F-3 in a steep climb through clouds, December 1939. (Grumman)

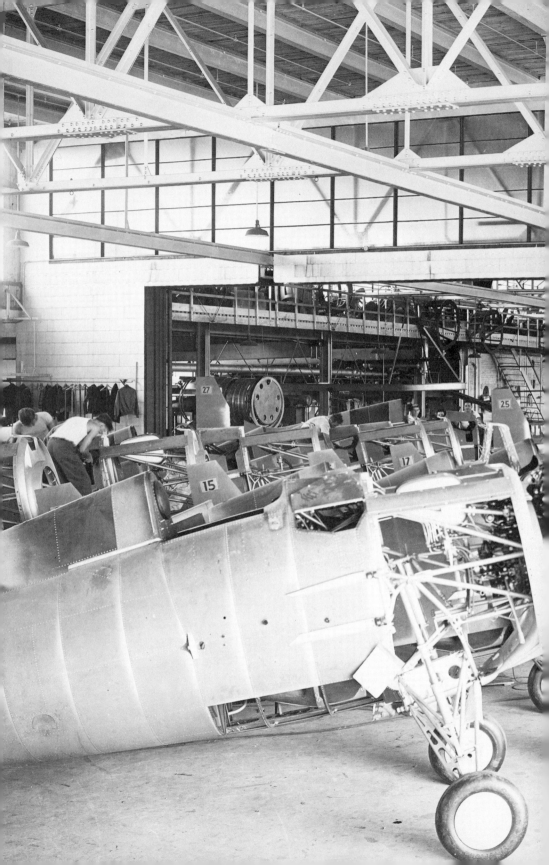

Fuselages of the first thirty-five F4F-3s under construction. (Grumman)

The second production F4F-3
(BuNo 1845) retained nose
guns and spinner hub, both of
which disappeared in subsequent aircraft. (Grumman)

An early production F4F-3
(with spinner hub, later dis-
carded) is trucked to the New
York World's Fair in May 1940.
This Wildcat was destined to
VF-4, as factory markings indicate. This is probably one of
the first two F4F-3s delivered.
(Grumman)

One of the original batch of F4F-3s delivered to Fighting Squadron Four in December 1940.
(Grumman)

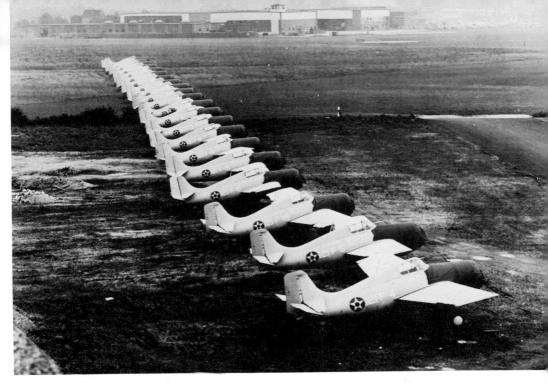

Marine Wildcats. F4F-3s of
VMF-121 awaiting acceptance
at the factory in early 1941.
(Grumman)

An Enterprise *plane handler*
directs a VF-6 F4F-3A into po-
sition for launch in mid-1941.
(Grumman)

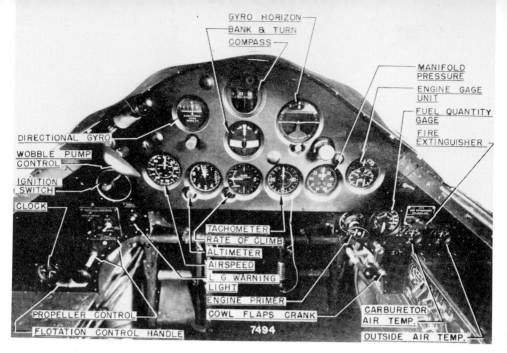

The F4F-3 instrument panel. (Grumman)

Marine Corps F4F-3s of VMF-111 participating in Army maneuvers in Louisiana in November 1941. Note that underwing bomb racks are installed. (USN/Tailhook Assn.)

Wildcat's claws. An excellent view of the .50-caliber M2 Browning installation in the F4F-3. Easily seen are the manually operated charging cables leading from the cockpit to each gun. (Grumman)

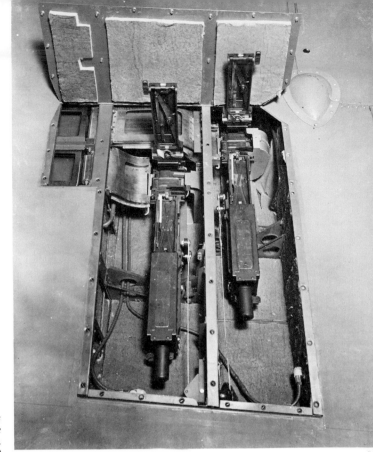

59

A Grummanite demonstrates ammunition insertion into the port wing of an F4F-3. Each ammo box contained 450 rounds. (Grumman)

The shape of things to come: an early F4F-4, featuring folding wings, with 100-pound bombs, in November 1941. (Grumman)

Grumman's production flight test office at Bethpage, Long Island, where factory pilots compared notes with management and engineering personnel. (Grumman)

On the eve of war, U.S. Navy F4F-3s share storage space with Martlet IIs at Grumman's Plant Number Two, 6 December 1941. (Grumman)

Factory pilot demonstrates life-raft deployment of the F4F-4. This feature was seldom used, since the aircraft usually sank before the pilot could get to the raft. Seat-pack rafts were more practical. (Grumman)

The Grumman Plant I in February 1942, with U.S. F4F-3s and a Britain bound G-21 Goose in the foreground. (Grumman)

Among early Wildcat squadrons was VF-71, nominally assigned to USS Wasp (CV-7). This dash three was probably photographed at Norfolk in 1942.

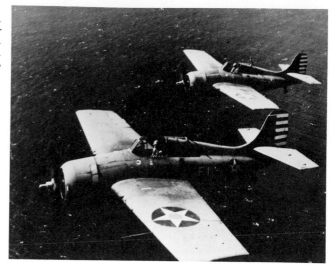

Lt. Cdr. Jimmy Thach and Lt. Butch O'Hare flying their assigned VF-3 aircraft following the defense of USS Lexington off Rabaul in February 1942. (Grumman)

64

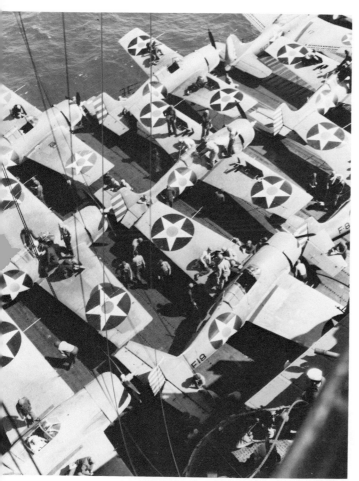

Enterprise *flight deck after Marcus Island raid of 4 March 1942. Ordnance men are disarming the F4F-3A Wildcats of VF-6. (National Archives)*

Fly One sends off a bomb-laden F4F-3 of VF-6 as the Enterprise *commences launch during early 1942. (USN/Tailhook Assn.)*

Fighting 6 was among the earliest recipients of F4F-4s. Enterprise *ordnancemen tend to the new six-gun armament in the spring of 1942. (R.M. Hill/Tailhook Assn.)*

An F4F-4 of VF-41 in early 1942, somewhere over the east coast. Originally VF-4, this was the first squadron equipped with Wildcats. Note the Wild Boar insignia beneath the cockpit. (Grumman)

Fighting Two's F4F-3s on Lexington's smoldering flight deck, 8 May 1942. "Lady Lex" was lost in the Coral Sea battle—first ever between carrier forces. (R.L. Lawson)

Enterprise during the lull between Coral Sea and Midway. Fighting 6 F4F-4s share deck space with SBD-3s on 15 May 1942. (USN/Tailhook Assn.)

F4F-3s and SBD-3s prepare for launch, circa mid-1942. (Grumman)

Grumman publicity photo making good use of the remains of a Mitsubishi A6M2N "Rufe." Note the pontoon on the truck. (Grumman)

THIS IS WHAT HAPPENS WHEN A ZERO *Meets a* GRUMMAN *Wildcat*

Lt. Edward "Butch" O'Hare of VF-3 earned lasting fame and the Medal of Honor for his defense of USS Lexington *from Japanese bombers off Rabaul, New Britain on 20 February 1942. (National Archives)*

This Wildcat has just received the "cut" signal from the LSO as a deck hand prepares to disengage the tailhook from the arresting wire upon landing. But one quarter of the carrier-based F4Fs at Midway failed to return. (Grumman)

Fighting 8 airplanes prepare to launch from the Hornet. The exact date is unknown but equipment and markings place the time frame during or shortly after the Battle of Midway. (USN/ Tailhook Assn.)

Portrait of a survivor. This F4F-3 was one of the VMF-221's ten returnees out of twenty-five which took off to intercept the Japanese carrier strike on Midway. Two other Wildcats were the only airworthy fighters left in the wake of the morning strike on 4 June. (USN/Tailhook Assn.)

This VF-3 Wildcat crashed on landing and ended up inverted on a dolly in the Yorktown's hangar deck on 4 June. (USN/Tailhook Assn.)

Lt. Cdr. "Jimmy" Thach, CO of VF-3, aboard the Hornet immediately after the Battle of Midway. Thach assumed command of the Hornet fighters in addition to his own when the Yorktown was disabled. His innovative fighter tactics were a major part of the reason for the F4F's success. (W.N. Hess)

Lt. William N. Leonard of VF-42 receives the DFC from Admiral Nimitz. Leonard saw combat at Coral Sea and Midway aboard the Yorktown and later flew with VF-11 at Guadalcanal, scoring a total of six confirmed victories in F4F's. (Tillman)

The rounded, elegant simplicity of the A6M5 (Zeke 52) silhouette shows a different approach than the angular, chunky Wildcat. F4F-3s and -4s engaged A6M2s in the early battles of 1942 but mainly fought A6M5s, featuring more powerful engines, in the upper Solomons. The Zero's outstanding maneuverability and climb rate, coupled with phenominal range, made it unique in the world in 1942. (Bowers)

Cactus Wildcats—Marine Corps F4F-4s on Guadalcanal. Note tents among palm trees and twin-mount antiaircraft guns behind nearest airplane. (USMC)

Ordnance specialists rearming an F4F-4, which carried two more .50-caliber machine guns than the F4F-3, but 360 fewer rounds. (Grumman)

Two divisions of Wildcats on patrol in typical tropic climate. (Grumman)

These five pilots of VMF-121 were credited with a total 53½ victories at Guadalcanal. Left to right: Lt. Roger A. Haberman (6½), Lt. Cecil J. Doyle (5), Capt. J.J. Foss (26), Lt. W.P. Marontate (13) and Lt. Roy M. Ruddell (3). Marontate was killed in action near the end of the squadron's tour in January 1943. (Grumman)

"The Cow Pasture," as Guadalcanal airmen called the fighter strip east of Henderson Field. (W.N. Hess)

This battle-damaged F4F-4 was photographed on Guadalcanal in November 1942. Apart from visible damage—bullet holes and dangling life raft—note that most of the instruments have been removed. (Perry N. Coley)

Lt.Col. Harold J. Bauer—"Indian Joe" or "The Coach" to his fliers—was one of the prominent fighter leaders at Guadalcanal. Arriving as CO of VMF-212, he eventually ran fighter operations and was awarded a posthumous Medal of Honor. This pre-war photo shows Bauer as a captain.(W.N. Hess)

The F4F-7 was designed as a photo aircraft, distinguishable from other Wildcats by the rounded one-piece windscreen and prominent fuel-jettison tubes below the rudder. On the 100 ordered, only twenty-one were actually delivered since the requirement was small. However, several dash sevens flew at Guadalcanal. (Grumman)

A surprise to naval aviators was the capability and aggressiveness of Japanese float planes. The Mitsubishi F1M, code-named "Pete," was first encountered over Tulagi by VF-42 in May 1942. Later Solomons operations threw Wildcats into frequent contact with the float fighters, often with results seen here. (Nick Wantiez)

Capt. Joseph J. Foss, USMC

Major Marion E. Carl

◄ *A good illustration of the Navy's tactical formation among fighter squadrons in the second half of 1942: four-plane divisions composed of two-plane sections. However, Wildcats usually carried external fuel by the time of Eastern Solomons and Santa Cruz. (Grumman)*

Major John L. Smith, USMC

◄ *Wildcats, Avengers, and Dauntlesses aboard an unidentified carrier—probably Enterprise—in late 1942. (R.L. Lawson)*

77

An F4F-4 clears the bow after a deck run, beginning a starboard turn to clear the way for the next aircraft. (Grumman)

Capt. Jefferson DeBlanc, USMC

Fighter One—Guadalcanal's first auxilary airfield—in February 1943, at the end of the island campaign. (USMC)

F4F-4s with drop tanks prepare to launch. Note F4U-1s with folded wings in background. Corsairs didn't operate from U.S. carriers on a regular basis until the end of 1944. (Grumman)

An F4F-3P of VMO-251 is serviced at Espritu in the New Hebrides in late 1942. None of the photo wildcats saw combat but 251 pilots helped fill the ranks of understrength fighter squadrons a Guadalcanal until the entire squadron became operational at year-end. (USN/Tailhook Assn.)

The pilots of VMF-112 on Guadalcanal. Fifty-eight victories for the "Wolfpack" date this photo at February 1943. The squadron transitioned to Corsairs in May. (Col. Archie Donahue)

Lt. James E. Swett of VMF-221 shot down seven Aichi dive-bombers in his first combat, 7 April 1943, tying the record for most kills by a Wildcat pilot in one day. Here he is seen in his Corsair later that year. Swett finished the war with 15½ victories and the Medal of Honor. (W.N. Hess)

This Wildcat's tailhook broke upon landing aboard the escort carrier Copahee in April 1943 when the hook snagged on the slightly raised elevator. (USN/Tailhook Assn.)

The Sundowners' Fox 27 nosed up on landing near Henderson Field following VF-11's tussle with Zekes on 30 July 1943. (Sgt. W.J. Wilson, USMC)

Capt. Bruce Porter, recently of VMF-121, shows fellow Marine Russel Isles one of the F4F-4s reportedly flown by Joe Foss. Porter, Isles, and the Wildcat were involved in the filming of Guadalcanal Diary at Mojave, California in December 1943. (Porter)

Major Robert E. Galer, USMC

able to go ashore to look over the new birds. Their folding wings and six-gun armament would require familiarization, but time was running out.

Based upon early experience, the fighter strength was boosted by 50 percent—from eighteen to twenty-seven planes in each squadron. But with extra weight imposed by more guns and armor, performance suffered. Said John Adams of VF-42, "We went from bad to worse when we picked up the F4F-4 for Midway. We had all kinds of extra weight and a real sluggish aircraft; six guns and less firing time. The reduction in rounds per gun with the six .50-calibers cut the firing time by at least five seconds. That doesn't sound like much, but can be a lifetime in combat."[6] He was right; 360 rounds really counted.

There was almost no time for familiarization; one or two short hops and the flight out to the ship was all. Even then, things only got worse for Fighting 3. When the air group flew aboard on 30 May, Don Lovelace was taxiing up the deck when the F4F behind him missed the wire, skimmed over the barrier and smashed down on Lovelace's Wildcat. The exec died almost instantly and two fighters were written off. Bill Leonard moved up to the number two spot in the wake of the tragedy, and Thach's squadron got on with the job at hand. Leonard characterized the "new" Fighting 3 as "well-knit, spirited, and well led."[7]

A good thing, for there was much to do in five days. The new dash fours' guns weren't even boresighted, so makeshift arrangements were taken. Wind battens were erected well forward and targets affixed. The *Yorktown*'s flight deck was about 200 feet short of the normal 1,000-foot boresight range, but the difference was taken into consideration. The crew raised the tail of each Wildcat in turn, leveled it up, and gained a quick-and-dirty sight setting. Other than some shooting over the side to check functioning (there were few stoppages), that was the extent of VF-3's gunnery practice for the Battle of Midway. Concluded Bill Leonard, "We burned the right incense."[8]

The other two fighter squadrons were more familiar with the F4F-4, though that didn't mean they were any happier with the heavier, less maneuverable Wildcat than Thach's people. Fighting 6 in the *Enterprise*, still under Lieutenant Jim Gray, had a full twenty-seven airplanes and a generally experienced group of pilots. The *Hornet*'s VF-8 also numbered twenty-seven Wildcats but the aviator experience level was low. In fact, the squadron was fleshed out with some torpedo pilots who'd been rapidly transitioned to fighters. Nobody in the outfit had been in combat, and that included the CO, Lieutenant Commander Sam "Pat" Mitchell and his exec.

The *Hornet* Air Group, if the truth were known, wasn't quite up to speed. The fighters' training syllabus remained incomplete and the CAG was a strict disciplinarian who'd grounded some experienced pilots for failing to rise when he entered the wardroom. The torpedo squadron was as gung-ho as they come, but lacked seasoning. Though both SBD outfits were good, and would prove it later, their contribution at Midway would not be decisive.

Midway's garrison fighter squadron was VMF-221. The Buffalo unit had been deposited there in December from the *Saratoga*, following the abortive Wake Island reinforcement attempt. It was a dull life, as the atoll's two islands—Sand and Eastern—were small, crowded spits of land. Many personnel lived underground, a distressing situation when the water level rose. The six-month routine consisted of two flights per day, with occasional bursts of excitement in the form of a passing Japanese submarine or patrol plane.

But in late May the Marines learned the Japanese were on the way, expected to strike on 4 June. Surprisingly, new aircraft arrived on 26 May aboard a ferry: sixteen SBD-2s for the scout-bomber squadron and, wondrously, seven F4F-3s to bolster the twenty-one Brewsters. The Wildcats were in need of some work but the new CO, Major Floyd Parks, happily added them to his command.

There was precious little time to spare. None of the pilots was very familiar with the Wildcat, but those fortunate enough to draw Grummans didn't complain. One was Captain Marion Carl, a lanky, easygoing Oregonian who was arguably the best flier in the Marine Corps. Carl logged only five and a half hours in F4Fs, all during the last week of May. But he felt it was enough. He had over 1,300 hours total time, much of it in fighters, and that was more important than time in type.

Actually, Carl and some other pilots felt there was relatively little to choose between the F2A-3 and F4F-3 as flying machines. The Brewster was widely considered more responsive, in some ways more fun to fly, but was harder to land and lacked the Grumman's stability. Therefore, as a weapon, the F4F offered more as a gunnery platform.

For six months the pilots of VMF-221 had been warming up their engines a half-hour before dawn, then sitting at readiness for an hour. Shortly before 0600 on 4 June, Midway radar detected a large formation inbound from the northwest, and everything flyable was scrambled: Marine, Navy, and Army planes crammed onto Eastern

Island in anticipation of this battle. Some 107 Japanese carrier aircraft were 90 miles out.

Twenty-six fighters were airborne in ten minutes, climbing into a cumulus-filled morning sky. But in the haste and confusion, division organization broke down, and one Brewster aborted with engine trouble. The formations consisted of a twelve-plane group under Red Parks (seven Buffalos and five Wildcats) which headed out to intercept the raid, and twelve (including one F4F) orbiting at ten miles.

What followed is not easily documented because so few Marines survived. What is clear is that the F2As were cut to pieces by the thirty-six Zeros escorting seventy-one carrier bombers. Of nineteen Brewsters which engaged, six returned.

Flying with Parks' group, Captain John Carey found himself nose-on to the Japanese strike with two other Wildcats flown by Marion Carl and Lieutenant Clayton Canfield. The F4Fs prepared to attack "an estimated seventy to eighty" dive and level bombers at 12,000 feet.[9] Thirty miles from base, the Wildcat trio rolled into a gunnery pass from 2,000 feet above.

Most of the Zeros were behind and below the bombers, evidently expecting to catch Midway's interceptors climbing to attack. That afforded the Marines "free admission" in the form of one gratis pass at the Aichis and Nakajimas. Canfield fired at the nearest bomber— probably a *Kaga* Val—and claimed a flamer. Carey also engaged a Val, but both Leathernecks were immediately set upon by "a pack of Zeros."[10] Carey's plane was hit by a deflection shot from port, and he took a bullet in the knee. There was no choice but to return to Midway, and somehow he got down safely without use of his rudder. Canfield's Wildcat was so shot up that it collapsed on the runway.

Most pilots fought a series of individual skirmishes. Marion Carl, during his pass at the bombers, suddenly saw Zeros everywhere and wisely turned away from Midway. The Zeros had literally climbed all over the Marines, and anyone caught at an altitude disadvantage was likely doomed.

Knowing that height meant survival, Carl climbed to about 20,000 feet, "wondering what one lone Wildcat was doing out there all by himself."[11] Headed back towards the atoll, he noted several Japanese planes below him, with no Americans in sight.

Abruptly an A6M latched onto his tail and started shooting. A couple of turns convinced Carl that he couldn't outmaneuver a Mitsubishi, as he heard bullets striking metal. "All we knew about the Zero was that it was supposed to be very maneuverable," he recalled. "I don't think we knew its relative speed, though it was just as fast as a Wildcat, if not faster, and it climbed better. It didn't do as well in a dive. If you had altitude, you could get away from a Zero normally by just heading that old Wildcat straight down."[12]

That's just what he did. Carl dived into a convenient cloud, chopped the throttle and crossed his controls, forcing the Grumman into a skid. The Zero overshot, and when Carl emerged the tables were turned. But in nosing down to line up his sights, all four guns jammed under negative G as he fired, and the bandit escaped with light damage.

At length the attackers set off, leaving Midway a smoking, flaming ruin. They had destroyed hangars, fuel tanks, the command post, and Eastern's powerhouse. Orbiting nearby, Carl could see the thick, greasy smoke of gasoline-fed fires. He also saw three widely-separated Zeros. Clearing his guns he decided, "I'll take on one of those." He made a high stern approach, closed unseen to gun range and squeezed the trigger. "I was on his tail and firing before he ever knew what happened," Carl said, and he watched the A6M spin into the water.[13]

Both of the Zeros Carl tangled with were probably from the *Kaga*. One returning Japanese pilot reported a one-minute inconclusive combat with a Grumman after the bombers attacked, expending 200 rounds. Only two Mitsubishis failed to return, and one of those was an *Akagi* fighter shot down while strafing Midway. The other missing Zero was from the *Kaga*, and nobody saw what happened to it.[14] The time and circumstances seem to fit Marion Carl's account, since the Zero he claimed was alone and evidently unseen by the other two in the vicinity. It was the first in a long string of victories.

Shortly afterward—about 0715—Midway ordered all fighters to land by divisions. When none did, the air ops officer radioed for 221 to recover individually. Of the twenty-five which had taken off barely an hour before, ten returned. Most of the planes which did turn up were flying wrecks, like Canfield and Carey's. Only Carl's and another F4F were fit to fly. Carl's Wildcat had taken about eight hits, though the other was undamaged, prompting some raised eyebrows among the survivors.

Except for a false alarm later that morning, VMF-221's battle was over. But Midway was at once a shock and a revelation to the Marines. The Zero was clearly superior to the Wildcat if an F4F pilot tried to play the Japanese game. Apparently that's what most of the 221 pilots tried to do. The Zeros had destroyed the squadron in under twenty minutes. Only one of the missing pilots turned up; the CO and exec were killed, and Midway had but two airworthy fighters left.

In exchange for thirteen Buffalos and two Wildcats which never came back, VMF-221 claimed seven bombers and four Zeros shot down, plus five planes damaged. Actual Japanese losses to all causes were ten planes shot down or ditched and fifty-five or so damaged to varying degrees. At best, it appears that Parks' squadron knocked down one Zero and two bombers, though the twenty-five Marines made an impression on the Japanese. All the interceptors were identified as F4Fs, and while no overall estimate of U.S. fighter strength shows in surviving reports, the four enemy air groups claimed over forty "Grummans" destroyed plus numerous probables.[15]

Now the action shifted seaward, where the battle would be decided.

The U.S. carriers operated in two task groups, neither of which was commanded by an aviator. Rear Admiral Raymond Spruance, a cruiser sailor, had replaced the ailing Halsey at the helm of Task Force 16 with the *Enterprise* and *Hornet*. Frank Jack Fletcher retained command of Task Force 17 with the *Yorktown* and her screen. Fletcher was senior and more experienced at carrier ops, but events would place Ray Spruance in charge of the battle.

PBY reports gave a reasonably good fix on Vice Admiral Nagumo's Carrier Striking Force early that morning, and all three U.S. flattops prepared to launch. The *Yorktown*'s scouts were still out searching, as planned, so Fletcher directed Spruance southwestward from his waiting position north of Midway. With knowledge of Japanese plans provided by CINCPAC intelligence, Fletcher and Spruance hoped to catch Nagumo off balance.

The *Enterprise* and *Hornet* commenced launching shortly after 0700, turning southeast into the wind under clear skies with scattered clouds at 4,000 to 5,000 feet. But as at Coral Sea a month before, American flattops employed varied procedures. The *Hornet* Air Group planned to fly outbound on 265 degrees true, but Lieutenant Commander John Waldron doggedly led Torpedo 8 on his own course, 240 degrees. Meanwhile, the CAG formed up his Dauntless squadrons in parade formation as launch continued and Pat Mitchell climbed into place with ten F4Fs. All this took time, and the launch dragged out for over forty minutes while the force was steaming away from Nagumo. The *Hornet* Air Group's insistence on formalized organization cut deeply into fuel reserves, and before the morning was over it would take three of her four squadrons right out of the battle.

The Big E's launch was also prolonged, though more to flight-deck delays than faulty doctrine. Her Torpedo 6 departed last, staying low to conserve fuel like VT-8, since the Devastators had shorter legs than SBDs or F4Fs. Jim Gray's ten Wildcats labored slowly up to 20,000 feet, expecting to cover Lieutenant Commander Wade McClusky's two Dauntless squadrons while keeping alert to calls for help from VT-6. Lieutenant Art Ely, exec of the torpeckers, had arranged a "Come on down, Jim" call if help were required from Gray.[16]

But somewhere early in the launch, Gray's fighters latched onto the wrong TBD formation. Much later it became evident that VF-6's escort flight attached itself to Torpedo 8, apparently due to confusion in looking down through the low clouds. So as Gray and Waldron proceeded on course to the southwest, they lost their respective air groups.

Viewed objectively, it was an understandable error. Less understandable was the behavior of the *Hornet*'s CAG, who flew more westerly than southwest and consequently missed Nagumo entirely. The forty-five-plane formation, impeccably precise and burning fuel at a terrific rate because of it, ended up somewhere north of the Japanese carriers. With no target in sight and fuel rapidly running low, the CAG split the air group and ordered squadrons to return independently. The SBDs either went into Midway or risked the longer flight back to the task force, and most of them made it.

Not so the Wildcats. Fighting 8's inadequate training in the YE-ZB homing system began to tell. The CO evidently couldn't pick up the signal, so Ensign John McInerney throttled to the front, tapping his earphones and patting his head in the "I have the lead" signal. The youngster had the signal from the *Hornet* and tried to show the way back, but it was too late. One by one the R-1830s began to cough, sputter, and then quit. Wildcats began dropping into the sea.

When McInerney's tanks ran dry his section leader, Lieutenant (jg) Johnny Magda, still had power. But Magda, later a Blue Angel leader, turned back, dropped hook and flaps, and splashed into a landing to stick with his wingman. The lead division kept going until it too ran out of gas and ditched together. Two of the ten VF-8 pilots were lost in this debacle (one crashed while landing downwind), just part of the tragedy afflicting the *Hornet* at Midway.

Meanwhile, Jim Gray's ten fighters had Japanese carriers in sight about 0915. Still believing Torpedo 6 was below, the *Enterprise* Wildcats orbited overhead, waiting for Art Ely's message. Of course, it never came. Torpedo 6 was still en route, several minutes behind. Gray later stated that he felt obliged to remain topside, keeping things clear for McClusky's SBDs unless specifically asked to drop down and help the TBDs. Twice before 1000 he radioed Red Base, informing the *Enterprise*, "We are returning to the ship due to the lack of gas. We have been flying over the enemy fleet. They have no combat patrol."[17] He reported enemy composition as eight destroyers and two battleships escorting two visible carriers. There were many more ships than that, and the Zero CAP was ferocious, but not all was discernable from 20,000 feet.

The second-guessers and professional critics have examined this phase of the battle for forty years. Some say the Wildcats should have descended to help with flak suppression if they believed there were no CAP, while others say the F4Fs wouldn't have made it home had they done so. Opinion seems divided among the surviving bomber and torpedo crews. Most say that nobody could have done anything to help; the odds were too great and F4Fs would have been lost needlessly. Others contend that the fighters were meant to protect the strike regardless of Wildcat losses—that's how the game is played. But confusion is the normal state of affairs in combat, and seldom does anyone have a clear picture of what's happening at any given moment.

As Gray led his F4Fs homeward, Torpedo 6 went in to the attack and met near-total destruction. Waldron's VT-8 was annihilated and only two of Lieutenant Commander Lindsey's fourteen Devastators survived. Two dozen Zeros against fourteen or fifteen unescorted TBDs at a time was no sort of contest, but it continued just the same. The *Yorktown*'s hodge-podge air group was also on the scene.

After recovering his morning search, Rear Admiral Fletcher followed Spruance southwest, preparing to launch a *Yorktown* strike. He decided to send off Bombing 3 and Torpedo 3 with a half-dozen F4Fs under Jimmy Thach. The fighter skipper wasn't sanguine about the prospects; six Wildcats were awfully thin protection for seventeen Dauntlesses and twelve TBDs. But the *Yorktown* wanted to keep its other nineteen fighters for task force defense.

The squadron leaders and air group commander held an impromptu war council. They decided to send the torpedo planes out immediately at 1,500 feet, just below the cloud base, while the Dauntlesses climbed to 16,000 and overtook them en route for a running rendezvous. Two fighters would stay low at about 2,500 while Thach's division flew at 5,000 to 6,000. The CAG, Oscar Pederson, consulted with the *Yorktown*'s meteorology department and concluded that Lieutenant Commander Lem Massey could navigate for the strike group by watching wind drift from the whitecaps. Everybody else would stay on track by watching the TBDs.

Pete Pederson further reckoned that Nagumo's carriers should be

155 nautical miles southwest. Jimmy Thach said he'd push it to 175 miles if necessary, which was being mighty generous. He'd have precious little fuel reserves for the return trip.

In any event, it worked. Launch commenced at 0845 with Massey leading his TBDs straight out while Lieutenant Commander Max Leslie orbited for twelve minutes, gaining height with his dive-bombers. Finally Thach led his five pilots off the deck at 0905, thereby conserving fuel. A running rendezvous was effected forty minutes later; a slick operation which made *Yorktown*'s the only American air group to operate as such in the entire battle.

Shortly after 1000, when Jim Gray was turning his VF-6 planes homeward, the Yorktowners spotted "three or four carriers" with numerous escorts to the northwest, distance 30 to 40 miles.[18] Turning starboard, the squadrons prepared to close the target and opened up on the radio to coordinate the torpedo and bombing attacks. But communications were shortly broken, and Max Leslie decided he couldn't wait any longer. Though he'd lost his bomb (as had three of his pilots) due to an electrical malfunction, he pushed over at 1025, marveling at the lack of opposition as he led Bombing 3 down on the nearest carrier.

The reason for VB-3's good fortune was Torpedo 3's misery. A gaggle of Zeros hit Massey's dozen TBDs at 150 feet less than 15 miles from Nagumo's carriers. In the violent, lopsided shootout which followed, ten went down. The other two ditched from battle damage or fuel exhaustion trying to get home.

Thach's Wildcats had almost no time to react. They heard Massey call for help, saw the Japanese guns open fire, then were swarmed by fifteen or more Zeros. The skipper's number four man, Ensign Ed "Red Dog" Bassett, was hit from astern and went down. Thach himself wracked into a hard turn to counter the attack, meeting one A6M head-on. He put his gunsight pipper on the Zero's nose and fired. His target flamed and dropped away. Then weaving in VF-3's patented defensive scissors, Thach saw Ensign Ram Dibb crossing his sights with a Zero in tow. It was a textbook deflection setup and the CO knocked the Mitsubishi off Dibb's tail.

Fighting 3 fought a desperate battle for survival. Things were complicated when Lieutenant (jg) Brainard Macomber's radio was shot out but he got in a burst while weaving on Thach and claimed a probable kill. The skipper bagged one more, but there was no chance to lend a hand to the TBDs. The top-cover F4Fs had all they could do just keeping in the air.

Meanwhile, the two-plane low element had its own troubles.

Machinist Tom Cheek and Ensign Dan Sheedy had a tough fight against odds. Sheedy took a hit in one leg but the Orange Section Wildcats dumped a pair of A6Ms plus one probable.

Then it was over. Three Japanese carriers gushed smoke and flames, the victims of a miraculously coordinated dive-bombing attack by VB-3 and Wade McClusky's two *Enterprise* squadrons. It couldn't have possibly worked so well if it had been planned that way. Nagumo's Carrier Striking Force, after repulsing sustained carrier- and land-based attacks throughout the morning, now had only the *Hiryu* to continue the battle.

Returning to the task force with his four remaining F4Fs, Thach realized the naval balance in the Pacific was changing hands. He wanted to make an immediate report to Admiral Fletcher, but at the same time a chilling thought ran though his mind. "My God, I've lost Torpedo 3."[19]

Caught at low level, outnumbered about three to one and forced to fight for their lives, the tiny Wildcat escort had absolutely no chance to protect the TBDs. The risk had been well understood before launch. But thirty years later—perhaps until he died in 1981—Jimmy Thach wondered what else he might have done.

After two and half hours aloft the F4Fs were back over the task force. Because of their low fuel state they were taken aboard first while Leslie's SBDs orbited nearby, but Tom Cheek's Wildcat hit the deck at an awkward angle. He actually cartwheeled over the barrier, fouling the deck temporarily. Thach was already on the flag bridge, telling Fletcher what he'd seen, but another VF-3 pilot had a worse time than Cheek.

Dan Sheedy was forced to land aboard the *Hornet*. He was in a bad way; wounded in one foot by shrapnel from a 20-mm hit in one of his scraps with a Zero. He'd found himself nose-to-nose with a Mitsubishi and wasn't sure if he'd shot it down or the Japanese had dipped a wing into the water. Painfully wounded and shaken by his close call, the young ensign evidently forgot to turn his gun switches off.

The *Hornet*'s LSO gave him the cut and Sheedy plunked his Wildcat onto the deck hard enough to collapse his right landing-gear oleo. The shock caused him to trip his trigger for two short bursts.

Ensign Henry Carey of VF-8 had just landed from a CAP when Sheedy smacked down behind him. A deck hand asked Carey if he needed ammunition, then gasped "Jesus Christ!" and dived off the wing head-first, nearly hitting the whirling prop. Carey heard the firing behind him and abruptly dropped his seat to gain whatever protection his armor plate afforded. At that distance, it wouldn't have done any good but both Carey and the deck hand were alright.

However, five men in the superstructure were killed. The skewed angle of Sheedy's plane due to its damaged landing gear caused his tracers to lace upwards into the island, and several sailors were horribly wounded by phophorus in .50-caliber incendiary bullets.

Cary's roommate was missing from the escort mission so Sheedy moved in with him. The *Yorktown* flier was disconsolate. Carey did what he could to alleviate the young man's misery, telling him, "It could have happened to any of us." Forty years later Henry Carey still says, "I wish I could tell Dan Sheedy that we didn't really hold it against him. We all took the same risks."[21]

For the moment, however, another risk was imminent. The CAP had been rotated throughout the morning at 90-minute intervals. Shortly before noon *Yorktown* radar picked up a bogie, and fortunately the ForceCap was relatively fresh. In the next few minutes it became apparent the contact was climbing, distance about 30 miles. The logical assumption was dive-bombers. Captain Buckmaster turned the *Yorktown* southeasterly, away from the threat, increasing speed to 30 knots. His screen of two cruisers and four destroyers deployed a repel air attack.

Fighting 3 had a dozen Wildcats airborne and the *Hornet*'s fighters were alerted to possibly bear a hand. Obviously, Task Frce 17 would be the target as the *Yorktown* was first in line of the raiders' approach. Fighting 6's CAP was held over Task Force 16 in case the Japanese tried to hit both carrier groups.

TF-16 fighter direction was handled from the *Enterprise*, call sign Red Base. The *Hornet* was Blue Base. Pete Pederson handled the *Yorktown*'s fighters from Scarlet Base. As the VF-3 sections were vectored to intercept at 15 to 20 miles, Pederson couldn't help calling, "Come on, you Scarlet boys. Get them!"[22] To a large extent they were his pilots, as he'd led VF-42 before moving up to CAG just as Wade McClusky had done in the *Enterprise*.

The *Yorktown* believed in maintaining a 10,000-foot CAP. This allowed fliers a fast dive to low level to cut off torpedo planes, but afforded a chance to intercept dive-bombers, given adequate warning to gain altitude. One of the last radio calls before tally-ho went to Scarlet 23 and trailing sections: "Many bogies, angels ten." The FDO followed with orders to "Arrow 305 at 10,000." Then a simple, "Step on it!"[23]

"Arrow" was the code for true course, in which the pilot mentally compensates for magnetic variation and the lesser deviation particular to his airplane. It was commonly used by TF-16, while the *York-town* used "Vector," a more useful term as it took the latter corrections into account and the fighter pilot merely flew the heading ordered. But with combat imminent and the pressure building, Vector wasn't always used by hard-pressed FDOs.

At this same time the leading F4Fs eyeballed the raiders. They correctly counted eighteen Vals but overestimated the four Zeros. Not that it mattered. The *Hiryu*, the only intact Japanese carrier, had launched her strike within half an hour of the devastating SBD attack. And two of her six fighters had taken damage from homing SBDs and aborted.

Fighting 3 hit the *Hiryu* formation like an aerial avalanche. Six planes went down in the first pass as the Wildcats picked their targets, dived into gunnery range and opened up. The Zero escort became embroiled with a couple of F4F sections; in particular Lieutenant (jg) Ed Mattson and Ensign Horace Bass. An A6M jumped Mattson's tail and hit his starboard wing, but Bass dutifully crossed over and put the skids to the Mitsubishi. But the Aichis were the priority targets. Mattson latched onto one, closed in and lanced his tracers into the canopy. Noting the rear gunner's hatch still closed, he shifted aim to insure the back-seater didn't shoot at him. Mattson was close enough to see the effect of his six .50s. With a queasy stomach he watched the Val plunge into the sea.

Doc McCuskey had picked up the eighteen bombers approaching head-on and bent the throttle, leaving his wingman in his wake. He spurted ahead, closing on Lavender Section—Bill Woollen and Bill Barnes—and followed them in a portside pass. In a fast couple of minutes, McCuskey sliced through two six-plane Vs, gunning three Vals as his sights came to bear. "It was just shooting from the hip," he later explained, "and I mean I was looking them right in the eye."[24] But when he turned his head to check his tail he found two nimble Aichis drawing a bead. So McCuskey dived out, recovered and started climbing again. But he was out of ammo. The dash four's limited ammunition capacity was proving troublesome in its first combat.

Another Fighting 3 pilot made excellent use of his 240 rounds per gun. Lieutenant (jg) Art Brassfield was an exceptionally proficient fighter pilot and leader of the fourth division. He selected three Vals and dumped them in sequence with precision flying and shooting. Then, noting another Val apparently strafing a ditched TBD, he spoiled the Aichi's sport with violent finality.

But Japanese air discipline—nearly always exemplary—withstood this assault. A *Hornet* division arrived to help out at the last

minute and bagged a bomber and probably a Zero, then part of
Fighting 6's CAP also piled in. Lieutenant Roger Mehle finally got
permission to extend his orbit the 20 or so miles westward, but his
gun solenoid failed and he never got off a round. Ensigns Tom Provost
and J. M. Halford double-teamed a Val but then the Aichis were past
the CAP, headed for the *Yorktown*.

Records are a bit hazy, but either seven or eight D3As arrived over
Task Force 17. The AA gunners knocked down two, but five are
known to have dropped. And having come this far, through a tough
fighter screen, the Japanese pilots didn't intend to waste the opportunity. From 70-degree dives at only 1,000 feet they pulled their release
handles. And they scored three hits. One blew a big hole in the
starboard side; the others both started fires and left the *Yorktown*
immobile.

The Wildcats had shot down eleven dive-bombers and three Zeros,
nearly all by VF-3. Only three fighters (including the two aborts) and
five Vals recovered aboard the *Hiryu*. But "Flying Dragon" had a
mini-strike of ten torpedo-packing Kates and six more Zeros ready to
go. They had orders to pass up the carrier hit by the first strike, and
try to knock a second American flight deck out of the battle.

But exceptional damage control snuffed out the *Yorktown*'s fires,
and she had steam for nearly 20 knots in two hours. And she was
ready to resume flight ops as soon as the ten-foot-square bomb hole
was planked over. It was a remarkable performance. And it insured the *Hiryu*'s second strike attacked the apparently undamaged
Yorktown.

Meanwhile, the airborne Yorktowners—including Bombing 3,
which hadn't gotten aboard yet—were diverted to the *Enterprise* or
Hornet. When the next Japanese raid showed on the scope about
1430, the *Yorktown* was refueling ten Wildcats on deck but had six
fighters overhead, including three VF-6 planes. A Fighting 8 patrol
orbited at 18,000 to reinforce the CAP.

Thus, TF-17 prepared to receive another strike; but things were
complicated by too many transmissions on the single voice radio
circuit. Consequently, fighter direction suffered. And it was compounded by giving back-to-back orders in conflicting phrases. At
1429, for instance, "Scarlet One from Scarlet Base, arrow 340." Then
two minutes later, "Scarlet 23, vector 340 distance 20. Large group of
bogies."[25]

Whether this was the actual reason for the initial missed intercept
is unknown, but the first division out (Doc McCuskey leading) passed

beyond the inbound Kates. At 1434 the flight was recalled, "Scarlet 21 from Scarlet Base. Return buster. You have passed them."[26]

Bill Woollen and Ensign Harry Gibbs made first contact. They jumped the Nakajimas in clouds at 4,000 feet from a 3,000-foot advantage. Woollen did the shooting, watching with satisfaction as his victim spun down. Then he continued ahead, ignoring the old warning against flying straight and level in a combat zone. A Zero surprised him from astern, holing his oil cooler. "I never did see the guy who got me," he said.[27] Noting the *Yorktown* headed into the wind, he proceeded five miles ahead and executed a safe ditching. Gibbs also splashed down, victim of a straight-shooting Zero pilot who tagged his engine. Fortunately both F4F pilots were rescued, largely avenged by McCuskey and Ensign Melvin Roach of VF-6 who splashed a pair of A6Ms.

The two task forces were now about 40 miles apart, limiting VF-6's support. The *Hornet* Wildcats at 18,000 feet were too high to help repel a torpedo attack in time. As before, the *Yorktown* was left to her own resources. Jimmy Thach was preparing to launch on CAP when the attack developed and had to lead a quick-and-dirty scramble at the last minute.

Refueling was far from complete—it had hardly begun—and with an attack minutes away, all gas lines had been secured. Only Thach and his wingman, Ram Dibb, had anything like full tanks. The other six pilots averaged under 30 gallons apiece. Bill Leonard grabbed a handful of operations documents and stuffed them in his pocket as he dashed out of the ready room. They were the only records of VF-3 to be saved in the Battle of Midway.

Thach hardly had time to crank up his wheels before the Nakajimas arrived. He turned hard right off the bow and met a Kate head-on, too close to draw a bead. Ensign Milton Tootle shot down a Kate, then was hit by "friendly" AA fire and landed in the water. A destroyer picked him up, and he was lucky. A VF-8 pilot was killed during the day by a direct hit from a 5-inch shell.

Thach turned back, selected another B5N and splashed it but was also set upon by a fighter. He evaded the tracers and awaited events. Leonard also pounced on a Kate and shot it down. Then the battle was over. It happened just that fast.

The CAP, including a division of VF-6, claimed eight Nakajimas and two Zeros during the *Hiryu's* second strike. Actually the Wildcats destroyed five and two, respectively, all but one by VF-3. But the

Yorktown had taken two torpedoes and was in a bad way; afloat but listing, she was shortly abandoned.

The Scarlet fighters pancaked at Red and Blue Base, regrouped, and resumed CAPs. A combined *Yorktown–Enterprise* SBD strike found the *Hiryu* late that afternoon and ended her career, but all F4Fs remained with the task force. The last CAP divisions landed after dark. Bill Leonard's flight was the final VF-3 patrol; he'd logged nearly six and a half hours this day. Fighting 6 had put up ten CAP flights.

Next day Jimmy Thach flew over to the *Hornet* to assume command of the fighters, which due to their cosmopolitan nature were called VF-3-8-42. The VF-8 CO was still missing from the previous day's escort and the exec had been committed to sick bay, in no condition to run a squadron. The pursuit phase of the battle lasted through 6 June, and just when it seemed the *Yorktown* might pull through, she was torpedoed by a Japanese submarine. When she sank on the seventh the Battle of Midway was over.

The F4F-4 was bloodied at Midway, and the experience provided a good indication of what fighter squadrons could expect for the rest of the year. Nobody was really happy with the new Wildcat in relation to the dash three, and all squadrons voiced similar complaints: reduced climb, range, and firing time. But more F4F-4s could be carried owing to their folding wings, so perhaps things evened out.

What was uneven was personnel performance. The fighter squadrons engaged at Midway turned in work ranging from magnificent to miserable. Because the *Yorktown* was the target of both *Hiryu* attacks, VF-3 was most heavily involved, with a total of twenty-three Wildcats actually engaged. This compares with about six each for VF-6 and VF-8, operating from the distant task force. The Japanese admitted twenty-four planes shot down in their two strikes, of which probably twenty-one fell to F4Fs. Thach's squadron seems to deserve credit for all these except two Zeros and three bombers. Therefore, without ignoring Fighting 6's generally good performance (which included two recon floatplanes during the fourth) one is still left to conclude that VF-3 with its strong core of VF-42 pilots handled task force defense almost by itself.

The matter of the *Hornet* Air Group was never properly addressed, even after the war. The captain, Marc Mitscher, went on to greater things as commander of the Fast Carrier Task Force in 1944–45, and is still recognized as perhaps the leading practitioner of his trade. But the bungled strike, loss of all escorting fighters, and a generally ineffective CAP performance still remain unexamined. The *Hornet*'s action report is sketchy and often vague, and none of her squadrons produced accounts. Perhaps the manner in which Torpedo 8 flew to glory overshadowed the larger failings, but a professional readership will do well to recall that such things can happen even in the U.S. Navy.

On the brighter side, the Wildcat had now taken the measure of the Zero. From a six-to-three deficit at Coral Sea, the F4F squadrons bounced back to outshoot the A6M eleven to five just four weeks later. Victory at Midway properly belongs to the Dauntless, but the Wildcat (to reverse an old saying) could now lick its weight in Zeros.

The 60-day respite between Midway and Guadalcanal allowed a much-needed breathing space. There was time to sit back, however briefly, and take stock; assess the developments of the first six months of the Pacific War and absorb their lessons. Tactically and strategically, certain patterns began to emerge. Some useful generalities could be set down as doctrine.

Perhaps the most obvious lesson was that carrier warfare was expensive, in ships, aircraft, and aviators. Coral Sea and Midway had cost the U.S. Navy two flattops and three other vessels, plus some 180 carrier planes and dozens of pilots and aircrew. After early June the well-established prewar air-group structure was a shambles. Attrition and necessary reorganization after Midway left none of the three remaining Pacific Fleet carriers with intact air groups. The *Lexington*'s squadrons were decommissioned after her sinking, their personnel mostly rotated stateside.

Of the Yorktowners only Scouting 5 remained active for awhile longer. Fighting 42 had lost its identity in the VF-3 merger and was disbanded on 22 June. Charlie Fenton's unit was the only fighter squadron to participate in the world's first carrier battles, though Jimmy Thach and his outfit's designation took precedence. Fighting 8, that unhappy *Hornet* squadron, lingered until August. Most of its pilots returned to combat before year-end and they acquitted themselves well. But it is significant that while the torpedo squadrons annihilated at Midway were rebuilt and deployed again that fall, VF-8 passed into oblivion.

Only two Marine fighter squadrons had seen action since 7 December. Both were write-offs, through no fault of their own; VMF-211 at Wake and 221 at Midway. The upcoming Guadalcanal campaign would provide more than ample opportunity for leatherneck squadrons to even the score.

The big reason for optimism on the grand scale was knowledge that the Imperial Navy had been severely crippled. The carrier exchange rate stood at five to two in the Americans' favor, and Japan lost 300 or more aircraft in the initial flattop duels. This, in context of successful defensive engagements, meant the United States could shift to the offense for the first time. That was the real significance of the Guadalcanal operation.

For the U.S. air groups there was also reason for optimism. The SBD, though considered obsolescent, had proven a superior dive-bomber. Well tested and available in sufficient numbers, it would remain the premier strike aircraft in the Pacific well into 1943. And while Midway had depleted nearly one-third of total TBD production, the new Grumman replacement was now operational. The TBF Avenger was largely untried but offered enormous advantages over the Devastator, and looked like a good bet.

The fighter squadrons were less sanguine about the F4F-4. No replacement appeared on the horizon, and in fact the first Hellcats were over twelve months away from combat. While many VF people (perhaps most) were emotionally attached to the rugged little Wildcat, intellectually and professionally they recognized its limitations. The folding wing was, in nearly every documented case, considered the only advantage over the dash three. While Coral Sea and Midway had demonstrated the value of increased fighter strength, the quality of that extra protection seemed diminished.

A case in point is the experience of Fighting 6. Recalled Jim Gray, "On several occasions we flew missions of over five hours in the -3A. At Midway, after climbing to 20,000 feet en route, our F4F-4s had used up over half a tank of gas in little over an hour."[28] Range and its flip side, endurance, both counted for a lot in the Pacific. A cursory examination of debriefs and after-action reports shows fighter directors constantly concerned about reinforcing the CAP due to low fuel state in airborne F4F-4s. External fuel tanks were badly needed.

Fighter direction itself is almost inseparable from the technical strengths or faults of the standard carrier fighter. Mistakes had been made both at Coral Sea and Midway, and they would be made again. But carrier warfare was a wholly new military art form. Nobody had ever done it before, and both sides learned as they went. The hitch was, most lessons were expensive. After Coral Sea, for instance, analysis of radar plots showed that several Japanese snoopers eluded the American CAP because FDOs hadn't allowed a radical enough vector to complete an intercept. FDOs, no less than duck hunters or fighter pilots, had to lead their targets.

Slow-climbing Wildcats had difficulty meeting high-flying bombers if not carefully pre-positioned. The initial tendency was to hold the CAP in close to the task force—generally within 10 or 12 miles—for better communications and control. But experience showed the wisdom of what became known as "forward interception." The farther out an enemy raid could be met, the better the prospects of breaking it up. However, if too much of the CAP were deployed at high altitude, it left the superior Japanese torpedo threat an opening which couldn't be ceded without excessive risk. But state-of-the-art electronics in 1942 were insufficient for reliable communication and identification at longer ranges. VHF radios were a full year away from fleet-wide service, and IFF sets remained both scarce and skittish.

The other major comment about the dash four Wildcat concerned its armament. About this time a correction was found for the nagging ammo-feed problem. Close examination showed burrs on many F4Fs aluminum feed chutes, causing snags which impeded smooth functioning. Grumman changed to stainless steel, heavier but much smoother, and the belt-feed problem largely disappeared.

Ammo box design was another fault, as an abrupt pushover induced negative G which lifted the belt to the top of the can. And from time to time, defective ammunition popped up. But the M2 Brownings established a terrific reputation for punch and reliability. Adequately maintained—particularly with proper headspace adjustment—they were the finest aircraft weapon of the war. Addressing a BuAer forum upon his return from the Pacific, Jimmy Thach spoke for the vast majority of Navy fighter pilots when he said, "I would prefer to have the .50-caliber gun to any other weapon I know of. I have, of course, never fought with a cannon, but I still feel that for a fighter, four .50-calibers are enough. The pilot who will miss with four .50-caliber guns won't be able to hit with eight. Increased firepower is not a substitute for marksmanship."[29]

It has been said that the guns are the soul of a fighter plane. If so, whatever the Wildcat's physical limitations, its soul was pure. But the addition of two more guns in the F4F-4 was, as Thach noted, not necessarily a benefit. It actually brought about a reduction in the amount of ammunition carried, and imposed a weight penalty with the extra weapons and their mounts. The -3 packed a maximum capacity 1,800 rounds (four guns, each with 450 rounds) while the new Grumman loaded 1,440 (240 rounds per each of six guns). Consequently, some F4F-4 pilots entered combat with two guns switched off. It not only conserved ammo, but provided a bit of "get me home" insurance. Eventually the Navy acknowledged that more isn't always better. The FM-1, FM-2, and finally the F8F-1 were all built with four .50s instead of the standard six.

However, on the plus side, combat pilots kept coming back to the Wildcat's terrific ruggedness. Again citing Jim Gray: "The F4F-4 was solid as a brick outhouse, almost a flying tank. It could take a lot of punishment, but I would have preferred the extra performance to the additional two guns. The -3 was easier to maneuver, but the tactics developed by Jimmy Thach more than made up for the superior maneuverability of the Japanese fighters. The Japanese were very vulnerable; we stayed in business after being hit repeatedly. I owe my very life to Grumman."[30]

Thus, Navy pilots learned quickly—especially after the initial contact with Zeros at Coral Sea—that dogfighting the opposition was pure folly. A cut-and-thrust turning contest in the classic tradition played directly into Japanese hands. Therefore, F4F pilots had to recognize the relative strengths and weaknesses inherent in each side's aircraft design philosophy and act accordingly.

During this early phase of the war, accurate information on Japan's newer aircraft types was limited. The pre-1940 designs were usually correctly identified since they'd been operational prior to Pearl Harbor. The Zero was another matter entirely.

Lieutenant (jg) Bill Leonard of VF-42 was among the first Navy fighter pilots to see Zeros up close. He recalls the initial impression that they must have been retractable-gear dive-bombers, owing to the unusually long canopy. Even then, rumors and spurious official data only clouded the matter. After-action reports throughout 1942 note supposed differences between the "Nagoya" and "Sentoki" Zeros. Nagoya, of course, was the site of Mitsubishi's main factory, and *sentoki* is merely the Japanese word for fighter, abbreviated as *Zero-Sen*. Furthermore, as late as the Battle of Santa Cruz there were reported sightings of Messerschmitt 109s off Japanese carriers. There were no 109s, of course, but pilots had been told to look for them, and in the confusion of combat they sometimes saw what they expected to see.

Aircraft identification was aided considerably in the second half of 1942 when the first air intelligence lists of enemy planes' code names appeared. Periodically updated, it reduced confusion and largely established standardization of Japanese aircraft types. Thus, the Zero became "Zeke," the Aichi 99 became "Val," the Nakajima 97 was "Kate" and the surprising G4M bomber passed into history as the notorious "Betty." Even so, U.S. aviators still studied profiles of "Mike" for some time—the widely-reported Japanese Me-109.

At the technical level, a debating point for much of 1942 was the Zero's forward visibility. Photos and drawings of the A6M2 showed the bulbous engine cowling, which American fliers felt must restrict the view forward. Therefore, many aviators believed that Zero pilots couldn't shoot accurately at wide deflection angles. Presumably the target aircraft would be obscured by that big cowl when the Zero pulled lead.

But in some early engagements Wildcats came back with holes in their sides and pilots exclaimed, "The Japs have some ace out there who's shooting deflection."[31] Later, when captured Zeros were flown, it became apparent that the A6M's forward visibility was better than anticipated. However, it wasn't quite as good as the Wildcat's, owing to the 6½-degree elevation of the Grumman's line-of-sight over the cowl. Aircraft designers call this subject "cockpit geometry," and it was as much a factor in surviving combat as guns or engines.

So much for the technical aspects of the early war period. Even more important was the human half of the equation. After six months of exposure, it was possible to classify squadron pilots into three broad categories. By far the largest was composed of those aviators who perhaps had little professional ambition, but would do their part to help finish an unpleasant business. They accepted each assignment as it came along, but generally preferred to limit their efforts to little more than honor required.

A far smaller group, including a few career men, quickly decided that this wasn't the job they'd imagined. Quite aside from the occupational hazard of being shot at were other wartime risks: stretching fuel to the limit on long escorts or patrols, landing on a pitching deck in darkness or rough weather. Such individuals frequently suggested that their valuable experience would be best employed in the training command. On occasion—not often, but inevitably when the home team could least afford it—a few of these men reported shadowy problems ranging from backaches (almost impossible to disprove) to malfunctioning radios, or rough-running engines. The only thing to do was grant their wish and send them home. They were useless in combat, and downright harmful in positions in leadership.

The third category outnumbered the second but was still substantially smaller than the first. These were the tigers: dedicated warriors who asked little more than a chance to ply their trade. Their motivation tended to differ, but broadly fell under two sub-headings.

There were career professionals who, finding themselves actually engaged in the activity for which they had trained most of their adult lives, naturally wanted to capitalize upon it. The high turnover of wartime personnel through attrition and rotation meant unprecedented opportunities for enhancement of professional reputations. This was particularly true of aviators, who at rock-bottom tend to be egotists anyway. An individual might not finish the war with three stripes and an air group, but if he were acknowledged by his fellows as a hot pilot, it counted for a great deal.

The smallest sub-species, and in some ways the most productive, frequently overlapped the ambitious careerists. But whether regular or reserve, there were in most squadrons a handful of men who relished combat. Some would privately confess that to them war became a global game, the most exhilarating of all bloodsports. For obvious reasons, a good many of these men perished. But others prospered. In an individual capable of distinguishing between foolhardiness and intelligent aggressiveness, mated with the pertinent skills, this personality made a superior combat pilot and perhaps the ideal tactical leader. He often fared poorly in civilian life or the peacetime military, but for the remainder of 1942 and the three years following, he was invaluable.

5. GUADALCANAL

"One of the blood-honored names of American history."
—James Michener

THE OFFICIAL NAME WAS Operation Watchtower. But eventually the Guadalcanal occupation became better known as Operation Shoestring. And not without reason. Throughout most of the bitter, bloody, six-month campaign, everybody was usually short of everything.

It started with considerable allotment of resources. The First Marine Division, reinforced, went ashore on 7 August, siezing beachheads on Guadalcanal's north-central coast and occupying the neighboring island of Tulagi. The real objective, however, was a not-quite-completed airstrip on The Canal's northern plain. It would serve as the aerial springboard up the Solomons chain in the U.S. offensive for the Southwest Pacific.

Supporting the 19,000 Marines were three fleet carriers and a substantial cruiser–destroyer force to cover the invasion transports. The *Enterprise*, *Saratoga*, and *Wasp* flew scores of search, strike, and ground-support sorties the first day, gaining local air superiority with little difficulty. Wildcats of VF-5, 6, and 71—totaling ninety-nine F4F-4s—destroyed some sixteen float and seaplanes in the area before most got airborne.

But the Imperial Navy's 25th Air Flottila at Rabaul on New Britain, over 600 statute miles northwest, was quick to react. Demonstrating a combat reach and professional competence which still

103

astonished some Americans, the Japanese had land-based bombers *with fighter escort* over Guadalcanal shortly after mid-day. They were twenty-seven G4M Bettys with seventeen Zeros, plus nine one-way Vals which lacked the fuel for a round-trip. Their goal was to sink the transports or at least drive them from the area, leaving the Marines stranded ashore.

Hard-fought combat ensued over the waters of what would shortly become known as Ironbottom Sound. But the Wildcat CAP was committed piecemeal and suffered accordingly. Fighter direction was handled by the cruiser *Chicago*, operating with the *Saratoga* and *Enterprise* to the southwest, and the first VF-6 division ordered to intercept took a reciprocal bearing and erroneously flew away from the fight.

Eight *Saratoga* Wildcats hit the Bettys during their bomb runs at 12,000 feet but were roughly handled by the veteran Japanese. One VF-5 pilot engaged in a spectacular dogfight with one of the Imperial Navy's best aviators, as Flight Petty Officer Saburo Sakai actually found an F4F turning with his Zero. Sakai, who claimed over fifty kills in his combat career since China, had never seen anything like it. Finally he gained the advantage and pulverized the Grumman from astern, watching the pilot bail out. Four other *Saratoga* F4Fs were lost in this scrap, including two pilots.

As the Bettys pulled away to the north over Florida Island, still largely intact, they were jumped by four VF-6 planes. Zekes engaged them and in a running fight up near Santa Isabell another half-dozen *Enterprise* fighters piled in. Altogether the Zeros gunned down four of Lieutenant Commander Lou Bauer's pilots in a wheeling, low-level dogfight. Five Bettys and two A6Ms had also gone down.

About an hour later the slower Vals arrived, hitting a U.S. destroyer, but elements of VF-5 and VF-6 intercepted. Ensign Donald Runyon off the *Enterprise*, a twenty-nine-year-old former NAP, claimed two kills. And though the F4Fs reported eleven shootdowns, none of the Aichis returned to base. But they hadn't expected to: four ditched, out of fuel.

Regardless of the respective claims, at the end of the day the 25th Air Flotilla was short sixteen airplanes. Vice Admiral Frank Jack Fletcher's task force had lost half the eighteen Wildcats actually engaged with the Bettys and Zekes, plus a *Wasp* SBD—all shot down by Rabaul's long-ranging fighters. The Marines were ashore, however, and off-loading of equipment and supplies was to continue the next day.

The Japanese also continued things next morning. Twenty-three G4Ms with Zero escort got within five miles of the U.S. ships before the CAP got the word. The low-level approach had succeeded, despite adequate warning from Australian coastwatchers further north. Three *Enterprise* Wildcats made a last-minute intercept, dumping three bombers and a Zeke, including one each by Don Runyon. The shipboard gunners put up a terrific performance, accounting for thirteen more bombers in exchange for damage to two ships.

So far, so good. But unloading proceeded slowly. Amphibious warfare was still new to the armed forces of the United States; the previous such operation had occurred during the Spanish–American War. Time was needed to get the vital supplies ashore, but time was fading with the setting sun on the evening of 8 August.

A formidable Japanese cruiser–destroyer force entered the sound in the early hours of the ninth and sprang another of the unpleasant surprises for which the Imperial Navy was famous. Without noteworthy damage to his own force, Vice Admiral Mikawa overwhelmed five Allied cruisers, sinking four and leaving the fifth crippled. The only blessing he left in his wake was a disinclination to finish off the easy-meat transports.

The dramatic reversal of fortune imposed a hard decision on the Americans. Without adequate surface protection the transports couldn't remain in hostile waters a day longer. And Vice Admiral Fletcher, forever computing his fuel state and obliged to reserve his CVs, refused to remain in the area. Citing the loss of twenty-one Wildcats to all causes in the previous three days, he was already withdrawing southwards. Rear Admiral Kelly Turner, responsible for the transports, glumly informed the Marine commander, General Archer Vandegrift, of the situation. Then Turner upped anchor and departed, taking most of the First Marine Division's equipment with him.

The Marines had landed, all right, but the situation was barely in hand. Since carriers were out, there was a screaming need for land-based air, and soon. The 25th Air Flotilla had taken severe losses—three-quarters of its available bombers so far—but Guadalcanal was scouted almost daily, without opposition. From the 18th on, bombing was regular. But help was on the way.

Marine Air Group 23, with two fighter and two dive-bomber squadrons, had been formed in May, only three months before Watchtower. Still based at the new Marine Air Station at Ewa on Oahu, MAG-23 was the obvious choice to provide air for Guadalcanal. But none of the squadrons was combat-ready in early July. The two dive-bomber outfits flew old SBD-2s and the fighter squadrons, VMF-223 and 224, were still making do with F2As.

But things changed, fast. Alerted for probable deployment, the forward echelon (VMF-223 and VMSB-232) engaged in an orgy of intense training and familiarization over the next few weeks. New pilots and airplanes arrived about the same time, and 223 hardly believed its good fortune upon finding itself the owner of twenty new F4F-4s.

Two-Twenty-Three's CO was a newly-promoted major, twenty-seven-year-old John Lucien Smith. A former artilleryman and dive-bomber pilot, he set out to train a fighter squadron for combat without having previously trained any unit for much of anything. This was his first command, but the Oklahoman intended to accomplish as much as time and endurance allowed. John L. Smith was widely considered a tough, abrasive character, determined and ambitious. But whatever flaws he may have possessed, combat leadership wasn't one of them.

Among the new pilots transferred in around the end of June were three survivors of VMF-221. These men, Marion Carl, Clayton Canfield, and Roy Corry, all had a smattering of combat experience from Midway. They lent a bit of expertise to the fledgling squadron, though there still remained an enormous amount to absorb in the coming four weeks.

First came about twelve hours of transition to F4F-4s, closely followed by carrier qualification. In mid-July VMF-223 listened as Captain Bob Galer, the skipper of 224, explained about field carrier landing practice. Galer was one of a handful of Marines qualified as a landing signal officer, and that particular skill had saved him from going to Wake Island with VMF-211 in November 1941. His advice was quickly put to use as each 223 pilot made about five landings aboard the *Hornet* during the 15th and 16th. One pilot ended up in the barrier, but nobody got hurt. However, 223's luck didn't hold entirely. A plane and pilot were lost when a second lieutenant apparently blacked out during a practice dogfight at 12,000 feet.

From 21 to 31 July, Smith had his pilots concentrate on tactics and gunnery. And in the limited time available, VMF-223 practiced hard. Gunnery was a fetish with Smith. He realized that no pilot, however skillful, was much use in combat unless he could get hits. It was part pragmatism, part pride. Those were the days when every Marine was expected to be a marksman.

By the end of July most 223 pilots had logged about forty hours in their new planes. On 2 August the squadron went aboard the escort carrier *Long Island* with nineteen officers, sixty-five enlisted men and nineteen Wildcats. The remaining thirty-two mechanics and ordnancemen embarked in the transport *W. W. Burrows*. Both ships were bound for Guadalcanal.

Sharing the *Long Island*'s crowded flight deck were a dozen SBD-3s of VMSB-232. The dive-bomber skipper was Lieutenant Colonel Richard Mangrum, a veteran aviator most frequently described by his colleagues as a recruiting-poster Marine, and a gentleman to the bone. Smith and Mangrum's thirty-one airplanes were to operate from a mysterious place they knew by two names—its proper name and the radio code word, Cactus. Thus they became the core of what would forever after be called the Cactus Air Force.

En route, the *Long Island* stopped at Efate in the New Hebrides for last-minute acquisition of supplies and exchange of some personnel. Smith traded his eight least-experienced pilots for an equal number of Major Harold W. Bauer's more seasoned VMF-212 men. They were mostly second lieutenants but included a valuable asset in a warrant officer pilot, Marine Gunner Henry B. Hamilton, a big Texan who would become the most successful non-commissioned fighter pilot in the U.S. Naval service. "Indian Joe" Bauer and his other pilots would have to wait, as advanced reserve squadrons were exceedingly rare. The only other fighter outfit in the region was VMO-251 at Espiritu Santo. Two-Twelve would be committed piecemeal as a replacement unit until the whole squadron arrived in mid-October, and 251 would perform valuable ferry service until its pilots finished tactical and gunnery training.

Meanwhile, 223 packed its Wildcats with everything which would fit into an F4F: spark plugs, starter cartridges, tool kits, even spare tires. Marion Carl was one up on everybody else. He'd acquired a Cushman scooter before leaving San Diego in December 1941 and sent it along with the equipment in the *W. W. Burrows*.

On the afternoon of 20 August, two days out of Efate, the *Long Island* steamed into a southeast wind off the southern tip of San Cristobal Island, southernmost of the Solomons. Launch commenced nearly 200 miles out from Guadalcanal. In a tedious, time-consuming process, all thirty-one planes were catapulted off the CVE's 400-foot deck. The lighter Wildcats went first, followed by Dick Mangrum's Dauntlesses. With launch completed, VMF-223 and VMSB-232 proceeded northwest along Cristobal's coast toward Cactus, an hour and twenty minutes away.

The fliers knew relatively little of what to expect at Guadalcanal.

Industrious engineers and a Navy advance unit for aircraft servicing had turned the incomplete Japanese airstrip into a usable facility. It was officially named Henderson Field after a Marine dive-bomber pilot killed at Midway.

Smith's and Mangrum's people learned soon enough how they would live and operate for the next eight weeks. Henderson Field was a 3,800-foot strip about 150 feet wide, covered mostly at this stage with pierced steel planking. The PSP afforded a margin of safety for aircraft operating in muddy, wet weather, but part of the field was merely packed dirt or gravel. The strip was oriented slightly northeast–southwest, barely inland from the coast at Lunga Point. In fact, its west end nearly ran into the east bank of the twisty Lunga River. The whole facility lay within a narrow, tenuous defensive perimeter.

Facilities were sparse, which is to say nearly nonexistant. No revetments were yet completed. A marginal supply of aviation fuel had been stashed with a skimpy assortment of parts and tools, but aircraft maintenance would remain a considerable test of American ingenuity and know-how. Throughout the next three months or more, aviators would find themselves chronically short of oxygen bottles and oxygen transfer equipment, all manner of parts and components, and frequently gasoline. Fortunately, ammunition seldom ran low, but the dive-bombers never had as many 1,000-pounders as they'd have liked.

Accommodations were primitive, though correspondent-historian Robert Sherrod was probably closer to the mark when he described them as "appalling."[1] Practically everybody lived in mud-floor tents or in dugouts, with handy foxholes nearby. Smith's personnel were given Japanese blankets and mosquito netting but usually ate from borrowed infantry messkits. What they ate was generally captured rice mixed with dehydrated food and the ubiquitous World War II contribution to American culture—spam. The diet and environment (featuring a splendid variety of tropical diseases) insured that men lost weight.

The only "permanent" structures were a few Japanese buildings: "the Pagoda," which became Henderson's operations center, and a hangar which eventually collapsed of its own accord. Best of all was an invaluable ice plant, "The Tojo Ice Factory," with a big scoreboard to tally the Cactus Air Force's record.

Communications were another problem, since the rag-tag assembly of aircraft which filtered through Cactus during the campaign only coincidentally had the same radio frequencies. With all this in mind the fliers went to bed that night.

And were awakened in the wee hours of the morning. A sustained volume of shooting came from the perimeter about 3,000 yards away, where newly-landed Japanese troops inaugurated the battle of the "Tenaru River." Actually, the American maps were wrong on many topographical features. The waterway was colorfully named Alligator Creek, where First Battalion, First Marines stacked up 800 Japanese.

Business picked up almost as if in response to VMF-223's arrival. During noon hour of the 21st, Smith's division tangled with a half-dozen Zeros over Ironbottom sound, near Savo Island. Smith saw them coming, 800 to 900 yards out and about 500 feet above. He turned into the attack, drew a bead on one Zero which banked away exposing its belly, and got in a burst. Then both formations split in a series of tail-chases. With two Japanese on his own tail, Smith poked his Wildcat's round nose down and headed back towards shore. The Zeros weren't having any of that; they broke off.

Returning to the Savo area, Smith regrouped two of his wingmen but his section leader, Sergeant John Lindley, had disappeared. Then the Zeros pounced again, putting some 7.7-mm holes in a couple of F4Fs, but the Marines found they could disengage as long as they had enough altitude to dive out.

Back at Henderson, Smith found Lindley's Wildcat a complete write-off. Hit in the engine, he'd dead-sticked in a wheels-up landing. But unidentified debris was reported in the water off Savo, and that was taken as evidence of a kill by Smith. During the day Lieutenant E. A. Trowbridge claimed two more Zekes, though no surviving Japanese records substantiate any of the claims.

In its first three days of combat, VMF-223 proved that fledgling F4F pilots could hold their own against the experienced Japanese. The claim stood at five kills for one loss, and whatever the real score, it boosted the Marines' morale. But the Cactus Air Force would have to continue to outshoot the opposition; the leathernecks could not afford to trade the Japanese one for one or even two for one at this early date. The Imperial Navy figured the A6M was the equal of three other fighters, even with its belly tank for the long, long round trip from Rabaul. In fact, the outnumbered Marines on The Canal would have to maintain nearly a three-to-one exchange rate just to hold the line.

The first meaningful test of Marine Corps fighters occurred on 24

August. Wake and Midway had proven the VMF squadrons had all the nerve and aggressiveness for the job, but in both cases the odds had been hugely stacked against them. However, the 24th afforded a reasonable evaluation in context of the first of two carrier duels fought during the Guadalcanal campaign. The *Enterprise* and *Saratoga* contested a major Japanese reinforcement attempt, sinking the light carrier *Ryujo* in the process. The enemy CVL's air group ran afoul of John L. Smith and company that afternoon.

The *Ryujo* launched six Nakajima bombers and fifteen Zekes with instructions to neutralize American airpower ashore. They were joined over the island by twenty Bettys from Rabaul. Forewarned, Smith was waiting with fourteen Wildcats over the water north of Henderson Field, between Malaita and Florida Islands. What followed has never been fully documented, owing to contradictory claims. But the Marines made their first big impression on Japanese airpower.

Evidently Marion Carl's decision made first contact. Flying the number four position was Second Lieutenant Mel Freeman, a VMF-212 pilot who'd only been on the island three days. He looked down, saw dark-painted twin-engine planes resembling Martin B-26s, and watched Carl peel off into "the most damned *beautiful* overhead passes I've ever seen."[2] Carl dumped one Mitsubishi, Trowbridge bagged another, then it became a free-for-all as the *Ryujo* formation arrived. Freeman tangled with a B5N, then a Zero. Lieutenant Zenneth Pond claimed a triple with two Kates and an A6M while Gunner Tex Hamilton claimed two Zeros. The other NAP, Johnny Lindley, gained a measure of revenge for his misfortune at the hands of Zekes three days before by shooting a Zero out of formation.

The engagement became a running gunfight as the F4Fs pursued the Japanese right over Henderson. The surviving bombers did little damage. Marion Carl made history this day, killing two more bombers and a Zero to become the Corps' first fighter ace. It all amounted to claims for twenty confirmed, including seven A6Ms. At most it appears 223 accounted for three A6Ms, three B5Ns and five Bettys, though all the *Ryujo* planes were lost when their ship sank.[3] On the debit side, 223 lost three pilots during the day. Two more were killed by the end of the month, with another missing.

But MAG-23's second echelon arrived on the 30th; Major Bob Galer with nineteen Wildcats of VMF-224, and a dozen Dauntlesses of VMSB-231. The reinforcements staged an appropriate if unexpectedly harrowing debut, arriving over Henderson amidst an air raid. Smith's crowd made Galer's troops welcome, explaining the hunting was good—too good, in fact—and that there was plenty for everyone.

That point was well proven this day. With the same warnings to 224 they'd received themselves ten days before (eat and sleep at every chance, and don't go into the jungle alone) 223 went back to the war. The squadron ambushed a Zero formation, claiming fourteen kills, including four to Marion Carl and three to John L. Smith. Enemy aircraft losses are not definitely recorded but it is known that the Japanese lost at least seven fighter pilots this date. Thus, the leading Marines were well into an approximately friendly rivalry, with the score currently pegged at eleven for Carl, nine for "Smitty." That night General Vandegrift wrote, "Lord, but these boys are fighters."[4]

But beneath the banter and shoptalk was a current of constant tension. Everyone was tired from lack of sleep (except perhaps Carl, who could nap anywhere) and the strain of combat and loss of friends began to tell. Somebody took time to figure the actuarial possibilities and concluded that VMF-223 would cease to exist in three weeks.

Different men dealt with it in different ways. Some brooded on their prospects for survival, and inevitably they were the first to go. Others lived day-to-day, keenly aware of their mortality but preferring not to dwell on it. Instead, they went swimming at night, swapped stories and opinions, and indulged in justifiable griping. Not the least reason for the latter was the perennial state of alert; Cactus seemed to exist in a permanent situation of Condition Yellow or Red.

But these were largely the younger pilots, the reservists who hadn't intended to make a military career. There seemed two kinds of effective professionals, perhaps exemplified by Smith and Galer. John L. was imbued with an iron will which, coupled with considerable self-confidence and ambition, kept himself and his squadron moving in the direction he wanted. Galer's approach seemed more low-key but yielded similar results. His pragmatic outlook was based upon the tenet of doing whatever was necessary to get the job done. One example: "We had little in the way of spares. We stole the only spare tailwheels we could get by robbing Navy planes in revetments at Pearl. Also stole the officer of the day's jeep."[5]

Galer led his pilots into combat the next day, 31 August. None had more than perhaps fifty hours in F4Fs and over half had logged only about 300 hours total time. Galer had some 1,200 hours in his logbook, including about 70 hours "in type," and his greater experience would quickly show. But the first lessons are often the hardest learned. Seventeen Wildcats intercepted an inbound raid, and fourteen pilots returned to Henderson, making no claims. One of the missing fliers returned a week later. The Marines were beginning to understand what the Fifth Air Force commander General John C. Kenney, meant when, speaking of the Japanese, he said, "You take on Notre Dame every time you play." Jimmy Thach agreed, noting "In all our battles it was anybody's game til the ninth inning."[6] However, on 2 September VMF-224 knocked down four raiders, with the CO accounting for a Zero and a bomber.

And so it went. The routine—if constant flying, fighting, and ducking bombs or naval shells can ever be routine—was now established. The Japanese seemed locked into a timetable, running the 25th Air Flotilla almost on an airline schedule. Nearly every day weather permitted, Bettys from Rabaul with escorting Zeros from Buin came down The Slot, the long stretch of water running the length of the Solomons. The raiders typically arrived between 1100 and 1300 hours, and the Marines were nearly always up and waiting. It wouldn't have been possible without the coastwatchers; resourceful, courageous Australian ex-planters, government men, naval officers, and missionaries. Stationed on most islands in the chain, equipped with bulky "portable" radios and aided by a few trustworthy natives, these men gave Henderson Field the precious time it needed to meet each major threat. "Thirty bombers headed yours" became a catchphrase, its terseness and phrasing symbolic of the very nature of the coastwatchers' work.

And crucial it was. The F4F squadrons needed about 45 minutes warning in order to scramble, form up, and climb to altitude. The dash four Wildcat simply couldn't reach 20,000 fast enough to "get out from under." Thus was born a fragile but durable relationship, a symbiosis of coastwatcher, aviator, and (by extension) rifleman. Each depended upon the success of the other.

Coastwatchers became best known to the American public for their aid in returning downed fliers and sunken sailors to safety. John F. Kennedy's PT-boat crew owed its survival to Reginald Evans on Kolombangara, but that was months away, well into the dim and distant future of 1943. For the present, most missing aviators who eventually turned up did so on their own or with help of local islanders.

Lieutenant Richard Amerine, the 224 pilot who walked back from the squadron's first mission, had a story to tell which would have pleased even Jack London, who wrote of "King Solomon's Isles" decades before. Amerine had parachuted into the jungle near Cape Esperance on Guadalcanal's northwest coast, 30 miles from base. He started eastward, and en route nearly tripped over a sleeping

Japanese. Careful to avoid making any noise, the young flier bashed in the soldier's head with a rock, then made off with his pistol and shoes.

Fortunately, Dick Amerine possessed an interest in entomology. He correctly identified an unappetizing variety of creepy-crawlies, the best of which were snails. It wasn't much, but it kept him going. Along the way he tangled with three more Japanese and was able to club two of them with his pistol, but had to shoot the other. When Amerine stumbled onto a Marine outpost on 6 September he'd nearly been given up as dead. Sick and exhausted, he was evacuated three days later. But he'd survived.

Another survivor was Marion Carl. In early September he'd come down with dysentary for two days and used that time to get his scooter running. On the ninth he took over from John L. to lead an intercept when the CO's Wildcat became mired in Guadal's ever-present mud. An estimated three dozen Bettys went after a convoy in the channel, and in the frantic hassle which followed, the aggressive Oregonian shot down two, running his string to thirteen. But an unseen Zero got below and behind Carl's pet Wildcat and shot out the oil lines. The first indication anything was seriously wrong occurred when Carl smelled smoke in the cockpit. With an in-flight fire amidst a swarm of unfriendly orientals, this was no time for sentiment. Carl rang up the for-sale sign at 20,000 feet, saying goodby to the F4F which had taken him to eleven of his victories.

Two-Twenty-Three claimed another eight kills this day, but Marion Carl's disappearance was hard to take. Sadly, the boys doled out his personal effects and assigned his bunk to a replacement.

Meanwhile, the object of this sympathy treaded water for four hours off tiny Neal Island. Finally a native boy paddled out and retrieved him. Carl was taken ashore to Guadalcanal, where a Fiji medic named Eroni made the visitor at home. After resting for a day, Carl followed Eroni and six others on a trek for Henderson Field. But they turned back on the 12th. There were too many Japanese in the area, and the group was almost certain to be spotted.

Neither Carl nor Eroni was ready to give up. A dilapidated motorboat turned up, and the Fijian helped the former farmboy get it running. Leaving in the early morning of the 14th, they putted into safe waters later that day. En route Carl saw three floatplanes shot down, professionally approving the efficient manner in which the F4Fs dispatched them. Actually, 224 claimed six of the pesky intruders that afternoon as Major John Dobbin and Lieutenant George Hollowell plucked a flock of Petes.

When Brigadier General Roy Geiger heard of Carl's return from the dead, he quickly sent for the popular young flier. The Cactus Air Force chief, in a jovial mood, informed Carl that Smith had pulled ahead in the scoring race. And indeed he had. In the five days Carl spent getting back, Smith had claimed five bombers and a Zero. Geiger asked rhetorically, "What are we going to about that?" Marion Carl knew the best way to redress the situation. Without a pause he looked Geiger in the eye. "Damn it, general," he said, only half in jest, "ground Smitty for five days!"[7]

Even though John L. had become top man in the league, Carl had to admit that things had improved. He counted fifty fighters on the field, and that "certainly looked good."[8] The increase was due in large part to the arrival of Fighting 5 off the *Saratoga*. Lieutenant Commander Leroy Simpler's twenty-four Wildcats nearly doubled Henderson's fighter population, and they were sorely needed. The two Marine F4F units were already understrength, and the Army's 67th Pursuit Squadron flew Bell Airacobras, of little use in aerial combat. The Navy pilots had come through the Eastern Solomons battle in good shape, but they were in for some hard knocks at the Canal. Their first combat came on the 12th when they put up twenty F4Fs with eleven Marines. Simpler's pilots claimed six shootdowns but lost their exec, wounded, and an ensign landing a damaged plane. At the end of the third day ashore, VF-5 had lost five pilots killed, missing or wounded.

About this time, congestion at Henderson became a problem and the Wildcats moved to a newly prepared strip a mile east. Built by Sea Bees on a grassy plain, it was officially the Fighter Strip (later Fighter One) but most people called it the Cow Pasture. There was also, at last, a radar station ashore. That was the good news. The bad news was that the station was only effective cut to 85 miles or so. And the Japanese had caught on to the fact that coastwatchers were radioing word of southbound raids, and took to flying dog-legs out to the east, sometimes avoiding detection by the vigilant Australians.

But nothing remained static on The Canal. Spare parts, fuel, airplanes, and fighter pilots were always in short supply. Joe Bauer's VMF-212 had been supplying replacement pilots since 223 first landed on the island, and Bauer himself arrived in late September. A popular, well-known character in Marine aviation, Bauer was an Annapolis man who'd returned to the Academy as an athletic instructor. Thus he was called "The Coach" by many. He flew alternately with 223 and 224 until the balance of his own squadron arrived. Intensely aggressive, he actually advocated dogfighting with Zeros.

But Wildcats were usually in shorter supply than Wildcat pilots. Innovative, hard-working mechanics cannibalized wrecked planes for parts, though sometimes that wasn't enough. Recalled Bob Galer, "I would say engines were the most critical. When a plane was shot up, you could usually salvage some parts, but normally the engine was heavily damaged."[9]

Mid-September saw the first large-scale reinforcement of nonassigned F4Fs. Previously, new Wildcats arrived with each squadron. But combat and operational attrition demanded a resupply of fresh fighters, and an unlikely combination delivered them: Marine photo-recon pilots off two aircraft carriers.

Most of the pilots of VMO-251 were new to carriers and none had been in combat. A few of the old hands had car-qualled years before, but the majority had never set foot on a flattop. Therefore, the CO, Lieutenant Colonel John Hart, instructed his troops in takeoff procedure: lock the brakes and run up the engine to full power. Select "manual" for the Curtiss Electric prop in full low pitch, which allowed a safe engine overspeed of 2,900 rpm when the plane reached about 70 knots indicated. With flaps down, a short deck-run was possible.

On the night of 12 September, 251 enjoyed hot showers aboard the *Wasp* and *Hornet*, then ate a civilized dinner in the wardroom, with linen tablecloths and genuine food: fresh salad, steaks, cake, and ice cream. Said Master Technical Sergeant Wendel Garton, "That was the only way to fight a war!"[10]

Just before dawn on the 13th the Marines launched with some seventeen Wildcats. The two-hour flight was made with each carrier's planes in separate formations, but within sight of one another. The pilots of VMO-251 received an eye-opening introduction to The Canal. Landing at Henderson as briefed, they looked for a parking area when a Marine climbed on each Grumman, instructing the pilot to proceed to the Fighter Strip. Since nobody had shut down his engine, the 251 gaggle took off, not even bothering to roll up its wheels.

Approaching the west end of the Cow Pasture, Hart's pilots were surprised to see a landing signal officer, paddles outstretched, working each plane in turn. It was Bob Galer, that enthusiastic if land-locked LSO, who'd expected Navy pilots from the carriers. Everybody got down safely.

But hardly had VMO-251 unstrapped and climbed out when a red alert sounded about 0800. One eager pilot, Lieutenant Rutledge, without benefit of orders or invitation, jumped into an unassigned F4F. But in his haste he'd not been able to to adjust the rudder pedals to fit his legs. Onlookers immediately knew the gung-ho newcomer was in trouble as the Wildcat accelerated down the grass strip. It began drifting left owing to insufficient rudder throw. Rutledge coaxed the runaway fighter into the air, barely clearing the trees at the end of the field. Then he stalled, snapped to port, and crashed inverted into the trees. His friends knew he was dead, an hour after landing.

Miraculously, Rutledge survived and recovered. But his misadventure was typical. Three of the other new Wildcats were wrecked or shot down before they were even assigned to a squadron.

Rutledge had barely been carted away in an ambulance when a piercing, high-pitched whine descended from the sky. Looking up, the 251 pilots saw an F4F-4 diving straight down, engine screaming. It plummeted into the trees south of the field, sending up a cloud of smoke. Obviously the Grumman had gone in from a tremendous height, and witnesses speculated the pilot had succumbed to hypoxia. Smith's squadron lost this flier and one other during the day.

That afternoon, following a Guadalcanal lunch of diced spam in Japanese rice, the new arrivals were treated to another spectacle. Two Zero floatplanes flew westbound through Henderson's traffic pattern as the last of four SBDs turned base leg at 500 feet. Machine-gunners opened fire at the Rufes but the Japanese took no action.

Abruptly, as if only then seeing the Dauntless, the Rufe leader cut across the pattern and made for the sitting-duck dive-bomber. The float fighter ripped a short burst into the Douglas, which rolled to port and went straight in. The Rufe pulled up, his wingman rejoined, and the intruding pair continued its leisurely flight. Nobody could believe it—the whole episode was surrealistic.

Another alert sounded ten minutes later, and this time most of the VMO pilots got airborne. Straining to join the VMF-223 and 224 pilots who had already scrambled, the 251 formation became strung out. Sergeant Garton had the best plane of the bunch and soon outdistanced his mates. "That F4F-4 I flew that day had the best engine supercharger capability of any Wildcat I ever flew," he recalled.[11]

Then Garton saw his first airborne hostile, a Zero above on the starboard beam. The flying sergeant rolled into a right-hand turn, anticipating a head-on shot when the Japanese committed himself. But the Zero turned away, joining a formation of Bettys to the northwest.

Garton continued to climb, having spotted a lone Wildcat ahead of him. Intending to join the stranger, Garton sailed right past the F4F since he had never done any high-altitude formation flying, and overshot. But by now the Bettys were jettisoning their bombs and turning back up The Slot. They were unmolested, but wouldn't escape intact. Garton passed the formation a couple of miles to port, topping out at 26,000 feet. With his 5,000-foot altitude advantage he initiated a high-side pass out of the westering sun. "I'm sure they didn't know I was there until my tracers started flashing through the formation," he recalled. "But of course, I had buck fever and started firing well out of lethal range." Then the Zeros, which had snuggled up to the Bettys for the trip home, took notice. They suddenly "popped up like rockets" and Garton remembered how alone he was up there. He rolled into a vertical dive towards Guadalcanal, leaving them well behind.[12]

All this might have been considered enough for one day. After all, the Cactus fighters had claimed eleven shootdowns for the loss of six Wildcats, including three from VF-5. But that night the men spent most of their time in foxholes, listening to the free-for-all to the south which became famous in Corps history as the Battle of the Ridge. At dawn the aviators could hear Japanese yelling just across Henderson Field, and some old-timers wished earnestly for their '03 Springfields instead of the .45 Colt automatics they were issued.

The 251 pilots were flown back to Espiritu Santo on the 14th. Their one day on The Canal was an education, but they'd be back for postgraduate work.

After the 14th, the equatorial weather closed down combat flying for almost two weeks. The Japanese made no serious attempt to bomb Henderson Field in that time, and the Cactus fliers certainly bene-fitted from the respite, though the driving rain and oozing mud rendered life no less miserable.

Still, there was time to regroup, after a fashion. The pilot shortage was as acute as ever, and at least one Army flier took up temporary residence in a Marine squadron. In one of those coincidences which occur only in remote places in time of war, Captain John C. Wilkins, USAAF, joined his old college classmate Marion Carl in VMF-223. They'd both graduated from Oregon State in 1938. But Wilkins' stint with the leathernecks was brief. He joined on the 19th and was detached the 23rd.

By the 17th Guadal's air strength was up to sixty-three planes operational, including twenty-nine Wildcats. Additional SBDs and TBFs landed later in the month as Lieutenant Colonel Al Cooley's MAG-14 people settled in. This included the first few pilots of VMF-121, ferried in by Grumman Duck on the 25th. Lieutenant Colonel Bill Wallace, previously the MAG-23 CO, was designated Cactus fighter commander while Cooley ran strike ops.

But the opposition had also restocked during this period. The 26th Air Flotilla provided Rabaul with no less than seventy-two bombers, sixty new Zeros and eight recon planes. Thus, the Japanese enjoyed a two-to-one fighter superiority. When the weather cleared on the 27th, they got on with the war.

At 1230 the New Georgia coastwatcher, Donald Kennedy, radioed Henderson Field. Eighteen Bettys with a strong fighter escort were headed down The Slot. The Japanese had avoided detection further up the chain, and as Kennedy was only 100 miles from Henderson, a late intercept was inevitable. But the Japanese had too much of a head start. Smith and Galer's sixteen pilots went for the bombers almost directly over the field while Simpler's eighteen fighters locked horns with thirty-eight Zekes.

The G4Ms bombed accurately, destroying or damaging ten SBDs and TBFs, but the Marines got among them and dumped six. In his first combat since being shot down, Marion Carl bagged one over the field and split a second with Major Kirk Armistead of 224. In all, the Marines claimed eight kills and VF-5 two.

Next day another twenty-seven bombers were back with an even stronger Zero escort, and the Cactus Wildcats claimed their biggest killing to date. This time the Marines had eighteen planes airborne plus fifteen from Fighting 5, and the coastwatchers let Henderson know in plenty of time. With thirty-three F4Fs waiting at altitude well forward, the two-to-one odds didn't matter much. That evening Marion Carl noted in his diary, "We really cleaned them out—23 of 26 or 27 bombers . . ."[13] The F4Fs hit the typically precise Japanese formation from above and scattered the bombers to the winds. Two-Twenty-Three claimed seven shot down, including one each by Smith and Carl to raise their respective tallies to seventeen and fifteen and a half. Galer's crew reported eight kills, the CO himself taking three to run his own string to eight. Flying a "guest appearance" mission was 224 was Joe Bauer, up from Efate for an idea of what his 212 could expect. The Coach got his scouting report, alright, claiming his first victim.

Fighting 5 returned without loss, though several F4Fs sustained damage, and determined it had shot down nine Bettys. While Japanese records indicate that perhaps only seven bombers went down, the inability of the Zero escort to protect the Bettys, and the way the Wildcats completely broke up the attack caused serious rethinking at Rabaul. When the Japanese came back for the third day of their latest blitz, they had a new wrinkle.

Donald Kennedy counted thirty-six planes overflying New Georgia the next morning, and informed Cactus accordingly. But something was different this time. Only nine bombers were escorted by twenty-seven A6Ms. Things became even more puzzling a little later when the Bettys returned, homeward-bound. What were they up to?

The Americans would later call this tactic the fighter sweep. It wasn't entirely unknown at the time, though it was new to the Solomons. Hurt and discouraged by the drubbing inflicted by Wildcats the day before, the Kavieng-based Zeros intended to draw the F4Fs into fighter-versus-fighter combat and wear them down by attrition. The Germans had employed similar tactics during the Battle of Britain, and Allied fighters would use the same procedure to defeat Japanese airpower in the northern Solomons during the coming year. But for now, Cactus took the bait.

Again, over thirty Wildcats climbed out over the now-familar geography: Guadal's northern plain, Ironbottom Sound, and the brooding monolith of Savo Island. But only VF-5 engaged, and Simpler's fourteen Wildcats broke even with the superior number of Zeros at one for one. Back on the ground at New Ireland the Japanese pilots estimated they'd tackled thirty interceptors and shot down eight, while in debriefing at the Fighter Strip the *Saratoga* fliers claimed four.

With more rain, air ops slacked off until 2 October. On that date the persistent Imperial Navy airmen repeated their ploy of the 29th, sending thirty-six Zeros down The Slot with nine Bettys which turned around within sight of Guadalcanal. The coastwatchers had missed this sweep, and Cactus radar couldn't make up the deficit. Of thirty-three F4Fs struggling up to altitude, six were caught at a fatal disadvanatge. Two-Twenty-Three lost two pilots in the Zeros' first pass as the Japanese made expert use of altitude, position, and sun. John L. Smith turned into a cloud, then poked his nose out and found a neat setup with a trio of A6Ms dead ahead. He killed one—a spectacular flamer—but the remaining pair turned as only a Zero could, and shot his plane full of holes. Somehow Smith evaded them and, losing power, eased his crippled Wildcat into a dead-stick crash-landing six miles southeast of the Fighter Strip. He hiked back to the Marine perimeter in about two and half hours, finding a smashed F4F on a hillside along the way.

It wasn't a good day for squadron commanders. Bob Galer recorded 224's only claims, with two Zekes. But the odds piled up and he was forced to jump over Tulagi. He'd ditched another Wildcat on 11 September, but, as then, he returned safely. Leroy Simpler made the only other claim of the day. The score was ominous. Cactus had seldom come out on the short end of things, but going four for six

boded ill for the future. Smith's squadron had now lost ten pilots—
over 40 percent attrition in 42 days.

The leathernecks exacted a measure of revenge next morning.
Twenty-seven Zekes flew southeast an hour earlier than normal on
the third, and Cactus radar noted the new procedure as the naviga-
tion Bettys reversed course. But 223, now "experienced ambushers of
Japanese formations," knew what to expect.[14] Marion Carl kept his
six Wildcats in close to the field, lest low-flying bandits elude detection as the F4Fs headed out. The Marines hit the Mitsubishis northwest of Henderson, and Carl bagged number 16. Then his guns
jammed. Lieutenant Ken Frazier dropped two, then had a losing
battle with more Zeros and bailed out of his crippled F4F. A vengeful
Japanese shot at Frazier's parachute but providentially he got down
all right. Frazier had proven himself the most adept pupil of Smith's
intense training program, running up twelve and a half credited
victories for third place in the squadron.

The replacements were also heard from. Two-Twenty-Three's attrition was such that 212 and 121 pilots now fleshed out most missions.
Lieutenant Floyd Lynch of 121 got a Zeke in this fight, but Joe Bauer
grabbed top honors. Leading Carl's second division, he was credited
with four confirmed and a probable. Thus, Indian Joe joined the
growing list of Cactus aces. He was so excited that he left his
supercharger in high blower even on landing.

The fracas near Henderson put a dent in the Japanese air fleet's
confidence in the fighter sweep. Wildcat claims of nine destroyed
exactly matched acknowledged enemy losses, so the Marines had
bounced back.

In the best tradition of the Marine Corps Hymn, VMF-223 had
literally been "first to fight" of the F4F squadrons on Guadalcanal.
But Smith's crew—or what was left of it—flew its last mission on the
10th. In a fitting farewell to The Canal, 223 accompanied SBDs and
TBFs on an unusually long jaunt out of the old neighborhood.
Japanese ships reported southbound near New Georgia had to be
stopped, and Smith led seven other 223 pilots as part of the escort that
evening. Flying rear cover, Smith glanced in his mirror and noted
black specks. Evidently there were about fifteen floatplanes, Rufes
and Petes, intent on executing a stern bounce.

The CO called his pilots' attention to the developing setup, then
abruptly broke formation, turning back into the threat. Incredibly,
the Japanese also reversed course and VMF-223 licked its collective
chops as the skipper radioed, "Pick your targets." In seconds the
Wildcats clawed through the formation, dropping six float biplanes

and three Rufes. Lieutenant Fred Gutt accounted for two, raising his total to four. As John L. circled over his own kill, number nineteen, he counted five parachutes descending toward the water.[15]

Two-Twenty-Four, led by John Dobbin, concentrated on the Guadal-bound warships bearing additional troops. Seven of his pilots shot up six men-of-war. When Lieutenant Howard Walter pulled out of a strafing pass he found a hostile airplane ahead of him. He triggered a couple of bursts and knocked the floatplane into the water.

Upon departure on the twelfth, VMF-223 had sustained some 43 percent casualties among its own pilots and a few more among "loaners" from 212 and 121. Smith's squadron claimed 110 victories in its tenure since 20 August, including 47 Zeros and just as many bombers. In fact, Smith and Carl shot down more twin-engine aircraft than any other Marine pilots throughout the war—ten and eight, respectively. Both would remain in the top ten among the Corps' aerial sharpshooters, and six other 223 pilots also ranked as aces. The exec, Major Rivers Morrell, narrowly missed the honor with four and a half credited kills.

Galer's 224 remained active for another several days but the second generation of Cactus fighter pilots had already flown its first missions. On 9 October VMF-121 landed en masse, ferried within launch range by the escort carrier *Copahee*. The CO, Major Leonard K. Davis, led twenty new F4F-4s into Henderson and learned the fighters were operating from the Cow Pasture. Rather than take off again, the newcomers merely taxied to their new home.

Duke Davis was a popular, easy-going leader who got results. Like Joe Bauer, he was an Annapolis graduate, and his leadership would make 121 the premier fighter squadron of the latter Guadalcanal campaign. In the process his exec would become famous.

Captain Joseph Jacob Foss, a twenty-seven-year-old South Dakota farmer, shared Marion Carl's passions for—and skill at—flying and shooting. Dark, rugged and straight-forward, Foss had joined the Marines because "I wanted in a fightin' outfit."[16] But his first fight was merely to get into combat.

Following a stint of instructing at Pensacola throughout 1941, Foss was assigned to a Marine photo squadron at NAS North Island, San Diego, flying F4F-7s. Aghast, Foss wanted "no part of it," intending to shoot something more tangible than pictures. With equal portions of persistence and bravado he jockeyed two unsympathetic senior officers to get his way. First was his squadron CO. Foss argued that photo pilots should be familiar with fighter tactics and suggested he be detached to the nearby Aircraft Carrier Training Group to gain such experience. At the same time he hounded the singularly unsympathetic commander in charge of ACTG into accepting him. The Navy flier harbored a king-sized prejudice against Marines ("They're nothing but trouble"), and wouldn't hear of it. But Joe refused to quit, even when the three-striper constantly pointed to the door and screamed, "Get out!"

Foss finally wore the man down by volunteering for "all the dirty jobs" at ACTG. This included the unpopular but persistent duty of arranging funerals for erstwhile student carrier pilots. But at least the Marine became carrier-qualified and proficient in the F4F. Flying six hours a day, he built up flight time at an amazing rate. Foss eventually logged 1,600 hours in Wildcats and remains devoted to the design, calling it "A very trouble-free aircraft."[17] With his quickly accumulated experience he became a hot prospect and joined 121 at Camp Kearney in August.

One of Foss' pals from North Island arrived at The Canal almost simultaneously. Lieutenant Herman "Hap" Hansen found himself a staff photo pilot for First Marine Air Wing. Equipped with two F4F-7s and suitable support, he was on call almost any time of day for recon missions around Guadalcanal and up The Slot. While VMO-251 had flown a few dash sevens from Espiritu (each carrier was nominally assigned one, which was inevitably put ashore) Hansen's ubiquitous activities remained the only combat use of the long-legged Wildcat.

And he alit on The Canal just in time to be of greatest help. Mid-October became a frantic period of move and counter-move as the Japanese intensified efforts to reinforce Guadalcanal. Cactus strike command ran a seemingly non-stop shuttle of SBDs and TBFs during the 11th and 12th, with as much fighter protection as VF-5, VMF-224, and 121 could contribute. Galer and company made its biggest score on the 11th, claiming seven bombers and four Zeros.

At no time durng the six-month campaign did either side have an accurate idea of the opposition's troop strength ashore. But it wasn't necessary to count noses in order to figure what was necessary. A temporary advantage of any consequence would decide the issue. Thus The Canal became a meatgrinder, a battle of attrition on land, at sea, and in the air. And the night of the 11th–12th saw considerable attrition in the dark waters around the Island. The Battle of Cape Esperance partially thwarted enemy plans to land troops and heavy equipment, but the "Tokyo Express" kept running with businesslike consistency.

Tuesday the 13th was unlucky by day and by night. The Japanese finally began double-teaming the Cactus fighters, sending back-to-back raids which prevented effective interception of the follow-up strike. At that, the initial raid got in range without warning from the coastwatchers, and Guadal's radar was too near-sighted to compensate. Though a record forty-two Wildcats and thirteen Army fighters raced out to attempt a last-minute intercept, two dozen of the Emperor's "sea eagles" unloaded on Henderson and the Fighter Strip. One-Twenty-One caught a retreating Betty and Zero, but the damage had been done—both runways pitted and, even worse, 5,000 gallons of avgas burned up. Additionally, one Wildcat was shot up by bomber gunners and the pilot had to ditch offshore.

Two hours later another fifteen G4Ms appeared while most F4Fs were still refueling. Nearly all servicing was done by hand-pumps, and it was a laborious, time-consuming process. Joe Foss led three divisions up to tackle the raiders, feeling "excited and good, like a kid waiting for a big dish of ice cream."[18] But some cagey Zero pilots were also smacking their lips in anticipation. Foss noticed his wingman signaling, figured his own radio was out, and wondered what happened when everybody peeled off, leaving him alone. He soon found out. The other 121 pilots dived to avoid a gaggle of Zekes which Foss hadn't seen. Now left with one potential victim, the Japanese ganged up on the lone F4F.

Foss didn't know how many Zeros jumped him, but there were enough for "a swarm." However, the enemy leader got overly anxious and pulled out of his gunnery pass right ahead of the Wildcat. Foss couldn't believe it. He barely touched his trigger and the Zero disintegrated. It was his first kill, and he felt like standing up and cheering.

Chased back to the field's perimeter, losing oil from a windmilling engine, Foss made one of the hottest landings ever seen at Henderson. In fact, they called out the ambulance, certain the cripled Wildcat would plow a high-speed furrow down the runway. But somehow Foss got the plane stopped. He'd learned his lesson. From then on, he vowed, the boys could call him "Swivel-Neck Joe."

That night Henderson took a pasting from two battleships prowling unchallenged in the sound, alternating with Japanese artillery and occasional bombers. Only a few stray bombs hit the Fighter Strip, but Cactus was deprived of nearly all its strike aircraft by dawn—destroyed or temporarily unflyable.

Considering Henderson neutralized, the Imperial Navy sent even more ships down The Slot during the next two days. Maintenance miracles and the timely arrival of some Navy SBDs just barely held the line. More bombardments, more nocturnal bombings, more sleepless nights and frantic, violent days of flying, fighting, shipping strikes and escorts, refueling, and rearming. Days and nights melded together in the tropical blackness until one was almost indistinguishable from any other.

Amid this chaos, the last of the old-line squadrons rotated south. On the 16th Bob Galer led his division on a strafing mission, shooting up beached transports which had delivered troops during the night. That afternoon the CO saw most of his people off the wretched, hateful island, and Leroy Simpler took VF-5 as well. During 224's stay on The Canal it recorded fifty-six and a half victories in exchange for seven Wildcats presumed or known lost in aerial combat. Galer led the pack by several lengths with fourteen, followed by John Dobbin, George Hollowell and Charlie Kunz who accounted for another twenty among them. Fighting 5 had claimed nearly forty shootdowns, losing five pilots KIA, three wounded.

That afternoon a much-welcome fast destroyer-transport hove to. She was the old four-stacker *McFarland*, bearing 40,000 gallons of fuel and a load of ordnance. Th last barge was heading to shore when an inconvenient flight of Aichi D3As appeared overhead. Lacking a better target, they dived on the stationary APD and one of the Val pilots planted his bomb on the fuel barge, which erupted like a seagoing volcano. The fireball and concussion staggered the *McFarland* and nearly everyone watching from Lunga Point.

As fate would have it, Joe Bauer led eighteen of his VMF-212 pilots into the Fighter Strip at this moment. After months of feeding replacement pilots up to Guadal, Bauer now had his unit intact. It had been a long hop up from Espiritu, and his fuel gauge read nearly empty, but The Coach had a full load of ammo and targets nearby. He wheeled out of the traffic pattern, going to full power, charging his .50s and turning up the gunsight rheostat.

Bauer preached aggressive fighter doctrine. He believed in hard charging, and his favorite motto was, "There's no way to make war safe. The thing to do is make it very unsafe for the enemy."[19] And he proved his point. In full view of hundreds of witnesses the lone Wildcat tore into the Aichis and dropped four in succession. With new fighters and additional gasoline, Cactus was back in business.

Late October brought more intense aerial combat as the Imperial Navy sought to coordinate with the Army a complex scheme to capture Henderson once and for all. On the evening of the 25th, Cactus possessed thirty-five F4F-4s and Herman Hansen's lone -7, but only a dozen of the fighters were operational. Ten had come to grief on the

Cow Pasture's wet, slick grass. Eleven of seventeen available Daunt-lesses were ready, and that was the extent of it. No TBFs had been made airworthy.

The carrier duel off the Santa Cruz Islands occurred next day, and as preparation for the grand sea-air plan to seize Guadalcanal, Japanese bombers raided intensively in the days leading up to the event. In a series of heavy air raids, VMF-121 became a leading distributor of Mitsubishi parts. Davis' pilots claimed eleven kills on the 23rd and another eighteen on the 25th. Foss was pushing himself and his two divisions hard in aggressive, close-in combats where most F4F pilots got plenty of shooting. "Swivel-Neck Joe" bagged four Zekes on the 23rd and two days later, in morning and afternoon interceptions, became the first Marine pilot credited with five kills in a day. This brought his personal tally to sixteen in only 13 days.

Foss attributed much of his success to his wingmen and section leaders, and rightfully so. He absorbed Bauer's and Davis's aggressive philosophy, relying on teamwork and gunnery to exploit any opportunities. Like Jimmy Thach, Joe Foss had grown up hunting pheasant, and wing-shooting experience showed. "Most of my shots were deflection setups," he recalled nearly forty years later. "I told my boys to fly their sights through the front of the target, and hold their fire until in range. Most pilots opened up too soon."[20]

Foss liked the pattern boresight in which two each of the F4F-4's six guns were sighted at 250, 300 and 350 yards. And though he sometimes switched off two guns to conserve ammo, he was one of the few fighter pilots who approved of the dash four's six-gun armament. The Marines received a lot of defective ammunition during this period (die-hard Republicans said FDR was reserving "the good stuff" for the European Theater) and malfunctions weren't uncommon. Therefore, Foss reasoned, with six guns instead of four, a pilot had 50 percent better prospects of keeping enough weapons on-line to do the job.

And so it went. Foss tied John L. Smith's record on 7 November when 121 waded into a flock of floatplanes covering a Japanese convoy 120 miles northwest of Henderson. Duke Davis' pilots splashed nine Rufes and Petes, including three by Lieutenant Bill Marontate, who was fast building a good score. Foss dumped two of the hard-turning, pugnacious Petes and flamed a Rufe, then abruptly found himself alone—that peculiarity of aerial combat in which one moment the air is choked with airplanes, tracers criss-crossing a cloud-flecked sky, and the next moment there's nothing but solitude.

Foss set course for what he thought was home, missing the now-

familiar landmarks due to a series of squall lines. By the time he
checked his compass and found himself 30 degrees off course, he was
out of fuel. He ditched off Malaita, the big island north of Guadalcanal, and spent the evening with the local coastwatcher. General
Geiger sent a PBY to fetch back the errant ace next morning.

Meanwhile, some badly-needed new blood had arrived. Bauer's 212
remained til mid-month, but many of his pilots had been on The
Canal far longer than the squadron as a whole. They were a tired
bunch of fighter pilots; the unit claimed only four victories after the
end of October. Cactus lost one of its senior fliers on the 21st when
Gunner Tex Hamilton was killed. He'd landed with 223 back on 20
August, scored four kills with Smith's unit and rejoined 212 to add
three more. His was the kind of experience which simply couldn't be
replaced.

The pace was telling on 121. Four pilots were lost on the 11th,
though Lieutenant T. H. Mann eventually turned up with a claim of
four Aichis. So the combat debut of VMF-112 that same day was the
best possible timing, as Major Paul Fontana led his pilots into a
formation of Bettys, knocking down one himself. The entries of new
names in the shootdown column of Cactus's sketchy record books
showed how the old order kept changing. Two-Twelve's veterans—old
pros like Fritz Payne and Loren Everton and eager youngsters like
Jack Conger and Bob Stout—were slowly replaced by up-and-coming
VMF-112 pilots such as Jeff DeBlanc, Gilbert Percy, and Wayne
Laird.

Now began a violent, frantic four days of incessant flying and
fighting. Japan's most ambitious effort yet to retake Guadalcanal
kicked off early on the 12th as the Bougainville coastwatcher, Paul
Mason, reported an estimated twenty-five southbound Bettys with
eight Zeros riding shotgun. Joe Foss led six other 121 pilots in a climb
to 29,000 feet, circling over the troubled, contested waters of the
sound where Rear Admiral Turner's transports were delivering fresh
Army troops to bolster the Marines. Meanwhile, the orbiting F4F
pilots peered to the northwest, squinting under the midday sun,
waiting for the bombers to appear in their usual impeccable
formations.

But the G4Ms didn't show up as expected. Cactus radar lost them
30 miles out, near the eastern tip of Florida as the big Mitsubishis
nosed down from 20,000 feet for a fast run-in below the American
CAP. Now it was obvious what they were up to. These weren't conventional bombers; they were torpedo planes going after the troop
transports off Kukum Point.

Looking down, Foss glimpsed the dark-green Bettys through some scudding clouds and realized what had happened. He hollered "Let's go, gang!" and dropped into a screeching, painful power dive with his six pilots close behind.[21] The rapid temperature change caused problems. As the Wildcats entered the warmer lower air, their canopies became glazed with frost, reducing vision. Foss's headlong dive at 300 knots created terrific pressure which blew out his canopy glass and peeled the walk strips from his wings. He hunkered behind his windscreen, scratching at the frost, and overhauled the Bettys as they started their runs.

Turner's transports and their escorts—some thirty ships in all—put up a terrific volume of flak. Mason had reported twenty-five Bettys, and the fact that there were "only" nineteen didn't help much. Foss and company, strung out in a stern chase, couldn't stop them all in time. But Paul Fontana had scrambled with eight VMF-112 Wildcats, and a like number of Army P-400s piled in. Even so, it was going to be close. The transports were beautiful targets.

Foss hauled into 100 yards of the nearest bomber, triggered a short burst which connected with the starboard engine, and pulled up as the Betty careened into the water. The other Wildcats and Airacobras were among the pack, hitting from above as the G4Ms skimmed the surface. Dirty white fountains erupted from the water as a succession of Bettys went down. Bill Marontate and Art Nehf of Foss's division each splashed two, as did young Jeff DeBlanc of 112. But one G4M wiped itself along the side of the cruiser *San Francisco*, inflicting casualties though no substantial damage.

Then it was a low-level ratrace as American fighters tangled with Zeros and picked off fleeing Bettys. Foss had his teeth into another bomber when a Zeke initiated a gunnery pass on him. In some spectacular snap-shooting, the Marine turned into the attack, quickly got his deflection, exploded the A6M just off the water, then turned back and flamed the Betty. He'd just become the first American to claim twenty or more victories in World War II. Paul Fontana added to his own bag, reeling in another Zeke for his third kill in two days. Circling the transports, the F4F pilots counted a dozen burning wrecks in the water around Kukum alone.

The Marines accounted for seventeen bombers and five Zeros, though shipboard gunners claimed five splashed as well. While two Bettys returned northward to tell the tale, and three Wildcats and a Bell went down, Admiral Turner's precious transports were safe. They continued unloading GIs so badly needed ashore.

Events were accelerating toward their climax. That same afternoon powerful elements of the Imperial Navy were pointing their bows southward from New Britain. An awesome bombardment group built around two battleships and a light cruiser with fourteen destroyers intended to wreck Henderson and the Fighter Strip, clearing the way for eleven transports packed with troops who would finish this business of the Guadalcanal sinkhole for good.

That night Rear Admiral Dan Callaghan's five cruisers and eight destroyers slugged it out in Ironbottom Sound, losing the *Atlanta* and four destroyers. But the intended bombardment was short-stopped, costing Japan two destroyers and immobilizing the battleship *Hiei*. At fearsome cost the Tokyo Express had been derailed for one precious night.

Nobody ahsore got much sleep, and dawn came artificially early. Brigadier General Louis Woods, who had relieved the ailing Roy Geiger as senior airman a week before, needed to know what was prowling out there in the darkness. The early-morning scouts lifted into lowering, rainy skies on their sector searches, and Joe Foss took off with them. He was airborne before 0600 with orders to scout the local area, and in the gathering light he found the sound littered with crippled and sinking men-of-war.

Throughout the day—Friday the 13th—Marine, Navy and Army planes worked over the floating derelicts. The *Hiei* was the primary target, of course, and the Cactus fliers relished the novelty of bombing and strafing a battleship only a few minutes flight from Henderson Field. The Japanese entertained desperate hopes of towing the dreadnought to safety and sent a passel of Zeros down to help out. In a tussle which ranged over the water and the island, pilots from all three Wildcat squadrons (including some VMO-251 folks flying with 121) claimed nine confirmed and a probable by 0830.

Cactus obviously was going to need some help, and it was near at hand. The *Enterprise*, the only U.S. fleet carrier still operable in the Pacific, bore bomb damage from the Santa Cruz engagement eighteen days before. But her Air Group 10 was the best bet for putting more aircraft into Guadalcanal, and at 0800 she launched six Wildcats under Lieutenant John Sutherland, escorting nine TBFs. Approaching from the south at 1100, the Navy fliers detoured westward by Cape Esperance in an impromptu search. There they spotted the *Hiei* with her distinctive pagoda mast, attended by four destroyers north of Savo Island. It was shocking to see an enemy battleship so close to the beach in daylight. But then it was apparent she was dead in the water, her topsides so much scrap iron from the night action and subsequent bombing.

Torpedo 10 swung in to attack, covered by Jock Sutherland's six F4Fs as his pilots craned their necks, looking for the Zekes which must be around. About eight Zeros did appear but were disinclined to fight—perhaps low on fuel. The *Enterprise* fliers landed on The Canal at an unenviable time. The heavy reinforcement convoy was known on its way and a cruiser-destroyer force seemed intent on conducting the postponed bombardment. The *Enterprise*'s two escorting battleships couldn't arrive in time to prevent it, so the Cactus Air Force spent the early part of that evening celebrating the sinking of the *Hiei* and preparing for yet another nocturnal shelling.

It came in familiar fashion. At 0130—just twenty-four hours after Callaghan's outgunned ships had taken on the *Hiei* force—a Japanese floatplane dropped marker flares which punctuated the tropic darkness with eerie greenness. But either the flares were poorly placed or Japanese gunnery wasn't up to its usual standard, for Henderson wasn't touched. The half-hour shelling hurt the Fighter Strip, however, leaving two Wildcats wrecked and fifteen damaged, though most of the latter were repairable.

Fighter Command started Saturday the 14th with fourteen airworthy F4Fs in addition to ten Army planes, including seven exotic newcomers—big, twin-boomed P-38 Lightnings. Beginning about mid-morning, hastily organized strike groups began hitting Rear Admiral Raizo Tanaka's eleven transports well up The Slot. Squadron organization was meaningless through most of the day as SBDs, TBFs, and even long-range B-17s from Espiritu pummeled the determined Japanese. A couple of ships hit in the early strikes turned back toward the Shortlands, but the only way to handle the others was to sink them. Several small formations of Dauntlesses and Avengers took off without fighter escort, and some were roughly handled. From about 1045 on, however, the Buin Zeros had to contend with F4Fs of VMF-112 and 121 over the southbound transports. The Marines gained and kept air superiority, claiming seven Zeros and a floatplane splashed during the next three hours.

The Navy Wildcats were also involved. About 1330 Jock Sutherland took his VF-10 division to keep station over the enemy ships on target CAP. Sutherland noted some B-17s, and upon closer inspection saw nearby Zeros. He pointed them out to his wingman, Lieutenant (jg) Henry Carey, and attached.

Jock Sutherland and Hank Carey had been flying together for months: Midway, Santa Cruz, and now The Canal. They were a potent team, and Sutherland cut out one A6M and dropped it as Carey covered him. But Carey had problems. He'd taken off in "an old clunker of a Marine Wildcat" which couldn't keep pace, and was surprised when his leader abruptly wracked up in a tight turn. Then Carey saw why—another Zeke was making a beam run.[22]

The Mitsubishi pilot was evidently as experienced as his opponents. He hit Carey's plane in a deflection shot from starboard, putting two 20-mm shells through the cockpit and a 7.7-mm bullet in Carey's leg. The shooting could hardly have been better. Wounded, with a damaged airplane and a cockpit fire, the former Ivy Leaguer prepared to jump. He shoved back the canopy, but on an impulse smothered the hydraulic-fluid fire with a gloved hand. He returned his well-worn loaner to the Marines, a bit more worn.

Additional help came from the Big E, but not without delay. Maddeningly persistent but inaccurate reports of Japanese carriers required the *Enterprise* air staff to hold something back during much of the day. The concern was justified, as the task force had been snooped by a Mavis the day before (Lieutenant Swede Vejtasa's division splashed it) and the CAP disposed of another shadower at 0920.

Therefore, the 0800 strike which launched roughly 200 miles southwest of Guadalcanal was concerned with finding the reported threat. Seventeen SBDs escorted by Lieutenant Commander Jim Flatley with ten Wildcats represented the major portion of the air group. But the Grim Reapers stayed tuned to the CAP frequency, and all but two missed the Dauntless leader's course change to hunt down the retiring enemy bombardment force. Flatley took his remaining seven pilots back to the ship while the SBDs found and sank the cruiser *Kinugasa*. The two-plane fighter section led by Lieutenant Stan Ruehlow stuck with the Dauntlesses as long as possible, but diverted into Cactus extremely short on fuel.

By mid-afternoon it seemed obvious that the Japanese carriers weren't going to materialize. Therefore, the *Enterprise* cleared her deck and launched the last eight SBDs with three fighter divisions, all under Flatley. Only eighteen F4Fs were kept aboard as the Big E swung southwards. Her air group was now committed to the final defense of Guadalcanal.

It was nearly two and a half hours to the advancing transports. When Flatley's formation got there, seven were still coming with daylight running out. An advanced thinker in matters of strike coordination, "Reaper Leader" set up as director 60 miles west of Savo and carefully allotted targets to his dive-bombers.

Zeros were still around, and though they weren't numerous enough to stop the persistent air strikes, they'd been a factor most of the day. When the A6Ms showed up, Ensign Whitey Feightner instinctively went to military power, expecting a brawl. But Flatley kept an eye on things and conserved fuel, turning into each threat while maintaining a consistent 1,400 rpm. Feightner couldn't believe the skipper's coolness.

But with the attack well-developed, Flatley led his fighters down to strafe and only then did the bandits prove aggressive. Ensign Ed Coalson was last man in one division and fell behind during the initial pass. Sandwiched between two pair of Zekes, he pulled into a loop—normally a sure-fire suicide tactic in a dogfight—and turned the tables. He avoided the two bandits ahead of him while coming down behind the trailing pair. Coalson shot down one from astern and the others made off.

About this same time, roughly 1615, more Marines came on the scene. Paul Fontana's VMF-112 locked horns with some Zekes and floatplanes, claiming eight without loss. Also along for the ride was Joe Bauer in a 121 Wildcat, flying with Joe Foss and Second Lieutenant T. W. Furlow. Bauer had been running fighter ops for two days and wanted a look at what was going on. General Woods said all right, but cautioned him to stay high, out of trouble. It was too much to ask. Bauer's trio was high cover for a mixed SBD-TBF strike and the colonel decided the bombers needed some extra flak suppression.

They went down to masthead height, machine-gunning the crowded decks, and pulled back up when Foss looked around and noted two Zeros jumping Bauer from above and behind. Bauer saw them, too, and turned hard into the leader, trading gunfire head-on. The Coach was on target, and the Zeke came apart under the combined impact of six .50-calibers.

Foss and Boot Furlow chased the other but lost it amid the milling ships and bursting flak. They turned back to rejoin Bauer but couldn't find him. Then Foss noticed an oil slick about two miles from the floating debris of the splashed Zero. He flew low enough to see Bauer near the slick, waving and motioning back towards Guadalcanal. Foss understood. The colonel didn't want attention drawn to his location. The two Wildcats bent their throttles, racing for Henderson in the growing darkness. Their repeated radio calls went unanswered or were blocked by other transmissions.

In a hasty conference with Major Joe Renner, an air ops officer, Foss told what he knew. Apparently, Bauer's F4F had been hit in the brief hassle, or antiaircraft fire knocked him down. At any rate, there was no time to lose. The two piled into a J2F amphibian, fretting while a formation of Army bombers landed, and finally took off. Darkness had fallen so Renner and Foss navigated by the glow of five burning ships, searching for their friend. But it was no use. It was too dark, and with a growing fear for Bauer's life they sadly returned to Guadalcanal.

The Coach was never found. Foss speculated that a passing Japanese ship had spotted the colonel. Tanaka's sailors had been under ruthless air attack all day, reducing their number to four transports and a lone destroyer. They wouldn't have been very chivalrous to a downed American flier.

At day's end Cactus counted twenty-four operational Wildcats, twenty-three Army fighters, sixteen Dauntlesses, seven Avengers and nine B-26s. It was almost an embarrassment of riches; seventy-nine available aircraft was an unheard-of number. But something more familiar occurred that night as U.S. and Japanese battleships indulged in the penultimate naval engagement of the campaign. There were heavy casualties on both sides but Rear Admiral Willis Lee's force prevailed.

The stage was set for the last act.

The four surviving transports had beached themselves during the night, discharging their cargo. It wasn't much: 2,000 troops, only one-fifth of the total embarked, mostly without food or equipment. Henderson-based bombers flew only 15 miles to wreck these ships while other formations mopped up the cripples from the day before.

On an early-morning flight Foss took two divisions looking for Joe Bauer when two floatplanes were spotted. Seven F4Fs ganged up on one, leaving the other to Foss. This Pete showed the same aggressiveness the type had demonstrated since VF-42's initial clash back in May. But after a short fight, Foss got in a good burst from 300 yards and flamed the biplane—his twenty-third kill. It was also the last claimed by Marine Corps fighters during this phase of the campaign.

The Navy got in a bit more shooting. That afternoon Jim Flatley had eight Reapers up on CAP when radar spotted bogies inbound. Flatley's two divisions were nearly "bingo," having been airborne for two and a half hours, but eight more were scrambled. Stan Ruehlow led them to 20,000 feet, and they didn't have long to wait.

An estimated eleven Zeros appeared over Savo, heading for Ruehlow's two divisions. This prompted some disagreement as to who had priority. Ruehlow had bagged an Aichi at Santa Cruz and was anxious to increase his score. He went for a single bandit when his wingman, Ensign Butch Voris, made threatening gestures towards the intended victim. Ruehlow cut him off: "Voris, that's my Zero. I saw him. Leave him alone!" Moments later he sang a different tune: "Somebody get this guy off my tail!" Somebody did.[23]

In all, the Reapers claimed six kills for one F4F ditched offshore. During the day another Wildcat nosed up on landing, blocking the Fighter Strip, and fourteen airborne planes landed on the beach. One P-39 landed too wide, wiping out its nose gear in the soft sand.

But that was the worst of it. Nobody knew it at the time, but the Guadalcanal Campaign had passed its crisis. The fighting dragged on for nearly three more months, but the defeat of the transports had convinced the Japanese that they couldn't retake Cactus. At dusk on 15 November 1942 the F4F's major contribution to winning World War II had been completed.

6. EASTERN SOLOMONS AND SANTA CRUZ

"Eternal vigilance or eternal rest."
—Lt. Cdr. James H. Flatley

TWO CARRIER BATTLES were fought as part of the Guadalcanal campaign—the third and fourth rounds in a new form of naval warfare unique to the Pacific. Both battles were fought as part of significant Japanese repostes at Guadalcanal. Eastern Solomons, coming only seventeen days after the initial Marine landings, represented the first major effort to reinforce Japanese strength ashore while presumably sapping American naval power in the area. That this reinforcement amounted to only 1,500 soldiers need not concern us; the carrier phase went ahead regardless of the number of troops.

Santa Cruz came in late October, eight weeks later. And though conditions had changed considerably, the strategic premise had not. The penultimate Japanese thrust at Cactus saw a combined army-navy effort which depended upon careful planning between troops ashore and the fleet at sea. The third and last effort, as we have seen, occurred in mid-November with the Battle of The Slot and its connected surface actions.

But the differences between these engagements are striking. Eastern Solomons was the only carrier duel of 1942 in which the U.S. Navy lost no flattops. Santa Cruz was the only one in which Japan's carriers all survived. Wildcats flew no escorts in the August fracas—

the only time F4Fs were all kept at home—but were back in the strike groups in October.

Despite the comparisons, one thing emerges at the bottom line. The naval balance, and hence the situation ashore, remained largely unchanged in the wake of both battles. This simply means that the carrier air groups preserved the status quo on Guadalcanal—a tenuous, uncertain status, to be sure, but a preservation just the same. In this important respect, both battles carry more weight than is sometimes accorded them.

Eastern Solomons shaped up early on 24 August with Vice Admiral Fletcher in overall command of Task Force 61, composed of the *Enterprise* and *Saratoga* with their screens. He was opposed by three of the Emperor's carriers in a situation not dissimilar from Coral Sea three and a half months before. Fletcher's old antagonists the *Shokaku* and *Zuikaku* formed the main carrier group under another old acquaintance, Vice Admiral Nagumo. A light carrier, the *Ryujo*, operated independently as had the *Shoho* at Coral Sea, but in a different role. The *Ryujo* was live bait, sailing well ahead of the main body to absorb Fletcher's attention while allowing the big-ship squadrons to operate largely unhindered.

The *Saratoga* flew a mixed air group: her own bombers and scouts plus the reorganized Torpedo 8. The fighter squadron was VF-5, originally of the *Yorktown* but displaced by VF-42 when Leroy Simpler's outfit was on detached service with the *Wasp* on neutrality patrol back in December 1941. Except for the original unpleasantries over Tulagi while covering the Marine landings two weeks previously, Fighting 5 was largely untried.

Fighting 6 in the *Enterprise* had more institutional experience, of course, but there were still operational problems. Like Sara, the Big E fielded a conglomerate of squadrons largely unaccustomed to working together: her regular bomber and fighter units, but also Scouting 5 and, ironically, the *Saratoga*'s VT-3.

Based upon Coral Sea and Midway, the U.S. Navy recognized the need of additional fighters. Consequently, the authorized strength was raised to thirty-six F4F-4s. But Lieutenant Lou Bauer, new skipper of VF-6, had just twenty-eight Wildcats on hand and Leroy Simpler had only twenty-seven. The *Wasp* had been detached by Fletcher to refuel to the south and consequently missed the battle. The twenty-eight Wildcats of VF-71, not to mention the rest of the air group, would have come in mighty handy.

Initial advantage went to the Japanese, not merely because of numbers but also due to reconnaissance. The Imperial Navy was always good at scouting, and at least three snoopers plotted Fletcher during the morning of the 24th. Two were shot down by the *Saratoga* Wildcats, one at 1100 and another at 1330; but Nagumo had a good fix. He closed the range.

That afternoon Fletcher's force steamed nearly 200 nautical miles east of Henderson Field, near the tiny cluster of dots on the map called the Stewart Islands. The *Enterprise* search planes probed to the north for the widely dispersed Japanese while the two F4F squadrons flew a series of CAPs, alternately landing aboard one ship, then the other.

Samuel Eliot Morison's account of Eastern Solomons contains several errors, but he vividly set the scene as only he could:

> Poseidon and Aelous had arranged a striking setting for this battle. Towering cumulus clouds, constantly rearranged by the 16-knot southeast tradewind in a series of snowy castles and ramparts, blocked off nearly half the depthless dome. The ocean, two miles deep at this point, was topped with merry whitecaps dancing to a clear horizon, such as navigators love. The scene, with dark shadows turning some ships purple and sun illuminating others in sharp detail . . . was one for a great marine artist to depict. To practical carrier airmen, however, the setup was far from perfect. Those handsome clouds could hide a hundred vengeful aircraft; that high equatorial sun could provide a concealed path for pouncing dive-bombers; that reflected glare of blue, white, and gold bothered and even blinded the lookouts and made aircraft identification doubtful. Altogether it was the kind of weather a flattop sailor wants the gods to spread over his enemy's task force, not his own.[1]

However, clear skies meant simplified intercepts for defending fighters. By late afternoon half of Fighting 6 was airborne plus a dozen VF-5 Wildcats over their respective roosts with others on standby. The *Saratoga*'s 1345 launch against the *Ryujo* had gone unescorted but the CAG, Commander Don Felt, got the job done without F4Fs. His Dauntlesses and Avengers swarmed over the CVL and left her sinking without loss of a single plane.

But it didn't work that way all day. Communications were terribly confused owing to use of just one radio channel. Consequently, some crucial contact reports never got through, resulting in missed opportunities. The *Shokaku* and *Zuikaku*, for instance, were located but poor radio performance meant Felt's strike couldn't be diverted from the bait. By that time Nagumo had launched twenty-seven bombers and ten fighters anyway, so the main event was on.

The thirty-seven Japanese planes approached from the north, headed for the *Enterprise*. She steamed in the middle of a 3,800-yard circle composed of six destroyers, a cruiser off either bow, and the battleship *North Carolina* astern. Ten miles southeast, on the disengaged side, was the *Saratoga* with a similar screen, minus the battlewagon.

Each carrier handled its own fighter direction. The *Enterprise*'s FDO was Lieutenant Henry Rowe, an erstwhile torpedo pilot who'd learned the fighter-direction business while understudying the Royal Navy in 1940. Hank Rowe was an acknowledged expert at his trade, ably assisted by Lieutenant Commander Ham Dow, a communicator without FDO training but possessed of practical experience at Midway. Sara's fighter direction was overseen by Don Felt with three non-flying officers previously trained by Rowe. The two carriers' CICs were in occasional contact, sometimes on the crowded tactical circuit but more often on the line-of-sight Talk Between Ships radio. The latter possessed the advantage of being immune from enemy eavesdropping.

Not until after 1600 did the Big E's CXAM radar show the first hostile blips on the scope. At first there was some uncertainty, as returning scouts and strike planes sometimes failed to use their IFF, but Rowe and Dow played it safe. They determined that the bogies flickered off the screen at 88 miles. According to their fade charts that meant an altitude of about 12,000 feet. The two carriers turned into the southeasterly wind to launch their remaining Wildcats.

Rowe deployed Fighting 6 stacked in altitude with the highest F4Fs out toward the inbound raid with a couple of sections low near the task force "as back-up." All the time he was mindful of the Wildcat's limitations: "Remember, the F4F was inefficient of fuel at altitude. The problem was to get them back, gassed, and rearmed, and back in the air when needed, so I landed fighters on either carrier. The carriers launched or recovered independently; we really operated as two one-carrier task groups. We were close on the Jap bombers' altitude but their fighters were higher, and I didn't give our fighters enough altitude advantage."[2]

When the Japanese closed at 1630, twenty-four Wildcats were airborne: eleven VF-6 planes over the *Enterprise* from 8,000 to 15,000 feet and Leroy Simpler with thirteen *Saratoga* fighters at 10,000 to 15,000. Seven minutes later Lou Bauer led four VF-6 divisions off Sara, followed at 1645 by six more *Enterprise* F4Fs, also from the *Saratoga*. At 1649 the bogies were back on the screen, still bearing northwest but down to 44 miles. Four sections, the equivalent of two divisions, were sent out to intercept as Ham Dow radioed, "Vector 320, angels 12 distance 35."[3]

There were now forty-six Wildcats up, but the CAP cycle had to be observed. Simpler pancaked on the *Saratoga* with his Scarlet One division at 1655 for a fast refueling. At the same time seven fighters— two of VF-6 and five from VF-5—launched from the *Enterprise*. At 1706 Simpler was back in his plane. He stood on the brakes, ran up the throttle, mixture, and prop controls, and booted in right rudder. Then he rolled down the deck, leading his three pilots back into the air after an eleven-minute turnaround. Four minutes later the first Vals began their dives on *Enterprise*.

Fifty-three Wildcats met the raid; all twenty-eight of Fighting 6 and twenty-five of VF-5. It appears that forty-six F4Fs engaged the thirty-seven raiders, largely because one division was vectored out on a 100-mile contact. Still, it was the largest fighter force yet to defend an American carrier group.

At 1625 the forward divisions made visual contact with the inbound Japanese at thirty-three miles. Most heavily engaged was Lieutenant Albert O. Vorse's Red Five division. Originally deployed at 2,000 over base, Vorse was sent out on 320 degrees with orders to 12,000. With .50s charged and gunsight rheostats turned up, Red Five eyeballed two bandit formations at two o'clock high. Climbing harder, they couldn't quite get to the dive-bombers before the Zeros came down. Consequently, Vorse and company had to fight their way upwards through the escorting A6Ms—a difficult chore at best. Somehow the Wildcats shrugged off the first pass by Zekes, but there was no way around them at 12,000.

Forced to fight, "Scoop" Vorse low-sided one Zero which was thought to hit the water burning. Ensign F. R. Register hit one Mitsubishi in a steep wingover and noted with interest that the pilot bailed out minus a parachute. Register then tagged another bandit, reputedly a "Messerschmidt 109."[4] Machinist H. M. Sumrall correctly identified his own opponent as made in Japan, for a Red Five claim of four kills. But Vorse eventually ran out of fuel and ditched astern of the *Saratoga*.

Other Wildcats pursued the Aichis toward their roll-in point, but probably no more than six attacked before the Vals dived. Another ten F4Fs followed the Japanese down, and while they may have upset some dive-bombers' aim, they couldn't deflect the bulk of the strike. The *Enterprise* was now vulnerable.

Leading the *Saratoga*'s Scarlet Four was Lieutenant Chick Harmer, an old hand in VF-5. Now squadron exec, he'd originally been gunnery officer when Simpler's troops traded in their F3Fs for Wildcats. Things had been so hectic that he'd found no Navy boresight pattern for the F4F-3 and had to consult Grumman for the information. Eventually he settled on a 750-foot boresight which provided a pattern of about ten feet. At first, gunnery scores were lower in the F4F than in the more familiar biplanes, partially to the Wildcat's rudder pressure changes in a dive. Now all that was past, and there existed only confusion.

"The strike planes and CAP were all talking on one frequency," Harmer recalls. He spotted the Vals at their push-over point above the *Enterprise* and made "a last-second intercept," meeting the lead Aichi as it dove. Somehow his three wingmen failed to follow him down, and the exec found himself the lone Wildcat at the Japanese rendezvous point. Still after the leader, he hung on and shot him into the water. Then Harmer tackled another, firing and seeing pieces fly off the fixed-gear bomber still in the RV circle. But an unseen bandit latched onto his tail at low level and hit the F4F solidly, wounding Harmer in one leg. He added power, accelerated away, and waited a chance to get aboard either carrier.[5]

In separate combats Harmer's other pilots claimed three Vals and a probable. But the three-plane Scarlet Six under Lieutenant Howard Jensen put up the biggest score: seven dive-bombers, a Zero and a probable, including three Vals by Jensen himself. In all, Fighting 5 claimed thirteen or fourteen Vals (one exploded from an AA hit as an ensign was also shooting) and three Zekes against the loss of three pilots and four planes. Harmer got his damaged Wildcat down on the *Saratoga* but went inverted into the barrier. Hardest hit was Lieutenant (jg) Jim Smith's standby division, as Smith and a wingman were both lost. The other casualty was from Lieutenant Dave Richardson's division. Somewhere in the combat, Lieutenant Marion Dufilho disappeared. Apparently nobody saw what happened to the luckless pilot who'd flown Butch O'Hare's wing off Rabaul.

Most of the action was fought almost directly over the *Enterprise*, as the intercepts came too late to disperse the Vals. Fighting 6 reported Nakajima torpedo planes with 20-mm cannon in the back seat, but no Kates launched on this strike. However, Lou Bauer's pilots came away impressed with the Val. An enlisted pilot, Radio Electrician T. W. Rhodes, claimed an Aichi in a high-side pass but remarked it seemed speedy and "much more maneuverable" than the F4F-4. Another *Enterprise* NAP, L. P. Mankin, confirmed Rhodes' report—one Val actually turned inside his Wildcat.[6]

Then of course there was the Zero. In one of the most impressive displays of the A6M's agility seen to date, Lieutenant V. P. dePoix noted a half-dozen Wildcats trying to corner a lone Zeke at 17,000 feet. The Japanese pilot didn't even shoot back; he merely evaded with elegant aerobatics.

A few other Zero pilots weren't so sharp. During the dive-bombing attack Ensign R. M. Disque of VF-6 spotted a Zeke harrying an SBD. As Disque dived to help out, the Zero saw him coming, wracking into a flipper turn. Disque anticipated the target's course, pulled deflection, and fired. He got a flamer and saw the Zero hit the water. Moments later Disque noticed a second Zero pulling away from three F4Fs. He cut the corner, pulling into range as the A6M continued a right-hand turn into his sights. When Disque fired, the Mitsubishi rolled inverted into the sea. However, Disque hadn't gotten off lightly. Somewhere in the hassle he took 7.7-mm rounds through his vacuum tank and cockpit. He crashed upon landing.

The raid cleared at about 1720, but the damage had been done. Proficient Japanese dive-bombing had put the *Enterprise* out of action. She took two bombs in 30 seconds within 20 feet of one another. A third hit in five minutes impeded steering and the carrier lost control for nearly 40 minutes.

With the Big E temporarily unavailable, most of her airborne fighers recovered aboard the *Saratoga*. Damage control brought things around, but she was still hurting. If several of the Vals which broke through the fighters and flak hadn't diverted to the tempting *North Carolina*, the *Enterprise* may not have survived.

But things weren't settled just yet. At 1600 the Japanese had launched a second strike of thirty-six planes, which showed on the radarscope bearing due west at 50 miles. The CIC watch gawked incredulously as the enemy search-strike flew to the southeast and finally reversed course. The Big E was drawing heavily upon her stock of good fortune, and when the crisis passed many sailors hankered for a cup of coffee. But one of the three bombs had exploded in a storage room where most of the ship's supply was kept. The result was frustrating. Hank Rowe remembers that the whole ship smelled of fresh-roasted coffee but there was none to be found.

Next morning the *Enterprise* sent off the rest of her planes to the *Wasp*, Guadalcanal, or Espiritu, retaining only six F4Fs and six SBDs. Eastern Solomons was over.

Fighting 6 claimed as many as twenty-six kills during the Japanese strike; record-keeping was confused in the hasty transfer to the *Saratoga*, and documents are contradictory. Fighting 5 recorded seventeen shootdowns, and of course the AA gunners on several ships chipped in with their share. Discounting the three snoopers destroyed by F4Fs during the morning, fighter claims ran to perhaps forty-three, more than the actual number of raiders.

Though nothing like the U.S. claims, Japanese losses were bad: some 65 percent of the aircraft launched. Eighteen of twenty-seven Vals failed to return, as did six of ten Zeros. Things are complicated by Japanese records which show five of the second strike bombers shot down, though other indications point to loss by ditching. Wildcat losses amounted to six, including five pilots.

Fighting 5 estimated that fifteen dive-bombers completed their attack on the *Enterprise*, and the figure is probably close to accurate, as late intercepts allowed most Vals time to dive. A survey of the thirty-eight Wildcat pilots aboard the *Saratoga* who participated in this action showed that only eleven engaged Aichis before or during their dives. Twelve were tied up with the relatively small Zero escort, and five never engaged at all.

The two fighter squadrons drew mixed conclusions from this scrap. Fighter direction and communications were foremost. Fighting 5 cited "the great amount of communication necessary between about 50 VF, the fighter director, and standby fighter director," which jammed the lone circuit. Separate FDO frequencies for each carrier were recommended, as well as more flexibility in CAP cycles. Leroy Simpler urged that pilots rather than FDOs determine when airborne fighters should be recovered. "No F4F-4 combat patrol should ever be required to operate on less than 80 gallons of fuel," he said, "unless contact is expected within 20 minutes."[7]

Shuttling F4Fs between two carriers worked well, with only two hitches. The *Saratoga*'s air department insisted on putting VF-5 pilots in VF-5 planes; a procedure Simpler thought was "of no consequence and completely sacrifices the most valuable experience obtained by combat teams working together."[8] He insisted that in the future, pilots of a particular division always be launched together, regardless of what squadron's planes they were assigned. The other recommendation called for a standardized arming procedure to load a live round in the chamber of each .50-caliber in order to reduce possible malfunctions in the air.

Again, the F4F-4 was deemed deficient in performance to the Zero. Chick Harmer described the dash four as "an overloaded clunker," and his skipper bemoaned the short cruising radius even with drop tanks.[9] Significantly, the Wildcat's strong points in both squadrons were considered the armor plate, Pratt and Whitney engine, and M 2 guns.

The Battle of Santa Cruz was fought in the same area as Eastern Solomons, two months later. The engagement takes its name from the fiercely malarial Santa Cruz Islands, thirty-odd sea miles southeast of the battle zone. But if the locale was similar to the previous bout, the lineup among U.S. carrier squadrons was entirely new. The *Enterprise* was patched up and flying Air Group 10, the first intact unit embarked in a U.S. flattop since Midway.

The fighter squadrons were now operating near authorized strength of thirty-six F4F-4s. Lieutenant Commander J. H. Flatley, formerly of VF-42, was the skipper of the Grim Reapers of VF-10. In the five months since Flatley postponed his stateside return in order to fly at Coral Sea, he had turned Fighting 10 into a competent, happy outfit. His pilots called him Reaper Leader in the air and Jim when off-duty. But he received that rare blend of familiarity and respect which marks great leaders. A devout Catholic with a strong commitment to the cause he served, Flatley could go drinking with the boys at night and still be all business next morning. His troops were devoted to him.

The *Hornet* still operated a scratch team built around her old bombers and scouts, plus the reorganized VT-6. The new fighter outfit was VF-72, ordered to the *Hornet* in early July following VF-8's debacle at Midway. Ten Fighting 8 pilots reported to their new CO, Lieutenant Commander Henry G. Sanchez, and they would perform well with him. They were men the quality of Jock Sutherland, George Formanek, and Henry Carey, who'd had little chance to show what they could do in VF-8, but would shine in 72. Four would perish.

Their new skipper took some getting used to. He was far more intense than their previous leadership, and possessed a different style from Flatley. "Mike" Sanchez was a tough, outspoken aviator who didn't mind letting superiors know where he stood on any issue. It may not have been diplomatic, but it did produce results.

So far, those results had been obtained in a two-week period dating from 5 October. On the fifth, the *Hornet* launched two strikes against Japanese shipping in the Shortlands near Bougainville. But rain and 800-foot ceilings conspired to thwart the raids, and the only noteworthy damage was inflicted by Sanchez and his wingman, who sank four flying boats and wrecked three Rufes on the beach. The small followup strike downed a cruiser-launched floatplane. During the day the

CAP splashed a flying boat and two Bettys, followed by six more snoopers from the 12th to the 16th.

But by the afternoon of 25 October Rear Admiral Thomas C. Kinkaid, with the *Enterprise* and *Hornet*, knew Japanese carriers were at hand. PBY reports indicated two big Japanese carriers 350 miles to the south, and at 1530 the *Enterprise* launched a forty-eight plane search-strike, including sixteen Wildcats. Ordered to fly 200 miles outbound, Air Group 10 cruised at 17,000 feet as the shadows lengthened below. They didn't know it, but Vice Admiral Nagumo had been spooked into reversing course by the Catalinas. Consequently the Big E's aviators droned on, sucking 100-percent oxygen through their masks for over three hours without sighting a thing. Scheduled to return at sunset, they didn't arrive for another hour. Few were night-qualified, and a VF-10 pilot crashed about 40 miles out. Three SBDs and three TBFs ditched in the landing pattern, but everyone else got aboard.

By now the pattern was well-established: knowledge of the enemy's presence the day before the engagement, overnight preparations, and last-minute checks of aircraft and equipment. But this time the odds were longer than normal. U.S. carriers had been outnumbered three-to-two at Coral Sea and Eastern Solomons; four-to-three at Midway. This time the Japanese fielded four flattops against Kinkaid's two. Nagumo had the *Shokaku, Zuikaku* and CVL *Zuiho* with his Striking Force, and the *Junyo* operated with Vice Admiral Kondo's Advance Force. In terms of carrier-based airpower, the Japanese enjoyed a numerical advantage of about 210 to 170. Clearly, the Wildcats were going to be a crucial factor, for in war as well as in football, you may not win based upon a strong defense, but you can surely lose without it.

Santa Cruz was a confused, complex battle characterized by multiple strikes airborne from both forces. But the actions of the two F4F squadrons are somewhat less bewildering. Both VF-10 and 72 launched divisions on escort while retaining most of their fighters for CAP. The *Hornet* sent her first strike against Nagumo at 0830 as Mike Sanchez led his division to protect Lieutenant Commander Gus Wildhelm's fifteen SBDs and Lieutenant J. C. Bower's four Wildcats covered six Avengers. Thirty minutes later Air Group 10's CAG, Commander Richard Gaines, set course with eight TBFs, three SBDs and two Grim Reaper divisions under Jim Flatley and Lieutenant John Leppla, some 200 nautical miles from their target.

However, the Japanese were already off the mark with a sixty-two plane strike from Nagumo's force and forty-four more spotted for launch. The *Hornet*'s second attack group departed about the same time as the *Enterprise*'s, this one composed of eighteen bombers with a three-plane VF-72 division under Lieutenant W. W. Ford shepherding the SBDs and Lieutenant Jock Sutherland's four assigned to the TBFs. Sutherland, with his former VF-8 wingman Lieutenant (jg) Henry Carey, first spotted trouble. The *Hornet*'s planes were about 75 miles en route when Sutherland noted an unusually large formation at 16,000 to 20,000 feet, headed for Task Force 16. Sutherland immediately called out the sighting, giving altitude, course and composition of the bogies but neither carrier acknowledged. Looking down to starboard, the VF-72 pilots saw a burning plane crash into the water. They could do nothing but continue on track of 305 degrees.

The Reapers were climbing at 115 knots indicated, "feeling quite secure at 5,000 feet and only 60 miles from our base," when the roof fell in.[10] Nine *Zuiho* fighters executed a professional portside stern attack on the *Enterprise* group, shooting down the TBF leader and knocking two other Avengers out of formation. John Leppla, responsible for protecting the TBFs, immediately turned into the threat but it was too late. About six of the Zeros hammered away at his four Wildcats, now beyond mutual support of Flatley's division. It was a dismal situation—some *Enterprise* pilots hadn't even turned on their radios and a few F4Fs were caught with their guns uncharged.

Actually, Leppla should have continued ahead, drawing the lethal Zekes within weaving distance of Flatley, but the decision had been made in an instant. The price was heavy. Leppla was thought to have bailed out but somebody said his chute failed. Ensigns Raleigh Rhodes and Albert Mead also went down, eventually picked up by the Japanese. Ensign Willis "Chip" Reding, now terribly alone, ran for it. He had no other choice. His F4F was perforated by 20-mm and 7.7-mm shells and his electrical system had been shot out, leaving him no guns, prop control, or radio. Somehow he kept the stricken Wildcat airborne for three and a half hours, until things settled down.

Jim Flatley's division on the starboard side of the formation was momentarily surprised. Then the CO went to work. The Wildcats dropped their external tanks and Flatley noted a lone Zeke setting up a run on the remaining TBFs. He fired at full deflection from a diving turn. Though he missed, the Zero was startled by flashing tracers and pulled up to find itself hemmed in by four F4Fs with altitude advantage. Flatley's next pass was from six o'clock at extreme range, but he scored hits which drew smoke. His third pass was a high-side which dumped the Zero into the water.

The remaining A6Ms disengaged but they'd done their job. Three Avengers and three Wildcats were lost, and another TBF soon aborted with engine trouble. The Big E's little group continued awhile longer, but without external tanks the F4Fs couldn't stick it out. They watched the TBFs ineffectively attack a battleship, then turned for home.

Meanwhile, the *Hornet*'s first strike found the same target at 1000: two battleships, four cruisers, and destroyer escorts steaming south of Nagumo's three carriers. At least nine Zeros tackled the *Hornet* formation, and Mike Sanchez had his hands full trying to keep the interceptors off Widhelm's Dauntlesses. While fighting the Zekes two of Sanchez's pilots were shot down and another was wounded, later lost in ditching near the task force. Bombing and Scouting 8 shot their way through determined fighter opposition to rock the *Shokaku* with at least three hits. She was out of the battle, but her planes were now closing Task Force 16.

The four enemy air groups put up nearly 140 planes in an hour that morning—twice the total number of F4Fs. The result was the longest sustained carrier-launched air attack against a U.S. task force until the Marianas eighteen months later.

Under gray skies with lowering dark clouds and fequent rain squalls, the first Japanese strike got within 50 miles before painting on *Enterprise*'s radar. It included twenty-two Vals and eighteen Kates, which would have been hard enough for the thirty-eight available Wildcats to handle in addition to eighteen Zeros, but the Grummans were placed too low for an early intercept. Lugging around their drop tanks cut heavily into rate of climb; some pilots said they couldn't make more than 1,200 feet per minute. But it was a no-win situation if the F4Fs lacked adequate altitude, because without its external tank no dash four had enough loiter time on station. Cycle times would be shortened unacceptably.

Red Base handled the original vectors but no clear picture emerged. After a series of sometimes contradictory and confusing orders, most fighter pilots became suspicious and tried to follow their own instincts. Finally Blue Base assumed control of its own fighters as the *Hornet*'s FDO came on the air. Regaining contact with two VF-72 divisions, Blue Base had a handle on the situation and, said one pilot, "with just one vector sent us slam-bang right into them."[11]

Initial contact was made by Lieutenant Ed Hessel's division, 20 miles out. Few *Hornet* planes were over 18,000 feet, but even at that, they were higher than most *Enterprise* fighters. Trouble was, the Vals were at 17,000. Hessel and his wingman each claimed a dive-bomber, and there's evidence at least one Aichi was destroyed at this point. But the number four man in Hessel's flight was shot down and the rest of the Vals were nose-down, scooting past most of the still-climbing Wildcats to reach their push-over point above the *Hornet*.

Number four in Lieutenant R. W. Rynd's VF-72 division was Ensign George Wrenn, a drawling southerner who anticipated a busy day. He'd shared a patrol plane previously and knew the value of conserving ammo, so he switched off two guns "just to get me home" and followed Rynd down on an estimated forty bandits.

The Wildcats met the Vals on a quartering angle from the front, milling around for perhaps two minutes unfettered by Zeros but unable to come to grips with the single-minded Aichis. Somewhere in the hassle Wrenn became separated from his section leader, finding himself "almost in a loop," diving down through the dive-bombers. At that point he saw the torpedo planes and decided to continue his descent. First one F4F, then another from different divisions joined him in an impromptu effort to head off the dark-green Nakajimas.[12]

As the Kates spread out for their run-in, Wrenn overhauled them from astern. He drew a bead on the nearest, shot it into the water and flipped over to the next. That one went down, too. Wrenn's two squadronmates claimed probables before the speedy Nakajimas plunged into the wall of flak but the Wildcats banked away as the *Hornet*'s screening vessels opened up.

Wrenn hung around at low level, spotting two Kates emerging from the gray-black sky around the task force. Each turned in his direction, perhaps not seeing him until too late. That made four. But in chasing down the second he was drawn in range of the *Enterprise*'s screen, and the *South Dakota* did her best to shoot him out of the air. "The whole deck was ablaze with AA fire," Wrenn vividly recalled, as her battery of 5-inch and 40-mm erupted in orange-yellow lights. But he wasn't finished just yet. A fleeing Val "right on the water" passed by, and Wrenn just about fired out his four guns' remaining ammo to destroy it. He was even happier now that he'd conserved his two outboards, just in case.[13]

The *Enterprise*, 10 miles away, benefitted from a passing rain squall which concealed her for about 20 minutes. But a few of her Reapers tangled with the Vals topside which mauled the *Hornet*. One VF-10 division caught the Aichis just as they dived. Lieutenant A. D. Pollock's Red Two had been orbiting midway between the two task forces at 23,000 and managed a last-minute intercept as the Japanese attacked. Dave Pollock, even more conservation-minded than George Wrenn, used only his two outboard guns and took the nearest Val from behind, apparently killing the gunner. But the D3A pilot continued his dive on the *Hornet* so Pollock activated all six .50s, dived in closer and pressed the trigger. He scored a sure kill as the Val flamed and fell into the water.

Pollock's section leader, Ensign Steve Kona, had trouble with his drop tank. He couldn't get rid of it at first, and only managed to tear it loose after diving to 15,000 feet at an indicated 250 knots. Kona dived after a Val and finally caught up at about 7,000 feet, by which time the flak "was getting pretty hot."[14] But Kona spotted three Vals recovering astern of the *Hornet*, so low they almost ran their fixed landing gear along the choppy water. Kona made high-sides on two, unable to observe the results because of necessarily steep pull-ups. He claimed them as probables. Then a Zero intervened, attacking from six o'clock high. Without diving room, Kona could only weave and watch his wingman, Ensign F. J. Fulton begin a defensive scissors—good lad!

Evading the Zeke, with only a quarter of his ammo remaining, Kona led Fulton back towards the *Enterprise*. But abruptly Fulton broke off, reversing course for the *Hornet*. Kona followed, uncertain what was happening, and tried to catch up but his number two plunged into a cloud and was never seen again.

Another Reaper division, Red Seven, had also made contact. Eleven VF-10 pilots were scrambled when the raid first appeared, joining the dozen already airborne. Red Seven was led by a former VS-5 pilot, Lieutenant Stanley Vejtasa. Like John Leppla, Vejtasa had been recruited by Flatley from a Dauntless squadron because both showed VF potential at Coral Sea. Blonde, blue-eyed Swede Vejtasa was a Montanan with the westerner's traditional talent for straight shooting, and today he proved it in spades.

Leading his three pilots straight out in a running rendezvous to 12,000 feet, Vejtasa was ordered to investigate a five-mile contact. He looked up to see six or eight Vals in loose column; evidently some of the last dive-bombers of the first strike, since the *Hornet* was still under attack. One nosed down, emerging from clouds at Vejtasa's level and Swede flamed it in a high-side run. The others passed overhead.

Lacking specific orders, Vejtasa dropped down and found two more Aichis outbound. He burned one while his number four, Ensign Leder, torched the other. Red Seven then climbed, awaiting developments. Vejtasa's engine abruptly quit and his fuel pressure gauge dropped to zero. He'd been feeding off his drop tank, preferring to burn his external fuel first, and now it was dry. But the troublesome fittings were causing more headaches than usual. Vejtasa finally had to yank on the release with both hands.

By now Nagumo's first strike had departed, sustaining heavy losses (about twenty-five of fifty-eight actually attacking) but leaving Hornet savaged by three bomb hits, two torpedoes and the impact of one aircraft. The *Shokaku*'s dive-bomber commander, hit by AA fire, had crashed into the *Hornet*'s island.

Then the second strike arrived. Actually it was two formations within several minutes of each other: twenty *Zuikaku* Vals trailed lower by a dozen *Shokaku* torpedo planes, plus Zero escort. The incredible confusion of varying orders, intense flak, thick clouds and seeming hordes of raiders at all altitudes resulted in bedlam. More *Hornet* fighters returned about this time from the escort led by Mike Sanchez and some of them got in considerable shooting. Jock Sutherland's division claimed four Vals and part of another, in addition to three Zeros as a result of the strike escort and the action over their own base. But this time the Japanese concentrated on the Big E, now devoid of her cloaking squall line.

Many F4F pilots—perhaps most—were now spectators owing to empty ammo cans. Fortunately for the *Enterprise*, Swede Vejtasa still had .50-caliber to spare. His second section under Lieutenant Stan Ruehlow had investigated another contact when Ensign Leder, number four, called "Tally ho, nine o'clock down." Looking low to port from 13,000 feet, Vejtasa had no trouble distinguishing eleven shiny green Kates at about 7,000 in three vics of three with one two-plane section. Vejtasa led Lieutenant Harris into a 350-knot power dive to overtake the Kates before they attacked the *Enterprise*.

The geometry worked, but just barely. Vejtasa and Harris narrowly arrived in position for a steep high-side run as the Nakajimas bored closer to the Big E at about 250 knots, passing through scattered low clouds. On their first pass the two Reapers each flamed a Kate. Then another F4F jumped in and the Japanese formation disintegrated, several raiders trying to evade into clouds.

Now alone, Vejtasa latched onto an intact three-plane element in heavy cloud. Through the mist he closed to killing position directly astern and exploded one wingman with two short bursts. He shifted aim to the leader, shot off the rudder and set the B5N afire. Number three flamed after a sustained burst. Vejtasa had a go at another torpedo plane but missed in a low-side pass. This Kate suicided on the destroyer *Smith*, smashing into her forward turret and causing fifty-one casualties.

Wary of the AA gunners, Vejtasa orbited outside the flak zone waiting for something to turn up. He earnestly wished for more ammo—he was having a day like no American fighter pilot had ever had—but would make do with what remained. Soon two more Kates emerged close to the water. A lone Wildcat jumped one so Vejtasa took the other. Firing the last of his .50-caliber load, he saw the Kate skid violently, catch fire, and eventually splash. It was Vejtasa's seventh kill of the mission.

Regrouping Red Seven, Vejtasa asked to come aboard but the *Enterprise* had taken two bomb hits and a damaging near-miss. At that, she was better off than the *Hornet* and only elegant shiphandling by Captain Hardison had prevented a spread of torpedoes from disembowling the Big E. With yet another raid inbound, flight ops were impossible. The result: "We circled just outside the screen for an hour and 20 minutes," noted Vejtasa.[16]

So did everyone else still airborne. The *Hornet* had been taken under tow by a cruiser but two subsequent Japanese raids forced her abandonment, and she sank that evening. This left the *Enterprise* as th eonly available flight deck, despite her damage. It also left numerous pilots with precious little margin for getting aboard when things let up.

One was George Wrenn, who'd made two passes and was waved off due to inbound hostiles or local thunderstorms. On his next circuit he saw the carrier beginning a hard turn—another raid, probably—and he never expected to make it. Wrenn was almost resigned to a ditching when Robin Lindsey's outstretched paddles sliced down to give him the cut he had to have. Forty years later Wrenn still insists, "Robin Lindsey was *the best.*"[17]

Crammed to the rafters with *Hornet* orphans and her own birds, the Big E turned southward. The Battle of Santa Cruz was over, a tactical victory for Japan but a strategic win for the United States. The Marines ashore held Henderson Field's perimeter against the land portion of Japan's two-pronged thrust at The Canal. In effect, little had changed.

The two Wildcat squadrons received some hard knocks. Fighting 72 counted noses and found twenty pilots aboard the *Enterprise*, plus two later transferred from a destroyer. Another was reported safe in a hospital ship. Five were known shot down on strike escort or CAP and another six were missing, probably out of fuel. Of the twenty *Hornet* F4Fs recovered in the *Enterprise*, seven were damaged; one so badly it was jettisoned.

The Grim Reapers lost fewer aircraft but more pilots. Eleven VF-10 Wildcats were shot down or ditched, and only four of these pilots were rescued. It wasn't known at the time that two of Leppla's division had been picked up by the Japanese.

Between them, Flatley's and Sanchez's squadrons lost twenty-six F4Fs aginst forty-nine claimed shootdowns and twenty-seven probables. The confirmed credits amounted to twenty-two Vals, fourteen Kates and thirteen Zeros. Swede Vejtasa and George Wrenn counted twelve kills between them—the first time two carrier pilots had bagged five or more planes in a single engagement. (Flatley endorsed a Medal of Honor for Vejtasa, but in the end a Navy Cross was awarded.)

The overall fighter claims were undoubtedly exaggerated, but apparently not by much. Japanese carrier plane losses amounted to ninety or more from all causes, not least of which was the startling American flak. The *South Dakota* optimistically reported a bag of twenty-six raiders for herself, but while she showed the way to the future of task force air defense, she remained unpopular with fighter pilots. Aviators from both F4F squadrons commented bitterly upon her inability to distinguish between friendly and hostile aircraft.

There were other bitter comments. Mike Sanchez, never one to mince words, blasted fighter direction, task force doctrine, and the F4F-4 with equal venom. The VF-72 pilots who saw the *Enterprise*'s radar plot all agreed that the *Hornet*'s had been "extremely superior" due to its integrated layout. The Big E was an older ship, and her CIC was a make-do affair, putting personnel and equipment where room existed. In fact, *Hornet* pilots concluded that if their ship had handled radar control, the task force would never have sustained such grievous damage.[18] But now nobody would ever know.

In his summation Sanchez hammered away at two weaknesses of the dash four Wildcat. First was reduced ammunition capacity. He wrote that if more ammunition had been carried, shootdowns would probably have increased by 50 percent. And in a jab at the F4F-4's increased weight the skipper noted, "The American movie *Flight Surgeon* ended with the sage commitment (sic) 'The nation whose planes can fly higher and faster will win the next war.' In the Pacific the Japanese are always flying higher and faster. Well???"[19]

Jim Flatley's comments were similar, if less colorfully phrased. He estimated that at least eight of his planes were lost to fuel exhaustion after nearly five hours in the air. There had never been a sustained attack upon a carrier force such as at Santa Cruz, but more fuel was a crying need. The Curtiss Electric prop was "subject to numerous failures," and an electrical problem inevitably left the pilot with a propeller in full high or full low pitch, either of which rendered the plane "practically useless." Hydromatic props were strongly recommended.[20]

Fighting 10 was happy with its guns—again, few failures were reported—but Flatley considered the F4F-4's reduced ammo capacity "the glaring deficiency in this battle." Most of his pilots had empty guns for the last ninety minutes, and "Needless to say, it proved to be extremely embarrassing."[21]

Both squadron commanders agreed that the CAP was positioned too low and too close to the task force. This was the result of the dash four's poor climb and altitude performance as well as inexperienced fighter direction. Sanchez said that radar control of fighters, once the expected salvation of carrier aviation, had failed to live up to its promise. In large part that was true at the end of the Wildcat's fourth and last carrier battle. But the lessons learned (including those regrettably relearned) in 1942 would make American task forces nearly impregnable to conventional daylight air attack a year later.

Meanwhile, the F4F-4 would remain the U.S. Navy's shipboard fighter. With all its faults, the underpowered, short-winded, over-gunned little Grumman was still the best airplane for the job. It was all there was.

7. Song of the Solomons

"... exile in the isles of death."
    —Mary Ashley Townsend

THE CRUCIAL PERIOD OF the Guadalcanal campaign ran from 20 August to 15 November: from VMF-223's arrival to the defeat of the transports. Historians customarily draw the line at the end of those eighty-seven days, for what followed was, in retrospect, inevitable. The failure of Japan's major reinforcement attempt and her subsequent withdrawal from the island marked a watershed in the Pacific War.

But nearly three months of fighting remained before The Canal was declared secure. And the successes achieved so far had been won at no small cost. Six F4F squadrons (five Marine, one Navy) had operated from Henderson Field or the Fighter Strip during the important twelve weeks from August to November. This excludes VF-10, which arrived at the last minute, so the above-mentioned squadrons employed about 126 Marine and 34 Navy fighter pilots as near as anyone can tell. Record-keeping never received much priority on The Canal. Aside from a physical shortage of paper, weary operations officers (who also flew combat missions) simply lacked the time or energy for much documentation. Many accounts were created from hastily scrawled notes and reconstructed from memory after leaving the island.

But some fairly representative statistics can be complied. The odds of being killed or seriously injured were one in five for all Wildcat pilots. There were two ways of looking at the odds. Across the board, if a pilot were going to become a casualty, it occurred in his first seventeen days ashore. If he were an optimist, he might breathe a sign of relief at midnight of that day. If he were a pessimist, he would decide that from then on he was living on borrowed time.

In truth, however, anybody could get the chop. Smith, Galer, Carl, and Foss were all shot down. Each was fortunate enough to survive and come back for more. But of the thirty-eight pilots killed or seriously injured during this time, no less than eight suffered misfortune in their first two days. Another nine succumbed within the first seven days. In other words, nearly half the F4F pilots killed or injured met with grief in their initial week of combat.

In the context of aerial warfare history, this is not surprising. Those aviators who survive their first few combats stand an immensely better chance of finishing their tours than the newcomers. All proper training is aimed at getting the novice through his initial brushes with the enemy. After that, he's on the way to becoming productive beyond the basic task of staying healthy.

For a fighter pilot, of course, "productive" usually means shooting down enemy airplanes. That was Cactus Fighter Command's job, pure and simple. There were few strikes to be escorted during most of the campaign. Fighting defensively, the F4F squadrons had only to find the enemy and engage him. Since the opposition frequently operated directly over the Wildcats' home drome, it was often a painfully simple task. Yet only a handful of Cactus F4F pilots became "producers." Marion Carl, who has good reason to know, estimates that perhaps one fighter pilot in four or five remained combat-effective over the long run.

But that handful was enough. Marine Wildcat squadrons claimed some 395 shootdowns from 20 August through 15 November, while VF-5 and VF-10 added another 45 or so. This aggregate of about 440 F4F claims is wide of the estimated 260 Japanese losses to Guadalcanal-based aircraft but roughly meets the historical rule of thumb which allows two shootdowns per three claims.[1] Even with reduced claims, the Cactus losses of 101 aircraft in combat resolves to a better than two-and-a-half-to-one exchange ratio.

However, simply counting the score has seldom been a realistic measure of the actual situation. There's too much room for error in tabulating combat results. What did matter was who controlled the sky. Over Guadalcanal in late 1942, if the Wildcats didn't own the airspace outright, they'd certainly made a substantial down payment.

Things remained relatively quiet in the air war through the end of the year. The Kukum strip, better known as Fighter Two, became operational in mid-December because it offered better drainage than Fighter One.[2] But both auxiliary fields remained in use. Maintenance was upgraded to a considerable extent with arrival of more mechanics from unassigned squadrons. For instance, when VMF-221 set up shop, its aircraft were serviced by personnel from VMO-6. They kept 221's Wildcats at about 75 percent availability.[3]

Only thirty-one victories were claimed by Marine fighter squadrons from the mid-November crisis to year-end, and VMF-121 was rotated to Australia for a badly need rest. Disease, fatigue, and attrition had all taken a toll. While "down under" Joe Foss addressed three Spitfire squadrons recently assigned to the air defense of northern Australia. The RAAF wing commander was Clive R. Caldwell, credited with twenty Axis planes in North Africa, and many of his pilots were combat-experienced against the Germans and Italians. But Foss detected an air of complacency among the Spitfire pilots, and attempted in his direct (that is to say, undiplomatic) way to set them straight. "I understand that several of you guys are aces," Foss began. "Well, congratulations. But what worked against the Germans won't work against the Japs." He paused and felt more than heard a murmur run through the room. Then he plunged on.

"I know what you're thinking. You think that if a stiff-necked American can shoot down twenty-three Japs in an 8,000-pound airplane with 1,200 horsepower, then you're really going to clean house in a 6,500-pound airplane with 1,500 horses. Well, it doesn't work that way. If you try to dogfight a Zero he'll eat your lunch."[4]

When asked how he handled a lone Zero, Foss made no better impression upn his hosts. "We have a saying up at Guadalcanal," the Marine replied. "We say that if you're alone and you meet a Zero, run like hell because you're outnumbered." One Australian asked if that wasn't quite sporting, was it? Foss shook his head. "It may not be sporting, but it's smart." He left the meeting as a friend of Caldwell, admiring the Aussies' spirit, but fearing for their future.[5]

His fears were well founded. Cutting through the wartime claims, a comparison of RAAF and Japanese records shows that the Darwin Wing came out on the short end of an eight-to-one exchange ratio in its early combats.

While VMF-121 was rotated south, VMO-251 under Guadalcanal veteran Joe Renner arrived intact. The photo pilots had completed their tactical and gunnery training, and began flying as a squadron in December. However, early that month some were still filling in for other units. Lieutenant Mike Yunck got things off to a fine start during a strike to Ramada Bay on the north coast of New Georgia on the third. Flying with VMF-122, he picked off three float biplanes.

When 121 returned for its second stint at The Canal, the new CO was Major Don Yost, a thirty-year-old career aviator from Pennsylvania. The squadron had claimed 107½ victories during its first stretch at Cactus, and from late December through the end of January 121 ran up 54 more. Yost himself became top gun this second time around, bagging six planes in two days.

On Christmas Eve the new CO led a division as part of the escort for nine SBDs in a follow-up strike to Munda. Hunting had been good the day before when 121 claimed five Zekes; two by Yost. Next morning when the Army-Marine formation arrived, four Zeros were up and waiting, with an estimated twenty more ready for immediate takeoff. The thirteen Army fighters and four Marines tangled with a total of fourteen Zekes while the Dauntlesses smeared the remaining ten where they sat. Don Yost returned with claims for four kills and his wingman, Lieutenant Ken Kirk on loan from 251, tallied three more.

As the Solomons air war reached farther up The Slot, the limiting factor was fighter range. Bombers needed escorts for any chance of success, and the available fighters needed external fuel tanks. In this respect, the Wildcat was a short-legged competitor—a sprinter which found itself engaged in a marathon.

Based upon her early wartime experience, the *Enterprise* noted this situation in March 1942. The obvious solution was a new fighter, but no Corsairs were forthcoming until the following February. Therefore, the next-best fix was a field modification allowing Wildcats to carry drop tanks. The Big E's air group recommended the idea for close consideration.

But then came Coral Sea, closely followed by Midway. Not until that fall, with the Guadalcanal operation in full swing, did anyone have time to devote to drop tanks.

Carl Anderson was one of the Grumman engineers assigned to the drop tank project. Designs were on hand for the tanks, brackets, and fuel-system modifications, and Anderson worked day and night preparing drawings and data on internal wing changes to accommodate the additional plumbing. Such was the demand that Anderson's drawings went direct from his board to the shop, without benefit of blueprints. Forward and aft sway-braces were employed, at first secured with bolts but later with rivets. The extra fuel line and valve were mounted in front of each forward Y-brace; "a crude installation in a hurry" was how Anderson characterized it.[6]

The tanks themselves were 50-gallon capacity, made of hemp in upstate New York. The release mechanism was operated by a hefty tug on a T-handle in the cockpit, though some pilots had to brace both feet on the instrument panel and pull extra-hard to disengage the toggles. When the tank fell, it broke the fuel connection and took the sway braces with it, leaving the bracket ready to accept a replacement tank.

Manufacturing the items was one thing. Getting them where they were needed was something else. Ordinarily the Navy would have sent a plane to pick up the sketches and hardware, and take them to the west coast. But by the time everything was ready, fog had closed down Bethpage. So Grumman trucked the goods to Floyd Bennett Field, New York's naval air station, where the Navy forwarded the load to California. Anderson recalls that a clipper was detailed to overtake a westbound aircraft carrier and transfer the much-needed materiel en route. He eventually received first-hand confirmation of the initial shipment's arrival, for his brother was on Guadacanal when the first drop-tank F4Fs arrived.

The extra range and endurance came in handy during the second half of January. On the fifteenth, two strikes against shipping in the New Georgia area spurred heavy combat which resulted in claims for twenty shootdowns by VMF-121 and 251. The morning mission went for a reported nine destroyers, coasting five fighters and an SBD. The evening strike (like the first, composed of Dauntlesses escorted by F4Fs and P-39s) attacked a cargo ship northwest of Munda, and returning pilots claimed seven kills for one loss. In this scrap Joe Foss ran his string to twenty-six by splashing three Zekes, as did Captain F. E. Pierce. The other victory went to Foss's teammate Bill Marontate, credited as his thirteenth. But Marontate's was the missing Wildcat—his squadronmates thought he'd collided with a Zeke and lost a wing. In any event, he never returned.

By month's end 121 had finished its second Solomons tour. Under Duke Davis and Don Yost the squadron claimed 161½ victories in 122 days at Guadalcanal, losing twenty pilots to all causes. When the reorganized unit returned to combat later in the year it was equipped with F4U-1s, and would remain the top fighter outfit in the Corps.

The last two days of January ended the month with a bang. Late in the afternoon of the 30th, the *Enterprise* was back in the area, providing CAP for the cruiser *Chicago* which had been torpedoed the previous night. Under tow by a tug near Rennell Island, the wallowing cruiser was jumped by a dozen torpedo-packing Bettys east of Rennell. Jim Flatley, that tireless aviator, had a division of VF-10 over the force when the threat developed. Lieutenant MacGregor Kilpatrick's six planes blocked the Bettys' path to the Big E so the Mitsubishis swung back north to pick off the cripple.

In simplified terms, it was a race. A race between the Bettys and the Grummans to see who got to the *Chicago* first. And it was pretty much a tie. Kilpatrick and his wingman had the angle on the Japanese, diving into gun range from 10,000 feet in high-side runs. They dropped three G4Ms in succession as the task force flak opened up. Flatley's division tried to stop the nine survivors, and the combined efforts of ten Wildcats clawing around in bursting flak trimmed the odds considerably. Between the Reapers and shipboard gunners, seven more Bettys cartwheeled into the water. But four had dropped torpedoes which connected; the *Chicago*'s starboard side was split open and she went down in 20 minutes.

Thus ended the last action fought by carrier-based F4Fs. It was argued that a faster carrier fighter could have prevented the *Chicago*'s loss. And perhaps Hellcats and Corsairs might have succeeded where Wildcats failed. But for the present, the F4F-4 remained the only horse in the stable.

One of the top jockeys put in a stellar performance the next day. Lieutenant Jeff DeBlanc, a Louisana pilot not quite twenty-two, led a six-plane division of VMF-112 on a bomber escort to Kolombangara on the 31st. Intercepting Zeros tangled with the Wildcats in a dandy set-to at 14,000 feet as the Dauntlesses and Avengers went after Japanese shipping. Two Zekes went down in this scrap, tieing up the interceptors until the SBDs and TBFs got away.

But the Solomons nemesis of Allied aviators—aggressive, ubiquitous Rufe float fighters—pounced the SBDs at low level on the way out. Responding to a call for help, DeBlanc disengaged and poked his Wildcat's nose down, found the fracas and broke up the Rufes. At this point the bombers had hauled off and DeBlanc could have called it a day. Instead, he stayed to shoot it out with the Rufes. An experienced combat pilot with three kills to his credit during the previous two months, he calculated the odds carefully. Ignoring his alarming fuel state, he outflew the floatplanes and shot down three of them. But in the process he'd sustained damage and turned for home. Hardly had he settled on his southeasterly course when he spotted two Zekes pouncing from six o'clock. With little option but to accept combat, he turned into them and engaged in a spiraling fight over Kolombangara.

Both sides scored, and though the lone Marine claimed two more kills, he found himself with a Wildcat falling apart in his hands at treetop level. He went overboard, parachuting into the water just off the Japanese-controlled island. Fortunately, coastwatcher Henry Josselyn on nearby Vella Lavella received word of two fighter pilots down on Kolombangara, and his scouts found DeBlanc and Staff Sergeant James Feliton. The Marines had been befriended by natives who exchanged the two fliers for a sack of rice—"a deal which still makes DeBlanc wonder how much a fighter pilot is really worth."[7] The United States Government considered DeBlanc worth a good deal more, and gave him the Medal of Honor. He and Feliton were two of 118 fliers known saved by the Solomons coastwatcher network.

Aside from bread-and-butter fighter missions, Wildcats performed another mission during the latter portions of the Guadalcanal campaign. Hap Hansen's photo outfit had arrived in October, and seldom has a twenty-two-year-old aviator enjoyed such latitude and independence. Nominally assigned to First Air Wing headquarters, Hansen pretty much ran his own show.

For support, Hansen possessed a jeep, several mechanics, and a photo processing unit with ten technicians. He also had two F4F-7s ("all mine") which were eventually destroyed in air raids, but they were replaced one at a time. Carriers destined for the South Pacific generally embarked a dash seven, but since the flattops had no need for such aircraft, the photo birds were put ashore at Espiritu. VMO-251 flew these aircraft for a while, and evidently they became the source of Hansen's equipment.

In any event, Hap Hansen's little command was kept busy since it owned a monopoly in the photo-recce business. Local flights around The Canal generally lasted one and a half to two hours, but were accomplished without fighter escort. Since the F4F-7 was unarmed, if Japanese aircraft turned up, Hansen ducked into cloud cover or hid behind the island's main mountain range.

As the campaign moved up The Slot, Hansen ranged farther afield. He had all kinds of endurance—up to seven and a half hours if needed—and sometimes accompanied strikes to Munda and beyond. This was an ideal setup. It afforded the natural cover of a built-in diversion while allowing F4F-4 escort if needed. As before, he shunned combat. "We had opposition," Hansen said, "but my job was to avoid all contact. Just run and hide."[8] But he always brought back the pictures.

After nearly 100 missions Hansen contracted malaria and was sent to New Zealand. His industrious photo-gathering activities over a five-month period won him a DFC from the Army-Marine command, but he'd be back with guns next time. When VMF-112 transitioned to

Corsairs that summer, Hap Hansen led the pack as skipper. Though the remainder of his wartime flying was done in F4Us, he remained fond of the F4F-7; "It was a fine airplane."[9]

Guadalcanal was declared officially secure on 9 February. A successful series of evacuation runs by Rear Admiral Tanaka's destroyers—a sort of Tokyo Express in reverse—removed most surviving Japanese troops by that date. Only one destroyer was lost in this tricky operation.

Yet the departure of the Japanese from Guadalcanal served to inaugurate more Navy F4Fs to combat in the arena. At the end of January three escort carrier squadrons—VGS-11, 12, and 16—were detached from their ships at Nandi in the Fijis. Sent up to Cactus, they arrived just in time to participate in strikes against the last runs of the Express.

The most successful—and longest in service by the time it was all over—was VGS-11, formerly embarked in the *Altamaha*. Lieutenant Commander Charles "Whitey" Ostrom's Wildcats flew into Fighter One almost immediately and logged their first mission on 2 February. Next day the CVE squadrons were reinforced with seventeen additional F4Fs from VF-72.

On 4 February Ostrom led twenty-one of his own planes to Munda as part of an Army–Navy–Marine strike against enemy destroyers. Claims amounted to two DDs sunk and one damaged (in fact, no Japanese ships were lost) but the newly-arrived Wildcats tangled with Zekes and returned with claims for seven downed; five by VGS-11. Four Avengers and an F4F didn't make it back. An afternoon restrike cost VGS-11 two more Wildcats in exchange for five Zekes.

On 1 March the VGS units were redesignated composite squadrons, but in mid-May another change occurred. VC-11 became VF-21, still under Ostrom, and VC-12, flying TBFs, was renamed VT-21.

Continuing Allied success in the air and at sea that spring provoked an uncommonly heavy response from the Japanese. Photo missions up The Slot showed a startling enemy buildup during the first week in April, especially on the airfields at Kahili and Ballale. Therefore, it was unsurprising when coastwatchers radioed word of exceptionally large Japanese formations headed southeast on the afternoon of the seventh.

The official count was 160 raiders, and for a change it was too conservative. A staggering escort of 110 Zekes led 67 Vals, bent on wreaking havoc with U.S. shipping around Guadalcanal. By the time the magnitude of the raid was appreciated, "only" 76 fighters were able to scramble, and Cactus radio described the conditions as *"Very red."*[10]

The huge Zero escort soaked up nearly all the Cactus interceptors. Captain George Britt's VMF-214 Wildcats made one of the early contacts, and in the squadron's only combat of its first tour, claimed four Vals and six Zekes. The heaviest fighting was reported by VMF-221. Eleven of Captain Robert Burns' pilots claimed kills, but only one division really got to the Vals as they tipped into dives on U.S. ships from 15,000 feet over Tulagi. The division leader was First Lieutenant James E. Swett, a twenty-two-year-old Californian who'd been on The Canal since late February. In six weeks he'd seen a few airborne hostiles but as yet hadn't fired his guns at any. Today, he had all the shooting a fighter pilot could want.

Sighting fifteen Vals preparing to dive, Swett led his F4Fs into the formation. American AA gunners already had the Aichis under fire, but the four Wildcats had to ignore the bursting shells. Confident in the F4F ("a marvelous gun platform") Swett flamed his first two targets easily.[11] He followed the third all the way down, through increasing volumes of flak, and finally exploded the dive-bomber after its pullout. At that point a "friendly" AA crew expertly put a 40-mm shell through his port wing.

Seeking temporary safety over Florida, Swett satisfied himself he could keep his Wildcat in the fight. He noted five Vals retiring northward in line astern and bent the throttle to overtake them. Approaching from six o'clock low, he got within range unseen and dumped the two tail-end bombers without difficulty. That made five. The next Val was some 1,500 yards ahead and, still undetected, the lone Marine flew in so close that he was rocked in his target's slipstream. He eased off, set his gunsight pipper solidly on the fuselage, and fired. Laced by tracers, the Aichi went down.

Most of Swett's shooting had been from astern at low deflection. The seventh Val of the day presented a beam shot, a textbook scenario. "We were taught to use the mil rings effectively," he recalled, "and granted that time was a huge factor, in a set-up shot we always used proper deflection and our kill efficiency was high."[12] And so it was. A perfectly placed burst dropped the target burning into the water.

The last retreating Val was fully alerted to the lethal solitary Grumman. The gunner drew a careful bead and neatly stitched a volley of 7.7-mm rounds into the engine and cockpit, smashing the canopy. Shattering glass badly cut Swett's face, leaking oil impaired his vision, and he pulled around from his pass without firing.

Knowing he was low on ammo, Swett carefully set up his next run and killed the sharp-shooting back-seater. Then he closed in, clamped down on his trigger and heard his last rounds pound away at the still-fleeing Aichi. The Val disappeared into a cloud, pulling a smoky banner, and Swett turned for home.

He didn't quite make it. Over Tulagi harbor his oil-starved engine gave out, and as if that weren't bad enough, zealous machine-gunners began shooting at him. He put the Wildcat down, splashing into a heavy landing, nearly drowned as the Grumman sank, and barely climbed into his raft. Wet, oily, and bloody, Swett awaited rescue by a patrol boat whose crew added insult to injury by asking if he were American. His profane reply removed all doubt.

Final evaluation of claims by VMF-213, 214, and 221 amounted to credit for twenty-eight shootdowns, plus eleven more by Army and Navy fighters. Actual losses were twenty-nine, including a dozen Vals, in exchange for seven Wildcats. There wasn't much doubt about Swett's claims, and in fact Japanese records admitted losing twelve dive-bombers. Swett's seven confirmed and one probable in 15 minutes amounted to a quarter of the Marine credits, and he became the fifth F4F pilot awarded the Medal of Honor in the Solomons.

The 7 April battle marked the end of Marine aviation's eventful association with the Wildcat. A few squadrons continued to fly the Grumman a bit longer, but VMF-221 and 214 recorded the last F4F victories credited to Marine Corps pilots.

By the end of May all VMF squadrons in the front lines were flying the fast new Corsair, and the others rotated up to the operational airfields by early July. Consequently, Air Solomons Fighter Command now involved Marine F4U squadrons and Navy F4F outfits, in addition to a leavening of Army P-38, P-39, and P-40 squadrons with a wing of New Zealand Kittyhawks for spice.

Navy reinforcements arrived in April, and they were warmly greeted. Air Group 11, at one time destined for the late lamented *Hornet*, set up shop at Henderson Field under the CAG, Commander Weldon Hamilton, erstwhile skipper of the *Lexington*'s Bombing Two. But Fighting 11, under Lieutenant Commander Charles Marbury White, plunked down on Fighter One with 34 F4F-4s. The Sundowners had to wait a while for an opportunity to live up to their name, but in the meantime they were fully occupied learning the neighborhood, like any new kids on the block.

By spring of 1943 Guadalcanal had grown into a greatly expanded air complex. Besides Henderson and its two satellite fields, there were two more strips to the east, just beyond Koli Point. These were

Carney One and Two. Additionally, F4Fs operated from Banika Island in the Russells starting in April. The local lingo was built upon the framework of radio call signs for these various facilities. Henderson, and Guadalcanal generally, was still Cactus. The U.S. fighter-director station was Recon and its New Zealand counterpart (highly regarded by American fighter pilots) was naturally Kiwi. Located on the north coast near Fighter Two, Kiwi became famous for turning up business when other radars had little to report.

Tulagi was Ringbolt, and the Russells were Knucklehead. The latter was a favorite watering hole and more than one CAP flight pancaked at Knucklehead under the real or perceived need to refuel. Actually, the fighter pilots simply wanted to patronize South Pacific Joe's, home of the only genuine hamburgers in the Solomon Islands.

By this time all the landing strips were paved with pierced steel planking. It made for safer operations, but increased the noise level substantially. Recalled one Wildcat pilot, "Whenever you landed your wheels made a most ungodly clanking, slapping, rumbling racket. On takeoff you didn't hear the noise above the engine at full power, but on landing there it was. In a way, it was really welcome after a long day in the saddle."[13]

Another sound was the call and squall of innumerable parrots. They made a perfect bedlam of the coconut plantation where most squadrons bivouacked. Marine pilots—being Marines—often got angry from sleep deprivation and declared war on the birds, using .45 autos or liberated Arisaka 6.5-mm rifles. A captured Japanese ammo dump nearby insured this "second front" never lacked for munitions. But the coconut trees were mature and tall, and the parrots made clever tactical use of height and cover so neither side gained much of an advantage.

When VF-11 moved into Fighter One the living quarters were unsatisfactory, to understate the situation. But things improved after a visit by Assistant Secretary of the Navy Artemus L. Gates who "unfavorably compared [the Sundowners'] accommodations with share-croppers' establishments in less enlightened parts of the Deep South."[14] Quonset huts and showers soon replaced the ramshackle previous arrangement.

Despite such improvements, some Navy fighter pilots were disappointed at flying Wildcats while the Marines stepped up to Corsairs. The F4F, even with drop tanks, lacked the range to escort heavy bombers all the way to Bougainville without staging through Knucklehead. But combat was increasingly found farther up The Slot, and most Navy squadrons had to be content with plying the

Russells–New Georgia area, which remained relatively inactive through mid-summer.

Things started slowly for VF-11, then went sour. White's squadron flew its first mission on 27 April and suffered its first loss five days later, when two F4Fs collided on an escort to Munda. One plane went down, its tail severed by the other Wildcat's prop, but the missing pilot turned up safe; one of twenty-two aviators rescued by New Georgia coastwatchers. The squadron lost another plane with its pilot near Rendova on 6 May, apparently to engine failure, and the CO was wounded while strafing Rekata Bay on the 26th.

After six weeks on The Canal, Fighting 11 still hadn't seen a Japanese plane. But after the drought, when it finally rained it poured. On a weather-aborted escort on 7 June Lieutenant Commander Gordon Cady proceeded with his division to Segi Point where an estimated thirty-two Zekes apparently awaited the diverted strike. The Mitsubishis pounced and caught three pilots. Two bailed out and one ditched but almost miraculously all three survived, despite being strafed in the water or ashore. Gordon Cady, dodging from cloud to cloud, twice came across lone Zeros and turned the tables. A noted gunnery expert, he'd developed the Navy's standard pattern boresight for the F4F-4, and with Bill Leonard posted the squadron's best scores in training. He shot down both Zekes, then raced home to collect help. His three wingmen were fetched back by amphibian and native canoe.

But the Navy pilots were learning. They'd already perfected cruise control, and found that a throttle setting of 1,500 to 1,800 rpm with 22 inches manifold pressure provided maximum endurance at altitude. Maximum range in the F4F-4, based upon a total fuel load of 144 gallons, was achieved at 5,000 feet. Using neutral blower with mixture in auto-lean and full throttle, pilots controlled speed by reducing rpm to whatever setting gave 140 knots indicated. After two and a half hours both external tanks were empty, allowing an increase of indicated airspeed to 160 knots, or 184 mph. Experience proved the fuel gauge unreliable, so pilots calculated remaining gas based upon 50 gallons per hour heavy and 45 gph after the external ran dry.

The drop tanks, in fact, were seldom dropped. For one thing, they were too scarce and for another, they didn't always separate. Ferry flights of 600 nautical miles were flown using these fuel management techniques, from the Fijis to the New Hebrides, and from Espiritu Santo up to The Canal.

The Japanese had learned things too. After a year and a half of trying, the Zero pilots decided they couldn't counter the four-plane, two-section tactics of the U.S. Navy and Marine Corps. Beginning about June the Imperial Navy fighters abandoned their long-standing three-plane division and adopted the world-wide standard of two pair. It was a case of the old adage, if you can't beat 'em, join 'em.

With new types such as the F4U and P-38 available in growing numbers, the aerial situation had turned round in the Solomons. The Zero pilots, believing their own grossly inflated claims, assumed they'd long mastered the F4F and considered it an easy opponent. The Lightning and Corsair were other matters, as their climb and dive performance equalled or exceeded the Zeke's, and when Hellcats appeared that fall, the Japanese realized they now sat behind the technological power curve. But however arrogant some Zero pilots may have been about the Wildcat, they still respected its armament. In fact, some of the better ones would have preferred six .50s to the mixed armament of their A6M5s, due to the American armament's greater range and denser pattern.[15]

In truth, the Wildcat still gave better than it got. Fighting 11 proved that during two days in mid-June. Bill Leonard had four divisions homeward-bound near the Russells from a PBY escort on the morning of the twelfth when the fighter director reported a large bogey closing. Leonard, who hadn't seen an airborne bandit in the 12 months since Midway, offered his services. The FDO worked the sixteen Wildcats for 35 minutes before eyeball contact was made: about three dozen Zekes in all, stacked above and below the Sundowner's altitude of 23,000. The F4Fs had been airborne now for over three hours, so it had to be a hit-and-run affair. Some quick mental calculations convinced Leonard his troops had fuel for one pass if they made directly for home, 70 miles southeast.

He shaved the margin razor-thin. Diving on the lower formation, Leonard drew a bead on two Zekes and exploded them both. By now some Corsairs were vectored in, and the engagement fell apart in a shambles. Leonard headed for Cactus, nursing his depleted fuel, and landed with about four gallons remaining. His number four man, Lieutenant (jg) Bob Gilbert, was right behind. Gilbert had barely extracted himself from a hassle involving Zekes, Corsairs, and Wild-cats, in which he claimed three kills. Both pilots' fuel gauges read empty. But Leonard's element leader didn't show up at all.

Lieutenant (jg) Vern Graham, a rugged Colorado pilot, became separated from Leonard in the first pass, and from Gilbert shortly thereafter. Going it alone, he pounced on a Zeke threatening a Wild-cat and shot it out of a slow-roll, flamed another in a high-side run and exploded a third head-on. Joined by two F4Us, Graham initiated an offensive weave in which he hit a Zeke as one Corsair dragged it across his sights. That was enough; he was nearly out of fuel and banked around for Banika. But yet another Zeke approached from twelve o'clock high, and Graham raised his nose, fired, and saw smoke from the bandit. Then his engine quit. The Marines from VMF-121 chased a pair of pesky Zekes off Graham's tail (one was Captain Bruce Porter, who'd cracked up his F4F-3 at Quantico on 11 December 1941) and the Navy pilot concentrated on a tricky landing.

Without power, a dead-stick Knucklehead landing was almost impossible. Graham unavoidably overshot the strip cut out of a coconut plantation and smashed into the trees at the far end. His Fox 23 was destroyed, and he was lucky to escape with injuries which sent him to the hospital instead of the morgue. Later, Vern Graham learned the rest of the story of his 33rd combat mission. The 121 pilots confirmed the destruction of the last two Zekes he engaged. He thus became the first ace of VF-11, and the last F4F pilot to bag five or more bandits in one day.

Another Wildcat ditched with battle damage but the pilot was alright. Fighting 11, in its first major combat, claimed fourteen kills against the loss of two F4Fs. The Marines accounted for five more victories. Vern Graham's services were lost to the squadron, but he eventually returned to flying—next time in Corsairs.

Four days later, 16 June, the Japanese launched another big raid at Guadalcanal. And again, VF-11 was heavily engaged. The Sundowners traditionally maintained a surplus of pilots on call in their ready tent at Fighter One. A few times previously they'd been able to scramble more F4Fs than requested by Fighter Command, but never before had the extras been so badly needed. Radar noted an exceptionally large bogey during the noon hour, and between 1310 and 1340 VF-11 scrambled seven divisions to patrol the shipping area from Cape Esperance to Tulagi. In all, VF-11 had twenty-eight Wildcats up and waiting when an estimated 120 Japanese planes arrived.

Actually there were twenty-four Vals escorted by seventy Zekes. They'd flown an unusual southerly route, avoiding interception near the Russells, and consequently approached the target area from the south at 15,000 feet. As Army P-38s and P-40s raced to join in, Lieutenant Commander White's pilots sized up the situation from an altitude advantage of 1,000 to 8,000 feet.

First to engage was Lieutenant Frank Quady's division, almost over its home field. Choosing a dive-bomber formation with Zeke escort on either flank, Quady's team hit the intruders from upsun in overhead and stern runs, claiming four Vals and two Zeros as sure kills. Then dark, good-looking Lieutenant (jg) John Ramsey took his division into the Zeke top cover. A half-dozen Zeros were thought splashed in this tussle, and though one Wildcat ditched with an unexplained engine stoppage, Ramsey himself got through the escort and bagged a Val.

By now things were a shambles. Wildcats, Vals, Lightnings, Zekes, and Warhawks tore into each other in a steadily decreasing combat as a handful of Corsairs belatedly engaged. But the single-minded Aichis continued for shipping in the sound, and they hit two vessels. White's division intercepted the Vals just as they dived, and the CO knocked two out of formation, claiming them as probables. Jumped by a Zeke, he wriggled away but when he looked for his wingman, there was no sign.

However, White's second section hit the aerial jackpot. Jim Swope and Charlie Stimpson were probably the most potent pair of jaygees in the Solomons. Swope was a superior airman, and the skinny "Skull" Stimpson possessed phenomenal eyesight—the medicos pegged his vision at 20/8. Swope as element lead followed the Vals into their dives and shot three into the water. Stimpson was right behind. He lined up four in succession and dumped them in turn. "I'm gonna be a hero when I get back to the field," Stimpson recalls thinking as he lined up number five. But an expertly flown Zeke injected itself into the proceedings, and "he crawled all over Jim and me, so we decided to call it a day."[16]

Three Sundowners never came back. One Wildcat pilot had collided with a P-40 and apparently the other two ran into each other. But the loss of four planes and three pilots had to be weighed against a claim of seventeen Vals and thirteen Zekes. The sixty-one Army and three Marine tallys brought the total to ninety-four, which was exactly the number of Japanese planes involved. But the results were impressive enough—nearly the entire enemy formation destroyed, versus two U.S. ships damaged and a total of six American fighters lost. It was the last time the Japanese raided Guadalcanal in daylight.

But it wasn't quite the last major Wildcat action. At month's end VF-21 matched Fighting 11's one-day total bag while covering the Rendova landings. As troop transports unloaded on 30 June, Lieutenant Commander Ostrom had eight divisions topside, waiting for the expected Japanese reaction. Lieutenant Ross Torkelson's Gold Three had one plane ditch when its engine refused to start after switching tanks. Then a New Zealand P-40 pilot asked, "what is that plane over there at 12,000 feet southwest of Rendova?"[17] The F4Fs shucked their tanks as Torkelson led his two wingmen to investigate; it was a Betty headed downhill to the southwest. Sailors always say a stern chase is a long chase, and so it was. Despite one tank which refused to release, Torkelson slowly overhauled the G4M and caught it on the water over 30 miles out.

Back over New Georgia, a bigger scrap brewed up. The top cover Wildcats came down out of the clouds at 18,500 feet in a spiraling dive to find F4Us, F4Fs, and Zekes everywhere. Commented one pilot, "I started shooting at Zeros, Zeros, Zeros,"[18] Another division broke through the clouds, saw Corsairs fighting Zekes above sixteen to eighteen single-engine bombers,and attacked the latter. "After making a firing run on them we saw they were SBDs and TBFs," a chagrined flight leader said.[19] In this phase of the battle VF-21 claimed two Zekes but lost two planes and a pilot.

During the afternoon Ostrom had twenty-eight Wildcats over Rendova between 10,000 and 15,000 feet when a Japanese formation came skimming in low for the vulnerable transports. Ostrom took his division down on the first four Bettys, and Gold One pilots knocked down three. One splashed close enough to a troopship to shower it with water and debris.

Then the rest of the squadron engaged. The Bettys, making an estimated 180 knots with Zekes overhead, pressed a determined attack. Ross Torkelson was back on the job; he claimed a Betty, then was hit by a Zeke which shot his tailwheel loose. As the Zeke climbed, Torkelson dived, picked another bomber and shot it down.

However, many of the Fighting 21 pilots were less experienced, and some of them wasted their precious ammo in flock-shooting. Instead of picking a single target—or better yet, a part of a target—they hosed down the entire formation. There were reports of "raking them up and down," or "I simply sprayed the sky."[20] With the limited ammunition capacity of the F4F-4, many guns quickly went empty.

But enough pilots concentrated properly and finished the execution. When it was over, VF-21 had claimed seventeen Zekes and ten Bettys. Yet amid the excitement and violence were some incredible moments of calm. Lieutenant (jg) Beasley, out of ammo and caught at a disadvantage, was approached by a Zeke. Beasley expected to die, but found himself instead with a Japanese wingman. For an agonizing 30 seconds the Zero flew close formation, apparently also out of ammo, before breaking off. On the other hand, some Zekes were seen shooting at parachutes floating on the water.

In his report, Ostrom praised VMF-213 for fine coordination with his F4Fs, and certainly the Corsairs had a good day: fifty-eight shootdowns credited, plus eleven for the P-40s. Fighting 21's total of thirty was tops, making a grand total of ninety-nine for Allied fighters. Air Sols losses amounted to fourteen, including four VF-21 Wildcats. Actual Japanese losses may have been as few as thirty to forty, but the Rendova landings succeeded.[21] The island-hopping trek up the Solomons was now in full swing.

Fighting 21 remained active through the next month. Flying from Guadalcanal and the Russells, Ostrom's F4Fs engaged in a series of July battles from Munda to the Shortlands. They claimed two dozen Zekes, Bettys, and Vals against five F4Fs lost in air combat, running their total to fifty-four for nine in twenty-six days. The Sundowners ended their eight-week Solomons tour in July with a box score of fifty-five against seven Wildcats known or presumed shot down by Japanese aircraft.

Fighting 21 departed in August, leaving three F4F squadrons in the Russells for a short time longer. These were also former CVE unites: VF-26, 27, and 28. They saw relatively little combat, though they provided a training ground for later, more intensive operations. One Fighting 27 alumnus was Lieutenant Cecil Harris, and erstwhile teacher who recorded his first two victories while flying in the Solomons. A year later he was flying Hellcats off the *Intrepid*, en route to the number two spot on the list of Navy fighter aces.

The Wildcat's tenure in in the Solomons lasted just about twelve months, beginning with the Guadalcanal landings in August 1942. By the following September there were no more F4F squadrons in combat. Thus, the northern Solomons marked the end of the F4F's operational career. The Corsair was now well established and the Hellcat was just arriving. The old order had passed.

From December 1941 through the fall of 1943 official Navy and Marine Corps records credited Wildcat squadrons—both land- and carrier-based—with 603 confirmed victories against an acknowledged loss of 178 in air combat. This was a kill-loss ratio of 3.3 to one, an exchange rate which had held steady since Midway. The actual ratio was probably closer to an even two-to-one overall (considering the nature of aerial combat, in which claims are inevitably inflated) but it was still impressive. Wildcats had continued to outshoot the Zero, despite the Imperial Navy's confidence that the A6M was equal to any three Allied fighters.

The Wildcat story was winding down in late 1943, but it was by no means ended.

8. OTHER ENEMIES

"Yes, quaint and curious, war is! You shoot a fellow down you'd treat if mete where any bar is, or help to half a crown."
—Thomas Hardy

THE NAVAL BATTLE OF GUA-dalcanal, with the attendant defeat of the Japanese transports in The Slot, marked the climax of the long, sanguinary struggle for that unhappy island. But half a world away another ambitious naval-air operation unfolded in North African waters. And Wildcats were there too, in abundance.

Operation Torch, the British landings in Algeria and simultaneous American occupation of French Morocco, opened the week before events peaked at The Canal. The U.S. Navy assigned four carriers to the Western Naval Task Force, supporting landings at Casablanca, Mehdia to the north, and Safi to the south. Embarked in these flattops were seven Wildcat squadrons totaling 109 F4F-4s, plus 62 Dauntlesses and Avengers.

Half the U.S. fighter strength rode in the *Ranger*. Lieutenant Commander Tommy Booth, the popular, easygoing skipper of VF-41, led a squadron which for this period of the war possessed considerable experience. Redesignated from Fighting Four which had received the first fleet Wildcats two years earlier, VF-41 had some pilots with over 500 hours in type. By comparison, the *Ranger*'s second fighter squadron had only been commissioned in the spring. Fighting Nine under Lieutenant Commander Jack Raby had trained hard at Bermuda, and his troops were enthusiastic. But they'd incurred several op-

169

erational losses, requiring resupply of new aircraft. Few VF-9 pilots had yet logged 200 hours in F4Fs, and most had only about twenty-five carrier landings.[1]

The *Ranger*'s partner in the center group off Casablanca was the escort carrier *Suwannee*, flying a mixed air group. The CVE contained four squadrons or portions thereof: twenty-nine Wildcats of VGF-27, twenty-eight and VGS-30, and nine Avengers of VGS-27. Why the six F4Fs of VGS-30 should have been designated a scouting unit, nobody seemed to know. Not that it mattered much.

Supporting the northern landing group was the CVE *Sangamon*, with twelve fighters of VGF-26 and 18 bombers. Guarding the southern flank was her sister the *Santee*, flying fourteen Wildcats of VGF-29. The CO was Lieutenant Commander John Thomas Blackburn, an experienced aviator, but his pilots were pretty green. Ten of the fourteen averaged only 400 hours total time, with eighteen carrier landings, and none had flown in two weeks.[2]

The main topic of conversation was the sort of reception the Americans would receive from the Vichy forces in Morocco. Technically, the territory represented unoccupied France—never mind that the regime was cooperating with Germany. If the scuttlebut in the *Ranger* was typical, all anybody knew for sure was that nothing was certain. In VF-41's ready room opinions were tossed back and forth. "The French won't fight . . . the whole thing will be a walkover."[3] "The French will fight anyone, and anyone means us this time."[4] In the end, Lieutenant (jg) Chick Smith of Fighting Nine summed up most pilots' feelings. "We thought of the French as traditional allies," he recalled, "and it was disappointing they resisted us as much as they did."[5]

Between the speculation and bull sessions, intelligence officers drilled fliers in all manner of topics: geography, communications and code, desert survival. There were lectures on Moslem culture and how to behave around Arabs. Expect two meals a day, take off one's shoes when entering tents, remember that distances were measured in a day's journey by camel. And stay away from Arab women. *Especially* stay away from Arab women.

Still, much was left unknown. A good deal of data came from such diverse sources as encyclopedias, travel brochures, and even back issues of *National Geographic*. Consequently, considerable information was probably dated.

Vichy air strength in Morocco totaled nearly 200 aircraft of the Armee de l'Air and Aeronavale. Based at seven airfields, they included seventy-eight bombers, seventy-eight fighters and thirty-six transport planes. The main bases were Casablanca itself with twenty Curtiss Hawk 75s (export models of the P-36) and thirteen Dewoitine 520s, and the naval air station at Port Lyautey with twenty-five Dewoitines and eleven Martin 167 bombers.

The battle—if there would be one—shaped up most peculiarly. Half the Vichy bombers and fighters were built in the U.S. and many of their pilots had combat experience against the Luftwaffe from 1939–40. In fact, several of the fighter pilots at Casablanca and Rabat-Sale were aces from the Battle of France. Now they prepared to ply their skills against American aviators. Perhaps most ironic of all, the aircraft of Groupe de Combat II/5 at Casablanca bore the famous Indian head insignia of the old Lafayette Escadrille.

Torch opened at dawn on 8 November 1942. Off the southern landing beaches at Safi, VGF-29 launched seven Wildcats from the *Santee*. The two divisions encountered light anti-aircraft fire and patrolled inland, seeking airfields. One pilot radioed in distress, reporting a severed oil line. Nothing more was heard from him, but his body was found in the wreckage several days later, 100 miles north of Safi. He may have been shot down by French aircraft.

Finding nothing to shoot at, Tommy Blackburn led his remaining five pilots back toward the coast and noted rain clouds out to sea. He turned to the *Santee*'s radio direction-finder frequency, trying to pick up the Morse letter N for that quadrant. Listening intently for the dah-dit pattern, he heard nothing. Rather than dead-reckon back to the ship, he called for a radar steer. The controller had him make a couple of identifying turns, then instructed the Wildcats to fly north-westerly.

After more than enough time, Blackburn radioed again. According to the radar man, the F4Fs were circling the ship. Blackburn realized the *Santee* had plotted another flight. With fuel running low, he told his pilots to head for the coast. They should find Mazagan Airfield between Safi and Casablanca.

But Blackburn's tanks ran dry and he ditched deadstick. Floating in his rubber raft for 60 hours, he finally flagged down a destroyer of the southern task force. Upon return to the *Santee* he learned four F4Fs had crash-landed ashore, their pilots briefly interned.

The *Ranger*'s squadrons found plenty of action. In fact, almost too much. Tommy Booth led eighteen VF-41 planes off to the southeast at dawn, climbing into good visibility except for clouds at 2,000 feet. Crossing the coast at 15,000 the fliers looked down on a peaceful countryside: grain fields, orchards, vineyards, and white houses with red tile roofs.

Orbiting Cazes airfield, which seemed empty, Booth's formation drew AA fire. Standing orders were to fire only if fired upon, as the Allies were anxious to avoid irritating the French. Now there was clear opposition and Booth radioed the prearranged signal, "Batter up!" The *Ranger* responded, "Play ball!"[6] The CO took his division down to strafe while the others remained upstairs awaiting their turns.

Cazes was a bomber and transport base, but French fighters were about. Lieutenant (jg) Charles "Windy" Shields made this unpleasant discovery when two red-and-yellow nosed D.520s bounced him from starboard. Shields saw them in time, turned into the threat, and while still at longish range, triggered a burst. His aim was good. The lead Dewoitine dropped into a dive and smashed into the ground.

Then Shields spotted three planes cutting right across the airdrome at what looked like zero feet. He dropped down to investigate and found Lieutenant Chuck August with two Hawks hard after him. August had already claimed two Vichymen, but this pair seemed intent on revenge. Shields heard August holler for help and jumped the French wingman, who proved slippery. But the Wildcat got a bead on him in a climbing turn, flaming him with a deflection shot. Meanwhile, August had chandelled back into the other Curtiss and nailed it head-on.

So far, so good. But headed for the rendezvous at 8,000 feet, Shields attracted two more Hawks which perforated his Wildcat. Again turning to engage, he clobbered one and watched the other break off. As if this weren't enough excitement, Shields then noticed a Douglas DB-7 taxiing for takeoff. He accelerated into a dive, overshot, and pulled around for another pass at Cazes. Shields came in low and flat—so low that when his .50-calibers exploded the bomber, his F4F was savagely rocked by the concussion.

By now Windy Shields had expended the last of his considerable luck. Four more Hawks hit him from above, shooting out his fuel lines and filling his cockpit with smoke. He pulled up, opened the canopy, unstrapped, and bailed out.

Then another Vichyman flew towards him. For a moment, dangling from his chute, Shields thought the Frenchman intended to murder him. But the Hawk merely flew close aboard, the pilot "wagging his wingtips and waving and laughing like hell."[7] Shields returned the sporting gesture, but some soldiers on the ground had different ideas about sport. They began potting at him as he descended. With no other option, Shields unlimbered his .45 automatic and returned fire. Now, a good man with a .45 can hit a standing opponent at 50 meters with the first round. But swinging from a parachute isn't part of the bargain. Neither side scored, and the shooting match seemed cancelled by mutual consent.

Meanwhile, Chuck August had his own problems. Like Shields, he was headed for the rendezvous when he became distracted. A lone F4F, strafing AA sites, dived steeply through the flak but never pulled out. August decided on just one more pass (famous last words in the fighter pilot trade) and got clobbered. With zero oil pressure at 1,100 feet, he slid back the canopy, rolled inverted, and fell free, hitting the stabilizer on the way out.

Yet another VF-41 pilot, Lieutenant Spanky Carter, ended up alone—temporarily. He soon acquired three unwelcome companions with red and yellow markings. Carter fought them as well as he could, damaging one which broke away trailing smoke, but the other two did a job on him. He glided towards the beach, closely escorted by a waving, grinning Frenchman. Carter ditched offshore, inflated his raft, and climbed in.

Back aboard the *Ranger*, Tommy Booth counted noses and found six missing. At the time he knew of one pilot rescued at sea. The others either made it or they didn't; there was no time for second-guessing. The Wildcats had succumbed to the individualist urge to engage in single combat, and that was the other fellow's game. The French pilots were often experienced professionals who (with Curtiss 75s, at least) could outmaneuver an F4F. Booth reminded his troops to stick together, emphasizing air discipline. Then he led a strafing attack against a pesky AA battery, but another Wildcat ditched from flak damage.

Meanwhile, VF-9 had put in a busy day. Jack Raby's gang went to Port Lyautey, where the skipper and his wingman noticed a twin-engine bomber flying towards a U.S. transport ship. They identified it as an LeO 45 and, at extreme range, exploded it from astern for the squadron's first victory. Actually it was a Potez 63.

Fighting 26 was also over Port Lyautey that morning, where the *Sangamon* Wildcats encountered six twin-engine aircraft and five D.520s. In the hassle which followed they claimed three bombers—probably Martin 167s—and a Dewoitine without loss.

But shortly before midday occurred another case of mistaken identity, and it didn't work out as well as Fighting Nine's encounter. A section of VFG-27 fighters off the *Suwannee* pounced on an un-identified twin at 2,000 feet and shot it down. They identified their victim as an LeO 45 but the victim was a Royal Air Force Hudson out of Gibraltar. It crashed at sea with only one survivor from the four-man crew.[8] Far to the east, Royal Navy Martlets made an almost identical error a few days later over Algeria.

So it went through the day, in a succession of launches and recoveries. Most of the F4F missions were strafing jobs, but they exacted a toll. Fighting 41's exec was one. Lieutenant Malcolm "Mac" Wordell, a six-foot New Englander, force-landed in a cow pasture with a damaged airplane and a leg wound. He was able to limp to a nearby wine shop, where the proprietor and his wife applied rudimentary first-aid, then poured rum and toasted Franco-American friendship.

Wordell shortly encountered a group of colonial infantry and had little choice but to surrender to the corporal. The Spahi wanted Wordell's pistol, which was reluctantly handed over, minus ammo. However, the exec intended to regain his .45, and requested a receipt. After consultation with his men, the corporal allowed as that seemed fair, but it posed one small problem. He was illiterate. Therefore, the wine vendor wrote a receipt and the African licked his thumb and sealed the deal by pressing it to the document. Wordell eventually joined other VF-41 pilots at French headquarters.

At day's end the landings were progressing reasonably well. The Wildcats had local air superiority, if not air supremacy, but it had been gained at some cost. Fighting 41 claimed six Hawks and three Dewoitines in the air for the loss of three F4Fs. Another three VF-41 planes fell to AA fire. Fighting Nine's one claim was balanced by the afternoon's loss to flak. But non-combat casualties exceeded those to enemy action, as operational losses boosted the total to twenty-three Wildcats. And this was only Day One.

Things got off to a bang-up start on the ninth. Two VF-9 divisions surprised sixteen Hawks which were apparently returning to base after escorting a bombing mission against U.S. shipping off Fedala. With crafty use of cloud cover, Jack Raby approached the rearmost eight Curtisses from above and behind, holding his fire until well within range. He scored hits and pursued his quarry as the H-75 tried to evade into clouds. But the skipper hung on, triggered another burst, and the Hawk exploded.

The next few minutes were frantic, with sea-gray Grummans and stripe-nosed Curtisses chasing one another in and out of the clouds. But the F4Fs stayed together better this second day, and won decisively. In all, Fighting Nine claimed five kills in exchange for one Wildcat, but the pilot was safe. Examination of French records showed Groupe de Combat I/5 lost four Hawks in this fracas.[9]

Meanwhile, some of the POWs enjoyed the hospitality of their "hosts" in the finest *Dawn Patrol* tradition. The French seemed to regard the events of the past few days as something of a lark. Perhaps it was merely the break in routine, but the chivalrous attitude displayed by Vichy pilots in the air, and their generally genial treatment of downed Americans, made for a peculiar situation. Chuck August, the dapper VF-41 pilot shot down the day before, was driven to a field where a tall, aristocratic French officer introduced himself as CO of the Escadrille de Lafayette. The Frenchman admitted to heavy losses, and other Vichy aviators asked August how many carrier planes had been shot down. August replied that he could only speak for his own Wildcat, and the French fliers undiplomatically allowed their disappointment to show.

Fighting Nine continued to experience mixed fortune. One F4F failed to join up after strafing Port Lyautey, and returning pilots reported a Wildcat's wreckage strewn all over the field. Two more were lost in strafing missions, though the pilot of one got out to sea and safety before his engine quit.

That evening VF-41 added another claim. This was allegedly a black Me-109 which had shot up the beaches at irregular intervals, causing considerable trouble. Two of Booth's pilots overhauled the "Phantom Raider" from astern and the leader, Lieutenant Wood, opened fire at 150 yards. He kept shooting until the fighter exploded, smearing the F4F's windscreen with oil. Wood assumed it was German oil.

However, the Germans weren't active in the area and no French planes were airborne at that time and place. But a photo-recon Spitfire disappeared that evening on a mission to Marrakech.[10]

Fighter missions weren't the only activity of the Western Task Force F4Fs. Fighting 41 had two Wildcats modified for aerial photography, fitted with 30-inch focal length cameras. Norfolk's overhaul and repair shop had fitted a camera in the lower starboard fuselage with a pulley-operated trap door. The Army Air Force had offered one of its two rotating cameras for Torch, which would have allowed an F4F to photograph while approaching and departing a target. But the Navy declined, noting the installation wouldn't work below 10,000 feet or so, owing to focal length.

The two designated pilots were Lieutenants (jg) Wally Madden and John Sweeney. Madden had been in the squadron since March 1939, and carried more influence than a jaygee normally did. The original intention was to remove the guns from each Wildcat, but Madden wasn't having any of that. He insisted that two .50-calibers remain aboard, and got his way. It was just as well, for though he never needed his guns, all photo missions were solo affairs. There weren't enough F4Fs to spare as escorts.

On one occasion, flying north of Casablanca, Madden crossed the lines at low level in lousy weather. Nervous GIs shot at him, and while their aim was reasonably good, they hadn't quite perfected their wing-shooting. Madden pulled up into the overcast, going on instruments. Back aboard the *Ranger* he examined his plane and declared, "There aren't any duck hunters down there, because all twenty-seven holes are in the tail!" He may remain the only naval aviator ever awarded the DFC for getting shot at by the Army.[11]

Down at Safi VF-29 was hard-pressed with its few remaining Wildcats aboard the *Santee*. Strafing missions abounded, and several pilots logged eight hours during the ninth and tenth. Three of Blackburn's pilots patrolling near Safi on the tenth noticed a bogey taken under fire by American anti-aircraft gunners, and the race was on. Fighting 29 hadn't yet seen an airborne hostile, but Ensign B. D. Jacques got there first and dumped it. He claimed a Bloch 174— another recognition error, but within limits. It was a Potez 63 from Chichaoua.[12]

When the French gave up, they did so early in the morning of 11 November. But it took awhile for everyone to get the word. About 0830 Lieutenant Harry Bass, acting CO of VGF-29, escorted a lone SBD-3 to Marrakech airfield. The Wildcat and Dauntless proceeded to shoot up the place considerably, with an estimated thirteen planes destroyed on the ground. In truth, they burned three Potez 63s.[13] Allied officers ruefully admitted to the French that the attack had been in error.

So ended Torch. On the geopolitical scale, it outflanked the Germans in North Africa and helped end the long desert war. Perhaps equally valuable were the long-term lessons for what Winston Churchill liked to call "triphibious operations." Farther down the chain of command, the Wildcat squadrons counted their successes and losses, and decided what they'd learned. Some things are only learned through hard experience, and the F4F pilots realized they'd just been through a short advanced course. Fortunately, the tuition in lives wasn't terribly high.

Most of the six losses to flak resulted from making low, shallow strafing passes. At least two F4Fs were knocked down when their victims exploded beneath them. As a result, pilots learned to make steeper gunnery runs with higher pullouts. The air-to-air score, however, was resolved well in the Wildcats' favor. All told, F4Fs claimed about twenty-two shootdowns (including one, possibly two, British planes) against five known losses to Vichy fighters. For once, the actual toll exceeded the claims, for French squadrons acknowledged twenty-five losses in the air.[14]

Against eleven losses to enemy action, the Wildcats recorded fourteen operational write-offs. This made a grand total of twenty-five losses to all causes; twenty-three percent attrition among the fighter squadrons in barely three days. The *Santee* was down to her last four Wildcats on the eleventh, and *Ranger* lost twelve of fifty-four. On the other hand, the *Sangamon* lost no F4Fs and only three of her eighteen bombers.

Many of the men involved in Torch went on to notable wartime records. Among the carrier skippers were Captains J. J. Clark of the *Suwannee* and C. T. Durgin of the *Ranger*. Both became task group commanders during the next two years; Jocko Clark after taking the new *Yorktown* to the Pacific, and Cal Durgin with CVE forces in both the Med and Pacific.

At the squadron level were lieutenant commanders such as M. P. Bagdanovitch with VGS-30's small contingent in the *Suwannee*. Thirteen months later he took Air Group 17 into combat from the fast carrier *Bunker Hill*. And Tommy Blackburn of VGF-29 shared a similar future. Like "Bags" Bagdanovitch, he helped shake down the *Bunker Hill*, then led VF-17 in the Solomons with new F4U-1As.

The execs of Fighting 9 and 41—Hugh Winters and Mac Wordell—would both lead air groups in the Pacific during 1944. Jack Raby's squadron had the brightest future of any engaged in Torch. Before year-end VF-9 received the Navy's first F6F-3 Hellcats and eventually made two Pacific deployments. Several of its "Africa Corps" veterans became aces in subsequent tours with Air Groups 9 or 12; among them Chick Smith, Hal Vita, Marv Franger, and Rube Denoff.

Meanwhile, there was work to be done in the Atlantic for the next year. The *Santee* and Air Group 29 remained active on U-boat patrol, frequently calling at Casablanca now that its status had changed for the better. Americans tended to envision that city in the romantic context of the eternally popular 1943 film, which suffered not a bit from the publicity afforded by world events. And if there really were no *Cafe Americaine* with a white-suited, cynical proprietor named Rick, at least it was still possible to ask the pianist to play *As Time Goes By*, clank glasses in a toast and intone, "Here's looking at you, kid."

But a bit of genuine intrigue was astir. On 6 November 1943 two VF-29 Wildcats became "lost" near the Azores and landed at Lagens

Field, Terciera. The flight leader was Brink Bass, who'd made the last-minute strafing mission to Marrakech twelve months previously. The Azores were crucial to closing the mid-Atlantic gap in the U-boat war, and after prolonged negotiations the Portugese government had allowed Britain access to air bases there. Bass's mission was to report on the Portugese reaction to an American presence in the Azores. He returned to the *Santee* with his wingman next day, completing the Wildcat's only known participation in the world of covert diplomacy.[15]

A break in the 1943 routine came in October. Operation Leader was a unique Anglo–American enterprise aimed at disrupting Axis shipping north of the Arctic Circle. The *Ranger*, with a reorganized Air Group Four aboard, joined a powerful unit of the British Home Fleet to launch strikes against the harbor and roadstead at Bodo in Norway's Saltfjord.

Fighting Four numbered twenty-seven F4F-4s under Lieutenant Commander Charles L. Moore, a Georgia aviator out of the Annapolis Class of '33. He had asked for FM-2s and hoped for F6Fs, but to no avail. He'd have to make due with Wildcats, and it caused some concern because Luftwaffe opposition was expected, and Bodo had recently based a *staffel* of Me-109Gs from JG-5. But German air strength in Norway had been substantially reduced. The major portions of two bomber wings, KG-26 and 30, had been withdrawn to Italy.

Launch was scheduled for 0700 on the fourth, but was delayed nearly 20 minutes due to light winds. But it shaped up as a fine day with only a few low, scattered clouds. By 0733 the first strike of twenty SBD-5s and eight Wildcats was skimming the water, on course for the 150-mile flight. Thirty minutes later another six F4Fs were airborne with ten Avengers as the *Ranger* turned west, steaming farther from the hostile coast.

Entering the leads, VB-4 split into pairs, selecting targets and attacking in shallow, fast masthead runs. As the early-morning light shone golden on the rocky shore, Dauntlesses pressed their attacks to 120 feet or less while two-plane fighter sections followed close behind, strafing AA batteries. Two F4Fs took flak hits. One pilot was wounded and returned to the *Ranger* with his wingman. Two or more 20-mm shells exploded in Lieutenant Commander Moore's fuselage, filling his cockpit with smoke, but he remained on hand, taking his remaining fighters to Bodo harbor, where more shipping was found at anchor. They hosed down the area with nearly 4,000 rounds of

(*Text continues on page 211.*)

Safe trap, as a VF-9 Wildcat engages the arresting wire during squadron exercises before the North African operation in late 1942. (R.L. Lawson)

This Ranger Wildcat, probably from VF-41, apparently suffered landing-gear failure upon engaging the arresting wire. (USN/Tailhook Assn.)

Aircraft and ordnance fill the Ranger's flight deck as Operation Torch opens in early November 1942. Note the tie-down dangling from the Wildcat's port bomb rack. (Tailhook Assn.)

F4F being moved into position on flight deck of the Santee during Moroccan landings. (Grumman)

◄ *F4F-3s of VF-71 prepare for launch from the Wasp during operations in the Mediterranean, May 1942. (Grumman)*

183

Deck hands move a VF-9 aircraft as the Ranger prepares for Operation Torch in October 1942. (USN/Tailhook Assn.)

Submarine hunters of an Atlantic escort carrier squadron: F4F-4s and TBF-1s in the gull-gray and white ETO color scheme, 1943. (R.L. Lawson)

The Wildcat's only combat with the U.S. Navy in northern waters occurred during Operation Leader, a shipping strike on Bodo, Norway in October 1943. This F4F-4 displays the same markings used by VF-4 aboard the Ranger at that time. (Grumman)

Another unpleasant surprise from Japan's bag of tricks was the superior B5N torpedo plane. Dubbed Kate by U.S. air intelligence in 1942, the Nakajima design was capable of carrying either bombs or a torpedo, and proved effective in both roles. Exceptionally fast, the B5N was difficult to defend against; she helped sink Lexington at Coral Sea and Yorktown at Midway. (Bowers)

An F4F-4, probably of VF-41, prepares for launch from the USS Ranger during Operation Torch. (USN)

An escort carrier squadron in early 1943, flying F4F-4s and SBD-3s. Such units formed the earliest carrier-based antisubmarine units until composite squadrons appeared that summer. (Grumman)

F4F-4's and TBF-1's aboard an escort carrier, 1942. (R.L. Lawson)

Composite Squadron 13 was among the most successful antisubmarine units in the U.S. Navy. This FM-2 patrols over the Atlantic with auxiliary tank attached in early 1944. (USN/Tailhook Assn.)

An FM-2 of VC-36 off the Core, one of the most successful U-boat hunters. By April 1944, when this photo was taken, the "Wilder Wildcat" had largely replaced the F4F-4 and FM-1 in the Atlantic. (PHoM N.E. Seehafer)

The first export Wildcat, this G-36A sports French Navy markings and U.S. civil registration NX-1. This model differed from the F4F-3 in engine (Wright R-1820 instead of P-W R1830), armament (note bay for nose guns), and instrumentation. (Grumman via David Anderton)

A batch of early Martlet IIs at the Grumman factory in October 1941. The plane at left rear is still in U.S. civil registry, apparently unarmed, and perhaps one of ten "stiffwing" Mark IIs. Note unusual position of pilot tube on the folding wing models. (Grumman)

An interesting shot of the G-36A cockpit, featuring bilingual instruments. The altimeter, turn-and bank indicator, and manifold pressure gauge are French or French/English. (Grumman)

With a new paint job the G-36As became British property as Martlet Is following the collapse of France in May 1940. English instruments and American armament replaced original equipment. (Grumman)

▲

Pilots of 805 Squadron in the Western Desert. Left to right: Lt. J.B. Musson, Lt. MacDonald, Capt. L.A. Harris of the Royal Marines, and Lt. Cdr. Alan Black. (C.F. Shores)

Martlet Mark Is in flight over England. Two Mark Is of 804 Squadron shot down a Ju-88 over Scapa Flow on Christmas Day 1940—the first Axis aircraft to fall to American-built planes in World War II. (Ken Dowell)

A section of 805 Squadron Mark Is takes off. The only visible support facility is a tent in the background. (C.F. Shores)

Martlets in the desert. The Naval Fighter Wing of the Desert Air Force comprised three squadrons, including Number 805 with its Martlet Mark Is in 1941. (C.F. Shores)

Taken nine months after the previous photo, this July 1942 shot shows two of the same aircraft (AM 966 and 968) aboard HMS Illustrious. (Grumman)

Kondor Killer. Sub-Lt. Eric M. Brown of 802 Squadron shot down two Focke-Wulf 200s while flying from HMS Audacity in late 1941. He later became the world-champion carrier pilot, with over 2,400 deck landings. (Brown)

U.S. and Royal Navy airframes awaiting completion at the factory in 1942. (Grumman)

A Martlet II of 888 Squadron aboard HMS Formidable *in the summer of 1942. Two pilots of this squadron shot down a Kawanishi flying boat in the Bay of Bengal on 2 August for the Martlet's only success against Japanese aircraft. By war's end "Triple Eight" had confirmed victories over German, Italian, and Vichy French planes as well. (Grumman)*

This Wildcat VI of 882 Squadron, British Pacific Fleet, has just made a heavy landing aboard HMS Searcher, *June 1945. (Grumman)*

Grumman employees pose with parts of the last F4F-4s before turning over Wildcat production to General Motors' Eastern Aircraft Division in February 1943. (Grumman)

D-Day invasion stripes adorn this Wildcat V from Squadron 896 in June 1944. During this period the squadron was nominally attached to HMS Pursuer. (Tailhook Assn.)

FM-1s practicing division tactics. (Grumman)

Composite Squadron 41 Wildcats over Makin Atoll during escort carrier airstrikes 20 November 1943. The aircraft are FM-1s in one of their earliest combat operations. (USN)

Impending trouble as a VC-7 Wildcat lands off-center and runs into the port catwalk of the USS Manila Bay en route to the Philippines. (USN/Tailhook Assn.)

The "tall tail" XF4F-8, which became the Eastern Aircraft FM-2 in production status. (Grumman)

Never a dull moment. This VC-83 FM-2 suffered a landing gear failure upon returning to the USS Sargent Bay. (Grumman)

*White triangles identify VC-4
aircraft from the USS* White
Plains *on 23 October 1944, the
day before the Battle of Leyte
Gulf. (USN/Tailhook Assn.)*

The number-one airplane of VC-79 caused a fouled deck aboard the USS Sargent Bay *during operations on 7 February 1945. (USN/Tailhook Assn.)*

Operational losses frequently exceeded combat attrition, as this VC-3 FM-2 demonstrated during the Marianas operation in June 1944. Other Kalinin Bay aircraft seem to have escaped damage. (USN/Tailhook Assn.)

The Gambier Bay loses a fighter as a VC-10 FM-2 is eased overboard following heavy damage in June 1944. Note that the gunsight and engine-access panels have been removed. (USS/Tailhook Assn.)

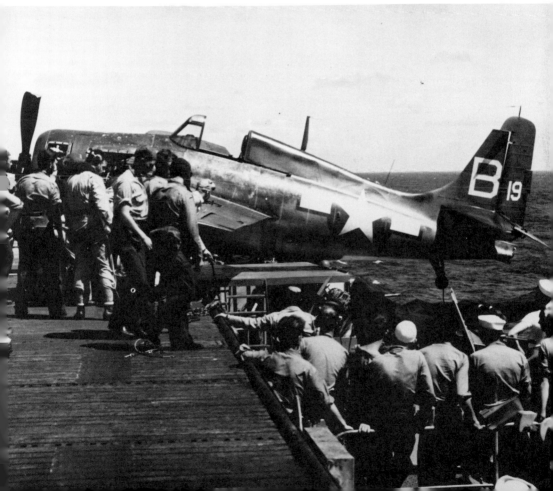

Here comes the crunch. A VC-70 Wildcat hangs nose-high before plopping onto the USS Salmua's deck, one week after V-J Day. (USN/Tailhook Assn.)

Escort carrier markings became standardized near the end of the war. Replacing geometric symbols and identification letters was a series of yellow and white bands or stripes, keyed to each CVE task group. This is a VC-99 aircraft aboard the USS Hoggatt Bay. (USN)

Jack Lenhardt of Hubbard, Oregon airborne in his FM-2 during 1972. This aircraft is now in the Naval Aviation Museum at Pensacola, Florida. (Tillman)

The Champlin Fighter Museum's FM-2 (BuAer 74560), FAA registry N90523 maintained in operational status. (Champlin Fighter Museum)

Rudy Frasca's FM-2 at Osh-
kosh, Wisconsin EAA Fly-In,
August, 1979. (Frederick A.
Johnsen)

207

Beautifully restored by the Marine Corps Museum at Quantico, Virginia, this F4F-4 (BuAer 12114) is the only Grumman-built Wildcat remaining in the United States. (USMC Museum)

Colonel R.B. Porter, USMC (ret.) with remains of the Vilu War Museum's F4F-4 on Guadalcanal, November 1980. (Porter)

.50-caliber before heading home. Two SBDs had been shot down, and one F4F's landing gear collapsed upon impact with the deck. Another Wildcat would require a major overhaul.

The *Ranger*'s second strike recovered at 1100, minus one TBF. The bombers had sunk or destroyed seven ships of some 21,500 tons and seriously damaged three more of similar gross tonnage. Leader was already a success, but now was the time to clear out.

At 1400 the task force was 200 nautical miles offshore, bound for Britain, but land-based bombers were expected. By 1430 seven F4Fs in two divisions were on CAP, orbiting at only 1,000 feet due to lowering clouds. Fifteen minutes later the fighter director had business for them. Lieutenant E. F. Craig's division was sent climbing to the northwest, then turned southwards. Lieutenant (jg) B. N. Mayhew, a Torch veteran, called a tally-ho from 6,000 feet. He'd spotted a dark-green Junkers 88 in the clouds at about 3,000 feet.

Mayhew high-sided the bomber from port, firing as the angle decreased from full to half deflection. Fighting Four's ammo was belted in sequence of five armor-piercing, three tracer, two incendiary, and the lethal combination smashed the port engine, which gushed smoke. Close behind was Lieutenant (jg) D. S. Laird who fired, saw hits, and noted the rear gunner was shooting.

Seriously crippled, the Junkers dived for a cloud but the F4Fs split up, making overhead runs from each side just as the 88 plunged into cover. Mayhew and Laird sped to the far side of the cloud, expecting to catch the snooper emerging, but the chase was over. They found a burning ring of gasoline on the water, 22 miles west of the *Ranger*. The Junkers had been from a reconnaissance group at Bardufoss, 150 statute miles north of Bodo.

Ten minutes later the FDO had another strange blip on his scope. This time it was Lieutenant Seiler's turn, as his three-plane division had missed the first chance. Seiler tested his guns, but then discovered his radio transmitter had failed. Unable to acknowledge the vector, he was out of luck. Craig's division was called in again. Steering southeast, the four Wildcats found a gray-green Heinkel 115 in a rainsquall at only 200 feet. The ungainly twin-engine, twin-float recon plane was clearly outclassed. It turned hard to port, seeking cloud cover, but was quickly overhauled. This time the whole division piled in from eight o'clock high. The rear gunner gamely popped away with his 7.9-mm free gun, but by the time Diz Laird had finished his run the Heinkel was burning. It smashed into the water thirteen miles from the carrier.

Seiler arrived moments later, circling low and noting three survivors amid the floating wreckage. He tried to contact the *Ranger* but his radio was still acting up, and he couldn't make his wingman understand his hand signals to call for a rescue. The seven fighters remained on station until nearly 1800, then came aboard. One landed slightly to port, crashed into the catwalk and went overboard. The Wildcat sank quickly, but the pilot scrambled out and awaited recovery by a British destroyer.

It was a good performance. The *Ranger* developed three radar plots and two were intercepted and splashed in sixteen minutes. The two snoopers became the first German planes shot down by U.S. Navy pilots; CVE-based Hellcats bagged eight more during the invasion of southern France in August 1944.

Fighting Four eventually added Japanese planes to its toll when the air group flew from the *Essex* in late 1944 and early 1945. By then the squadron had its sought-after F6Fs, and Diz Laird became the only Navy ace with victories against both Germany and Japan. But the Wildcat remained in the Atlantic for another eighteen months, where the U-boat war dragged on.

The U.S. Navy operated eleven escort carriers with fourteen composite squadrons in the Battle of the Atlantic from 1943 to 1945. These were specially-trained anti-submarine units with an average of twelve Avengers and nine Wildcats. They sank twenty-nine subs through the summer of 1944, and their escorts accounted for nearly twenty more. The wolfpacks had turned from hunter to hunted.

First of the "hunter-killers" was the *Bogue*, which appeared on the convoy routes in March 1943. Operating first VC-9 and then VC-19, her TBF-1s and F4F-4s harried U-boats all that spring and sank three of them. Next on line were the *Card*, *Core*, and *Santee*, all successful ASW ships. But the most spectacular squadron was VC-9, with tours aboard the *Bogue* from March through August and aboard the *Card* from September to November. With eight confirmed kills during the year, Lieutenant Commander William M. Drane's squadron finished far ahead of its nearest rivals. A ninth sinking came during a *Solomons* cruise in mid-1944. Tied for second by war's end were VC-1 of the *Card* and VC-13 of the *Core*, both with four sinkings.

Standard procedure called for one or more Wildcats to strafe a surfaced U-boat, suppressing or diverting its AA fire. Presumably an Avenger could then get in to make the kill with bombs or rockets. Failing that, if the sub pulled the plug and dived, an Avenger dropped a Fido acoustic torpedo which homed on the U-boat's propulsion noise.

But it didn't always work according to doctrine. In mid-1943, when

CVEs began closing the previous gap in Allied air cover for merchant convoys, Admiral Karl Doenitz took bold steps. He increased the AA guns on his submarines and directed his skippers to shoot it out with Allied aircraft. The intent of this fight-back technique was as much psychological as anything. Equipped with multiple 20-mm guns, and in some cases 37-mms, a U-boat could put up a terrific amount of flak. The sheer volume of firepower was often enough to keep aircraft out of range.

Frequently it worked. The first such boat, *U-758*, was caught running surfaced by a VC-9 Avenger off the *Bogue* on 8 June. The German's quad-20 battery fought off two Avengers and several Wildcats, though one F4F bored in through the ack-ack to shoot up the gunners. But they were quickly replaced and *U-758* got away, lending credence to the fight-back tactic.

On 13 July a *Core* patrol experienced a similar combat, but with a conclusion. An F4F and TBF of VC-13 surprised the tanker *U-487* and attacked. The Germans promptly rallied and shot down the Wildcat, killing its pilot. Momentarily stymied, the Avenger called up reinforcements which eventually sank the milch-cow, but it was now obvious that this form of warfare would involve casualties on both sides. Several other carrier planes would fall to U-boat gunners before the momentum swung to the Allies.

But swing it did, and by year-end the submarine campaign was well in hand. From May through December, CVEs and their screening destroyers had reduced Doenitz's inventory by twenty-seven boats. This was considerable in itself, but the constant aerial threat posed by Avengers and Wildcats rendered sub skippers' jobs infinitely more difficult. U-boat captains now looked back fondly on the heady days of 1940–41, the glorious "happy time" when convoys were ripe for plucking and tonnage scores accumulated with each patrol. Now, just surviving was more difficult than ever. Veteran U-boat commanders returning from the mid-Atlantic reported that aerial activity seemed even heavier than in the Bay of Biscay.

Not that there weren't reversals in Allied fortunes. One of the biggest setbacks occurred in May 1944 when the *Block Island*, with VC-55 aboard, was sunk by a vengeful U-boat. With three kills credited to her squadrons, she was an experienced anti-submarine unit but she remained the only U.S. carrier lost in the European theater.

However, in the next month occurred the most spectacular single incident in the history of U.S. Navy anti-submarine operations. The *Guadalcanal* already had two U-boat scalps on her lodgepole from the

March–April tour of VC-58. The task group commander was Captain Daniel V. Gallery, an immensely popular and colorful character whose main ambition in life was to capture a U-boat. His new composite squadron was VC-8 with twelve TBM-1Cs and nine FM-2s. The old F4F-4s had given way to FM-1s in the fall of 1943, and FM-2s had been active in hunter-killer operations since March 1944.

After two weeks of unproductive patrolling, Gallery was headed for Casablanca on 4 June when one of his five screening destroyers reported a sonar contact. She was the *Chatelain*, which initiated a hedgehog attack as two destroyer-escorts charged in to help. Circling overhead in blue skies with excellent visibility were two Wildcats. They had a clear view of a submarine and called the *Chatelain* back, fearing she'd passed up the spot. Actually, she was merely circling for a second pass but the fighter pilots didn't know that. They dived on the sub, firing into the water to pinpoint the location.

Next time around the destroyer laid down a salvo of depth-charges which punctured the sub's outer hull, violently rocking the boat. It was *U-505*, and her skipper surfaced to find himself the object of unwanted attention from three destroyers and two Wildcats. With a light northeasterly breeze and moderately high seas the Germans abandoned ship. Gallery seized the opportunity to put his capture plan into operation, and it worked. A whaleboat pulled alongside the now-deserted submarine and a small boarding party took over. Before long *U-505* was under tow for Bermuda. Wildcats had helped snap up the first enemy warship captured on the high seas by the U.S. Navy in 130 years.

The Wildcat's European war aboard American carriers lasted thirty-six months; from the *Wasp*'s Malta reinforcement in May 1942 until V-E Day in May 1945. It extended from the warm waters of the South Atlantic to the chilling temperatures of the Arctic Circle. In those diverse times and places, Wildcats had flown the full range of missions: CAP, fighter sweep, photo-reconnaissance, strike, and anti-submarine patrol. They'd shot down Vichy French as well as Luftwaffe aircraft, chased and sunk German submarines. Excepting the F4F-3, every other major Wildcat variant had been involved in the Atlantic shooting war: F4F-4s, FM-1s, and FM-2s. But now that part of the global task was ended.

Wildcats would finish their war in the Pacific.

9. MARTLETS

The fuselage is short and fat,
the plank-like wings are square and flat.
While out behind in foul or fair,
the Martlet's tail stands fair and square.
—Wartime verse

SCAPA FLOW HAD BEEN THE traditional base of the British Home Fleet since 1914. Back then, of course, it was the Grand Fleet; Admiral Beatty's powerful force which engaged the German High Seas Fleet in the two-day slugfest called Jutland. And it was at Scapa Flow in June 1919 that the remainder of the Kaiser's still-impressive navy had surrendered and defiantly scuttled.

Some 20 years and another war later, Scapa was still a crucial Royal Navy facility. Its 15-mile length and 8-mile width amid the Orkneys afforded a sheltered anchorage off Scotland's northern coast. So, not surprisingly, the Germans maintained a careful watch upon the comings and goings at the Flow. From Bergen, some 300 miles across the North Sea, Luftwaffe reconnaissance aircraft periodically intruded upon Scapa, photographing and observing what they could before cloud-hopping back for Norway.

On this particular Christmas Day a Junkers 88 attempted to take advantage of any holiday lull in British wariness. After all, it was well known that the Royal Navy was the most Christian of the world's warfleets, and the prospects must have seemed good to the staff planners of Luftflotte Five. But the crew of the twin-engine Junkers benefitted little from staff planning or optimism. Two fighter aircraft of a type no German fliers had ever seen intercepted with superior position, caught the bomber, and shot out one engine. The four-man crew bailed out and was captured just in time to share Christmas dinner.

Lieutenant L. V. Carter and Sub-Lieutenant Parke of 804 Squadron, Fleet Air Arm, had recorded the first success of the Wildcat in British service. The propeller from one of their Grummans was shipped to the United States in commemoration of the event; 25 December 1940.[1]

Strange as it seems, in the same month VF-4 received the U.S. Navy's first F4F-3s, the British were flying Wildcats in combat. Pearl Harbor was twelve months off.

Technically, the Fleet Air Arm fighters were neither F4Fs nor Wildcats. The factory designation was G-36A, export model of the XF4F-5, which became the Martlet I in British service. Named for the swallow family, the stubby little Grumman represented a major improvement in Royal Navy carrier aircraft. While British carriers were the equal of any afloat, their planes were often mere seagoing variants of Royal Air Force types such as the biplane Gloster Sea Gladiator and later the Hawker Sea Hurricane. Due to policy battles between the wars, the RAF exerted considerable influence in naval aircraft design and procurement. And the indigenous carrier fighters—most notably the Fairey Fulmar—were committed to a two-seat design philosophy. Therefore, Britain—which developed the armored and angled flight deck, steam catapult, mirror landing system, and beat the Americans in first flying jets off flattops—produced no built-for-the-purpose single-seat carrier fighters during World War II. By the time the Royal Navy retrieved full control of carrier aircraft from the RAF and established the Fleet Air Arm in 1939, it was far too late. War was only four months off.

However, the G-36 proved that blessings sometimes come in disguise. That same year the French government sent an aviation commission to the U.S., hoping to buy modern military designs. France's only carrier was the *Bearn*, completed in 1927 and capable of only 22 knots, but two newer flattops were anticipated. The emerging F4F looked like a good bet, and that fall—just as war erupted—the French ordered a batch of the new fighters. However, because of uncertainty in the continuing availability of Pratt and Whitney engines, a Wright R-1820 was selected. The 1820-G205A produced 1,200 horsepower, and its single-stage, two-speed supercharger afforded altitude performance not previously available in any carrier aircraft.

But such things take time, and not even the press of war in Europe could make the G-36A ready for testing until May 1940. Unfortunately for the original customer, that was just when France capitulated to the Nazi blitzkrieg which also drove the British Expeditionary Force off the continent. Fortunately for Britain, which had lost heavily in the Battle of France, the 36As were still available. The British Purchasing Commission took delivery of the initial Martlet I on 27 July; the first F4F-3s weren't delivered for U.S. Navy evaluation until the following month.

During the period through October, the Royal Navy took eighty Grummans while the follow-up order was processed. On 26 September Grumman accepted Job Order 127 calling for 100 basically similar aircraft, G-36Bs, except for folding wings and Pratt-Whitney engines.[2] This would become the Martlet II, leading to a total wartime delivery of nearly 1,100 Wildcats of all models to the Royal Navy.

HMS *Furious* took the first Mark Is to Britain that summer, where they were assigned to Number 804 Squadron, land-based at Hatston in October. The squadron had previously flown Sea Gladiators, and following a transition course to the new all-metal monoplanes, 804 began flying patrols over Scapa Flow. The results led to history, as we have seen.

Still, the Martlet Is were odd birds. They lacked the final equipment for carrier operation and consequently remained landlocked. Their instruments, reflecting the original destination, were calibrated in metric graduations, and the throttles worked in reverse— the pilot pulled back to accelerate—before modification. Solid rubber tailwheels were intended for shipboard use, requiring judicious use of brakes early in the takeoff run for directional control. A few months later pneumatic tires and lengthened tailwheel struts were installed, raising the tail nearly nine inches and affording adequate rudder control on takeoff.

The French intended to arm their Grummans with six 7.5-mm machine guns, and this too led to difficulty. Martlet Is were fitted with four .50-calibers, but the Brits found it difficult to maintain boresight due to the original mounts. In February 1941 British Modification 27 allowed installation of .303s, but Martlets retained their .50s throughout the series.[3] The Mark IIs and later models had no such trouble.

The Mark Is were fixed-wing, of course, but at this early period it was not much of a drawback. British pilots considered the U.S. radios better than those they were accustomed to using, and were impressed with the Grumman's overall performance. The initial climb rate was about 3,300 feet per minute—sensational in comparison to anything else the FAA had flown. And the Mark I seemed nearly as fast as a

Hurricane: 305 mph (265 knots) at 15,000 feet, and 285 mph (248 knots) at sea level.

Among the pilots in the second Martlet squadron was Sub-Lieutenant Eric M. Brown. A dapper, precise product of Edinburgh University, Brown had learned of the altered state of relations between his country and Germany while teaching in the Reich. Two SS men had banged on his door early that Sunday morning with the grim news and eventually escorted him to the Swiss border. Had they known of the twenty-year-old's future, it is unlikely they'd have observed the niceties of international law.

Brown was a junior pilot in 802 Squadron at Donibristle when he first met the Martlet. In view of his later record as the world champion carrier pilot (over 2,400 deck landings), his opinion of the Grumman bears considerable weight. "A venomous-looking little bumblebee of a fighter," was his first impression. Years later he recalled, "The Martlet was one of those few aircraft that I have encountered over the years with which I instinctively felt a rapport."[4] But Brown's attitude is representative of most British naval aviators. While the F4F had its detractors in the U.S. Navy as early as 1942, the Fleet Air Arm adored it.

The Mark II was welcomed, as any new aircraft was in the spring of 1941, but the new Martlet lacked the Mark I's get-up-and-go. With folding wings (except for the first ten aircraft) and a P-W R-1830, the Mark II was over a half-ton heavier than the Martlet I. Performance suffered accordingly, with a top speed of 295 mph (255 knots) at 5,400 feet. Nevertheless, 100 were delivered from March 1941 through the following April. And the Mark II became the first seagoing Martlet, for its tail-down launch position was previously unknown in the Royal Navy. Prior to the Grumman, British carriers used four-legged cradles to get their planes into a flying attitude off the "booster."

But the British had a wrinkle of their own. All Wildcats had two-position landing flaps, full down or closed. In order to gain additional lift on launch, Royal Navy pilots found they could achieve a half-flap setting by inserting wedge-shaped blocks in the flaps and hold them in place by selecting the "up" position. Once airborne they simply lowered the flaps, the blocks fell out, and flaps were raised again.

Additionally, the Martlet was an excellent gunnery platform. "If anything, too good," said Eric Brown, noting it was stable about all three axes and "definitely more so than the Spitfire or Hurricane."[5] Most combat pilots agree that the ideal fighter is slightly unstable about all three axes, making for better responsiveness. But with a steady aim and four .50-calibers, the Martlet represented a lethal opponent in a previously untried arena.

Another navy was also impressed with the Grumman. While Britain worked on the Martlett II contract, a Greek delegation sought F4Fs as well. Though Greece had repulsed an Italian invasion in October 1940, the Balkan situation became tenuous as Hitler moved to reinforce his ally. Under these circumstances the U.S. Navy agreed to turn loose thirty F4F-3As, though BuAer logically wondered what use the Greeks had for carrier aircraft. Popular wartime reportage had it that the head of the Greek commission observed that the Italians were known to have one or two carriers under construction. The Hellenic Navy, he insisted, would put its Wildcats aboard one of Mussolini's flattops before long.[6] It may have made good copy, but the assessment proved overly optimistic on two counts: Greece fell to the Germans in May 1941, and Italy's lone carrier the *Aquila* was never completed.

However, the thirty Wildcats were at Gibraltar en route east just then, and once again the British adopted the homeless fighters. The Royal Navy, unexpected beneficiary of Greece's misfortune, labled the -3As Martlet IIIs, and Fleet Air Arm squadrons in the Mediterranean used them during the North African campaign.

The workhorse Martlet squadron was Number 805. Re-equipped in Egypt following the British loss of Crete, it merged with two Hurricane units to form the Royal Navy Fighter Squadron, flying under RAF control from Dekheila along the Egyptian–Libyan frontier. Combats were rare, but on 28 September Sub-Lieutenant W. M. Walsh recorded the Martlet's second victory by downing a Fiat G-50. In the wake of Operation Crusader—the British advance into Libya—the Royal Navy units remained in Egypt to provide coastal patrol and convoy escort.

On one such mission of 28 December, Sub-Lieutenant A. R. Griffin was unable to take off with his flight owing to engine trouble. Griffin finally got started and proceeded to his patrol station over the convoy, but the other Martlets had spent their time on station and returned to base. With adequate fuel, Griffin remained overhead, the only fighter present when four trimotor Savoia-Marchetti 79s attacked with aerial torpedos.

Griffin dived to intercept, causing two Italians to jettison their loads. He shot another SM-79 into the water but the fourth pressed its attack. Shipboard AA guns opened fire, but Griffin radioed "Leave him to me." As the flak tapered off, the young reservist turned hard to converge, calling, "Good show!"[7]

The Italian hastily lined up a ship and dropped his torpedo, which went wide. But the SM-79 gunners had Griffin under fire, and shipboard observers saw his Martlet dive headlong into the sea.

Number 805 Squadron remained in Egypt until late summer of 1942. During this period the Martlets claimed three more shootdowns; a JU-88 in February and two more Savoias in July. Then the squadron moved to East Africa for coastal patrols over the Indian Ocean. Sometimes the settings were rather exotic—one pilot recalls lions in the back yard—but bases were changed frequently. Number 805 also flew in Abyssinia and wound up at RAF Nanuki in northern Kenya. There was virtually no combat in this backwater of the war, but the remote airfields and limited facilities afforded an excellent proving ground for the Martlet's maintenance potential.

"Both the Martlet airframe and the Pratt and Whitney engines held up marvelously," recalls an 805 veteran, Ken Dowell. "We had very little maintenance difficulty, and I should think our in-commission rate was generally high."[8] One of the few problems would have sounded familiar to any U.S. Navy fighter pilot of the same period. The .50-calibers proved erratic owing not to the guns, but poor-quality ammunition. There had been some difficulty with balky guns in the desert, but that was due to conventional use of lubricants. If the Brownings were only lightly oiled the gritty sand couldn't collect in bolts or receivers and cause wear or friction.

But elsewhere, blowing sand was far from the minds of Martlet pilots. In the maritime climate of the Atlantic, other Fleet Air Arm squadrons operated under vastly different conditions.

"Wartime expedient" is an oft-used phrase, but the manner in which the Martlet first went to sea was expediency itself. Recognizing the urgent need for convoy air defense, the British Admiralty authorized conversion of a 5,600-ton captured German steamer into an auxiliary aircraft carrier. HMS *Empire Audacity* (formerly the *Hannover*) was a pure expedient, with a 460-foot flight deck fitted above the hull. Surely it required audacity to turn a 14-knot steamer into a carrier. She had no hangar deck, only two arresting wires in place of the usual six, and a crash barrier. Intended to operate eight Martlet IIs of 802 Squadron, she rarely embarked more than six. Her career was short but eventful.

From September through December 1941, the *Audacity* made two round-trips escorting convoys from Britain to Gibraltar. On three of the four legs, 802's Martlets engaged Focke-Wulf 200Cs, the four-engine maritime patrol bombers which shadowed convoys, reporting their positions to U-boat wolfpacks. Frequently the huge Kondors themselves attacked, the aircrews of Kampfgeschwader 40 adding their own tally of sunken ships to the growing Atlantic toll.

The break-in period was brief but intense. Lieutenant Commander John Wintour, 802's CO, made the initial deck-landing tests and pronounced the set-up satisfactory. After that, the other pilots logged six "traps" each under the guidance of three squadronmates hastily appointed landing signal officers—"batsmen" to the Royal Navy.

But there was more than just flying. Wintour was a sharp professional, an excellent aviator, and expected his troops to keep abreast of things. He had a disconcerting way of tossing out unexpected questions, and one of the junior pilots became determined to provide the right answers. So Eric "Winkle" Brown started a personal dossier on the opposition.

Not much was known about the FW-200 other than it was the Luftwaffe version of the prewar Kurier civil airliner. It was bigger than a B-17, with a 107-foot wingspan and a maximum bomb load in excess of 2,700 pounds. Kondors were encountered as far west as Longitude 20, for their 2,000-statute-mile range put Iceland within reach. The Focke-Wulf was thought heavily armored, though reputed to have a rather weak empennage, and possessed substantial defensive firepower. Ventral guns, a 20-mm dorsal turret, and forward-firing nose guns made the Kondor a tough nut to crack. But Brown thought he had a method. By careful flying, it should be possible to tackle a FW head-on, keeping just above the boresight axis of the presumed forward-firing nose guns. It was worth a try.[9]

The *Audacity* left the River Clyde on 13 September 1941, headed for rendezvous with convoy OG-74. The merchantmen were laden with supplies for Malta, but the *Audacity*'s concern was to see the ships safely to Gibraltar. Yellow Section of 802 had been detached to HMS *Argus* for an Arctic convoy, but the other eight pilots remained aboard with six Martlets. Each two-man section rotated duty in turn: airborne; immediate readiness on deck; and standby status in the ready room. The fourth pair was at five-minute status, assuming two fighters could be readied for them.

Ordinary flight operations were tough enough in the carrier navy. On the *Audacity* they were complicated by the ship's lack of a hangar deck. Not only was maintenance performed in the open, but every time an airborne section returned to land aboard, the Martlets on deck had to be taxied forward, the barrier raised, and the homing fighters recovered. Then the deck was respotted for the next launch.

And in submarine water, each time the carrier left the convoy to turn into the wind for flight ops, she was left dangling like a prime piece of bait without support of escorts.

Still, things went smoothly despite low ceilings. No German planes appeared, but during a patrol on the 15th, Red Section spotted a sub. Sub-Lieutenant "Sheepy" Lamb, a sharp-eyed Scot of determinedly cheerful disposition, called "Tally ho! U-boat submerging on the starboard side."[10] Both Martlets dived, shooting at the disappearing periscope in the gray water.

Red Section—Lamb and Brown—spotted another sub the evening of the 20th, 12 miles west of the convoy, and during the night two ships were torpedoed. Rescue operations were in progress at dawn the 21st when one of the long-awaited Focke-Wulfs arrived.

The Kondor's aim was good. It straddled the rescue ship *Walmer Castle*, starting serious fires. Banking toward a nearby seagoing tug, the 200 was intercepted by Black Section. Sub-Lieutenant N. H. Patterson initiated a quartering pass, firing as the angle slanted to astern. He pressed his attack to near-collision range, the huge bomber filling his windscreen, and wracked the Martlet into a tight turn. Then Sub-Lieutenant Graham Fletcher connected with a beautiful full-deflection burst. He only fired 140 rounds, but it was enough to sever the Focke-Wulf's tail. The Kondor splashed into the sea as the Grummans circled low. A destroyer investigated, finding no survivors. The only trace was a set of coveralls floating on the surface.

Back aboard the *Audacity*, 802's mechanics celebrated in approved fashion. The Royal Navy still issued a liquor ration, and "Pat" and "Fletch" were treated to a tot of rum. But other business was at hand. At mid-day a lone JU-88 went after a straggling ship but was cut off by two Martlets. The Junkers narrowly avoided destruction, turning into a nearby cloud. This incident occurred 900 miles from Brest; extreme range for an 88. The Germans apparently meant to stop this convoy. Three more ships were torpedoed that night.

But even amid the grim reality of the Battle of the Atlantic, some harmless foolishness was possible. About this same time, a section of Martlets investigated a radar contact approaching the convoy at 8,000 feet. The *Audacity* boasted the most prestigious fighter-direction officer in the Royal Navy, former Cambridge don John Parry, and he put the fighters in visual range. They identified the stranger as a Boeing 314 flying boat, the *Dixie Clipper* on the Azores–Lisbon run. It was too good to pass up. The Martlets dived on the Boeing from astern, passed below, and pulled up directly in front, performing a series of slow-rolls "for the edification of the passengers."[11]

As if this weren't enough, one of the Grummans' guns accidentally fired during the aerobatics. Noted a quasi-official report, "That this was reprehensible must be admitted," but the results were memorably comic.[12] The Clipper fired a red flare, whether as a keep-away warning or in distress no one could say.

The actions of a female passenger were less conventional but decidedly more tangible. The distressed woman was seen at one of the cabin windows, frantically waving a white cloth at one of the Martlets now flying formation with the big clipper. Naturally, the slipstream snatched the improvised flag from her tenuous grasp and impaled it on the Martlet's pitot tube. A corrupted version of this story appeared in print, saying that the Grumman brought home a pair of bloomers as a souvenir. "Actually, the piece of materiel was not recognizable as any item of feminine apparel until converted to such by the aircraft's maintenance crew," recalls Winkle Brown. The mechanics employed "deft use of scissors and needle to produce an appropriate and hilarious squadron trophy."[13]

The *Audacity* escorted seventy ships back to Britain during the first half of October with little aerial activity. But before the month was out, OG-76 with twenty ships steamed for Gibraltar in steadily worsening weather. Black Section—Patterson and Fletcher, who had scored the squadron's first kill—scrambled for an alert on 7 November but found nothing to report. However, the sea conditions were abysmal upon their return. A sextant showed the *Audacity*'s stern pitching through a vertical arc of 65 feet, with the flight deck rolling 16 degrees. Visibility had dropped considerably as the ship wallowed through a rain storm.

Fletcher got aboard somehow, but Patterson's Martlet met the deck as the ship came up and his plane came down. The results was a spectacular evolution as the little fighter was tossed overboard to port. Unlike F4F-3s, the Martlet II retained the wing-mounted flotation bags and in this instance they performed as advertised. Patterson was pulled from the tossing sea by a skillfully handled escort.

Next day FDO John Parry's radar showed an unidentified aircraft nearby. It was a Kondor out of Bordeaux, plotting the convoy's position for Admiral Karl Doenitz. This time Blue Section was launched—Lieutenant Commander Wintour and his wingman, Sub-Lieutenant Hutchinson. They found the Focke-Wulf, and the CO made two quartering runs, damaging the Kondor and setting it alight. Satisfied with his gunnery, Wintour pulled level with his victim to watch it burn. It was a terrible mistake. The German gunner, with a steady platform and almost stationary target, opened fire. Wintour abruptly banked away, but too late. A 20-mm shell burst through his cockpit and the CO's Martlet went right into the ocean. Hutchinson finished off the bomber, but revenge counted for little. Said Winkle Brown, "John Wintour, the epitome of skill and airmanship, had fallen victim to overconfidence."[14]

Ninety minutes later Brown himself was shooting it out with another Kondor, flying a Martlet with a prop slightly bent in a deck-handling accident. But with only four fighters remaining, the pilots couldn't be too particular.

When it rains, it pours, for Red Section found two Focke-Wulfs. Lamb pursued his but lost it in the clouds. Brown dived abruptly from 4,000 feet toward his target from the port beam, fearful of losing sight of the giant at 800. But his closure rate was too fast, and Brown snapped out a quick burst before passing beneath the Kondor. There was no return fire; he'd caught the German by surprise.

Brown did better on his next two passes; one from the starboard quarter and another from port. His .50-calibers flamed the inner right-hand engine, but the big bomber kept heading for cover and plunged into a thick cloud bank. Brown caught occasional glimpses of the dark-green FW, then lost it completely. Despondent, he'd just about given up when the German abruptly appeared, nose-on and straight ahead.

Brown opened fire at long range—about 500 yards—and kept shooting on a collision course. He pressed the run to what seemed rock-throwing distance and saw the canopy disintegrate under his sustained fire. The Kondor pitched up, stalled and dropped into a flat spin. Impact tore off the port wing and the big Focke-Wulf began to sink. Circling overhead, Brown saw two survivors clinging to the severed wing. The head-on tactic really worked, and he'd have the chance to try it again.

The *Audacity* arrived at The Rock on 11 November, an appropriate date to note the safe passage of a merchant convoy without loss of one ship. In 1941 that was no small cause for celebration. The next convoy departed Gibraltor on 14 December: thirty-two ships and sixteen escorts plus *Audacity*. Number 802 Squadron still had only four Martlets, but another CO was assigned: Lieutenant Commander Donald Gibson. From the first night out, submarine contacts abounded. The dawn search on the 17th was uneventful until about 0900 when a returning Grumman reported a surfaced U-boat 22 miles on the convoy's port beam. A strafing pass forced the sub down, and destroyer escorts sped to the scene, gaining, losing, regaining sonar contact. Eventually another visual sighting developed and this time Graham Fletcher was airborne. He dived across the convoy at full power, closing the distance in hopes of engaging the U-boat and gaining time for the escorts to pile in.

The submariners saw him coming and decided to shoot it out. Fletcher opened fire, seeing geysers erupt around the U-boat just as 37-mm tracers curled upward. Then a flash winked on the Martlet's windscreen and the little fighter spewed smoke. Sailors on Commander Frederick Walker's escorts saw the Martlet smash into the ocean close aboard the submarine. But Graham Fletcher had gained the time Walker needed. Four escorts converged and shot up *U-131* for nearly 20 minutes before the surviving Germans abandoned.

The running battle continued during the 18th, with casualties on both sides. The *Audacity* narrowly escaped a torpedo which passed close astern. Captured U-boatmen told interrogators that the Germans knew the carrier by name, and she was a priority target. As war correspondent Ernie Pyle later observed, it's a tenuous honor, but a proud one.

The three remaining Martlets were kept busy. During the morning of the 19th Red Section found two Focke-Wulfs and Winkle Brown splashed one in a head-on pass. Sheepy Lamp shot pieces off another but the German evaded into ever-present clouds.

That afternoon 802 Squadron had one more chance at a prowling Kondor. The *Audacity* scrambled Yellow Section, Lieutenant Commander Jimmy Sleigh and his wingman. Guided by occasional AA bursts from a destroyer, the fighters gained contact and made several ineffective stern passes. Recalling Brown's success, Sleigh changed tactics and pulled in front of the bomber, closing to absolute minimum range, firing head-on. The 200 lurched and fell off, forcing Sleigh into a desperation pull-up with a windscreen full of Kondor. He felt a thump, but kept flying and recovered safely. When Sleigh alit from the cockpit he looked over his Martlet and hardly believed what he saw. There, dangling from his tailwheel, was part of the Focke-Wulf's port aileron.

The hunting continued throughout the 20th and 21st, bringing Martlet reports of surfaced U-boats. With only three fighters on hand, the convoy's air cover was stretched mighty thin, and the pilots rotated flights until dark. The aggressive German sub skippers penetrated the convoy that night, and frightened merchantmen fired star shells to try illuminating the raiders. All they accomplished was silhouetting the *Audacity* for the well-positioned *U-751*. At 2037 the former *Hannover* took a German torpedo aft. The *Audacity* stopped, unable to steer.

Twenty-five minutes later, while the sub lazed in the swell 200 yards to port, British sailors watched aghast as *U-751* took its time reloading for another salvo. This time two "fish" struck well forward, detonating aviation fuel. In minutes the little carrier was standing bows down, her single propeller well clear of the water. Aircraft, equipment, and men tumbled everywhere.

Winkle Brown was still dressed for flying and quickly scavanged the two items most important to him—his logbook and silk pajamas for his fiancée. Once in the water he sadly released his log, as it restricted his movement. He joined his wingman, Sheepy Lamb, with a group of about twenty other men and waited three hours for rescue by a corvette. When the ship hove to, only Brown and Lamb remained. The others, lacking life preservers, had drifted away in the chilling dark.

Loss of life was heavy, but 802 Squadron survived. With a month's survivor's leave Eric Brown finally married Lynn, his extroverted Irish girl. Then the five remaining pilots reformed 802 with Sea Hurricanes at RNAS Yeovilton in February 1942.

The *Audacity* and 802 Squadron represented a landmark in naval aviation. Though crude even by wartime standards, the combination worked smoothly, and clearly proved the efficacy of escort carriers. The Martlets had shot down five FW-200s, damaged three and driven off others. Nine U-boats had been reported by the Grummans, of which one was sunk in concert with escort destroyers. Admiral Doenitz, the U-boat master himself, knew the *Audacity* and later identified Convoy HG-76 as a distressing indication of things to come. Only two merchantmen had been lost against four U-boats.

However, it was over two years before the next British conversion joined the fleet. Meanwhile, American ship production increased by orders of magnitude, and by the summer of 1942 the first U.S.-built CVEs in Royal Navy service were plying the Arctic trade routes.

The Murmansk convoys were, if anything, even worse than anything the *Audacity* had encountered in the Atlantic. Martlet pilots in such baby flattops as the *Avenger* and *Chaser* in 1942–43 endured some of the vilest wartime conditions ever recorded. Wretched weather was normal, with extremely high seas, howling winds, and numbing temperatures. A man seldom survived more than a few minutes in the freezing water.

Rolling, pitching decks made almost every landing an adventure, and LSOs had to expertly judge each "cut" in order to bring a plane aboard just as the ship topped out in a swell. As weather worsened, Martlets sometimes had to assume anti-submarine patrols because Swordfish biplanes couldn't tolerate the landing gear stress of a high sink rate into a rising deck. Consequently, later marks of fighters (beginning with the Martlet V in mid-1943) were frequently fitted with three or four rockets under each wing to enhance their ASW capacity.

On top of this, fighter pilots had to fly in and out of snowstorms because the German bombers took advantage of low visibility to initiate surprise attacks. Guns were usually operated without lubricant, as oil could freeze and jam the bolts. And in the northern latitudes there were sometimes only two hours darkness in 24, leading to terrible fatigue. Many men never undressed in the course of a 12-day convoy. They were simply too tired, and too cold.

But the Martlet also went to war in other climes. In 1942 HMS *Illustrious* embarked 881 and 882 Squadrons, operating in the Indian Ocean. Supporting the siezure of Diego Suarez naval base on the northern tip of Madagascar, the *Illustrious* and *Indomitable* (with Fulmars and Sea Hurricanes) encountered Vichy French aircraft. The Martlet IIs strafed airfields in the vicinity on 5 May, stirring up airborne opposition the next day. Three 881 pilots claimed a pair of Potez 63 recon planes but on the 7th—opening day of the Coral Sea battle 6,000 nautical miles to the east—the opposition stiffened. Number 881 Squadron tangled with Morane 406C fighters over the anchorage. It was a striking example of the truly global nature of the Wildcat's war, and its more bizarre aspects: American-built fighters from British carriers fighting French airplanes off the east coast of Africa. At any rate, the *Illustrious* pilots had things largely their own way, claiming four Moranes in exchange for one Martlet which crash-landed on the beach. Later evaluation showed actual Vichy losses were two Potez 63s and three Moranes.[15]

Following consolidation of the British position on Madagascar, the *Illustrious* and *Formidable* departed Ceylon for the Bay of Bengal in late July. The latter embarked 888 Squadron, which made Martlet history within the larger framework of Allied grand strategy. The two British carriers were intended to divert Japanese attention from the 7 August landings by U.S. Marines in the Solomons. Sighted by an H6K flying boat, the Royal Navy force was duly reported. A second Mavis wasn't so fortunate. Sub-Lieutenants J. E. Scott and C. Ballard of 888 intercepted and splashed the big Kawanishi—the Martlet's first and only success against Japanese aircraft. But Royal Navy

Grummans had now engaged four Axis air forces, a record for American-built aircraft perhaps matched only by the Curtiss P-40.

The balance of 1942 operations were conducted against more familiar opponents. Martlets saw relatively little combat as carrier aircraft in the Mediterranean, but one of the exceptions was Operation Pedestal in August. All available carriers were concentrated to fight through a fourteen-ship convoy to besieged Malta, with considerable battleship and cruiser support. The *Victorious, Indomitable*, and *Eagle* provided air cover while the *Furious* ferried thirty-eight urgently needed Spitfires. The lone Martlet squadron was 806 in the *Indomitable*, a reformed Fulmar unit previously based in Ceylon. Actually, 806 wasn't quite a squadron. There were six Martlet IIs aboard "Indomit" plus twenty-four Sea Hurricanes of 800 and 880 Squadrons.

Pedestal started badly. The *Eagle* took four torpedoes from *U-73* on 11 August, and she went down in eight minutes. That evening saw the first of a sustained series of air attacks from German and Italian bombers. After all, the Med was *mare nostrum* to the Italians, and the Regia Aeronautica intended to keep it "our sea."

Summer in the Mediterranean is traditionally blessed with excellent weather. Or cursed with it, depending upon one's point of view. Clear skies prevailed on the 12th, affording no concealment for ships. Near the Sicilian Narrows, upwards of 100 dive-bombers and torpedo planes went after the Malta-bound ships in a succession of violent, hard-fought combats. Thirty Sea Hurricanes and eighteen Fulmars provided the bulk of Pedestal's air defense, but 806's half-dozen Martlets did their part, claiming two SM-79s, a JU-88, and a Reggianne 2000. In all, some thirty Axis planes were shot down in exchange for one Grumman and a dozen Hurricanes or Fulmars, but the bombers got through by sheer weight of numbers. The *Indomitable* took two bombs which inflicted serious damage, and the merchantmen suffered a beating. During the 12th and 13th they were whittled down until at last only five—including two in sinking condition—made Grand Harbor, Malta. But it was enough.

Fleet Air Arm pilots by now had enough experience to draw comparisons between the various carrier fighters. The Martlet was probably the most popular, as it had been designed and built as a proper shipboard fighter. The Fulmar, while effective, was handicapped by its two-seat configuration and poor speed; about 255 mph (220 knots) at 2,400 feet. Sea Hurricanes were faster than Martlets, making 340 mph (295 knots) at 22,000 feet. But the Hawkers were marginal carrier aircraft, with a harsh stall and bouncy landing gear. They lacked the Grumman's initial climb rate and endurance, but possessed an important tactical advantage over Martlets. Being more streamlined due to their liquid-cooled engines, they accelerated better in a dive. This was mainly pertinent to reaching sea level from altitude, since CAPs often had to beat a hasty path to the deck to intercept low-flying torpedo planes.

The glamorous, well-publicized Seafire had tremendous performance, especially at low level. But the elegant little thoroughbred took poorly to saltwater, and its airframe suffered considerably from the conventional stress of deck landings. This, combined with the generally inferior .303-caliber armament of most British fighters, made the Martlet a popular choice in the Royal Navy.

In November 1942 another Royal Navy carrier force supported a much more ambitious enterprise: Operation Torch, the Anglo-American landings at Algiers and Oran. This marked the first and probably only time that British and American Wildcats operated more or less in concert in the Atlantic/Mediterranean theater. The *Formidable* had returned from the Indian Ocean, now flying six Martlet IIs and eighteen Mark IVs of 888 and 893 Squadrons, while the *Victorious* embarked 882's eighteen Mark IVs. It made for a total of forty-two Martlets assigned to the Algerian landings plus 109 F4F-4s in four U.S. carriers off Morocco.

On 6 November, two days before the landings, "Triple Eight" launched a section from the *Formidable* to intercept an intruder. Leadng the scramble was Lieutenant D. M. Jeram, a Battle of Britain veteran with four kills in Hurricanes as an exchange pilot with the RAF. Jeram spotted a fast Vichy aircraft and closed to 250 yards. Noting the twin-engine, twin-tail configuration he identified it as a Potez 63 and opened fire. The hostile went down off Cape Kramis. Actually, it was a Bloch 174 from Oran, externally similar to the Potez.[16]

Neutralizing enemy airfields was a prime chore of the carrier planes, and during one such mission on the 8th occurred one of those peculiar events not uncommon in war. A flight of 882 Squadron off the *Victorious* capped Blida Airfield southwest of Algiers that morning, but while the dawn mission had drawn light AA fire, now the Frenchmen were waving white handkerchiefs. The flight leader, Lieutenant B. H. C. Nation, radioed the *Victorious* for further orders, and after awhile he was told that one Martlet could land to investigate.

Nation himself took the job. Taxiing to the hangars, he was received by French officers with elaborate courtesy and escorted to the base commander—"a nice old boy and very friendly."[17] The elderly gentleman turned over a handwritten note certifying that the field was available to the Allies, and the impromptu Anglo–Franco entente continued amicably until American rangers arrived. Thereupon Lieutenant Nation climbed back in his plane, took off, and rejoined his flight. It was undoubtedly the only time a Royal Navy pilot "captured" an airfield single-handed.

Next day the Germans interceded, disrupting the fragile truce. Bombers raided Algiers, and 882 Squadron downed a Heinkel 111 and damaged a JU-88. Later in the day Lieutenant Jeram and his wingman added to 888's bag, exploding another Junkers.

On 11 November, 893 Squadron experienced one of war's greater tragedies. The *Formidable* had four Martlet IVs airborne and they intercepted a pale-colored twin-tailed aircraft tentatively identified as an SM-84. Three pilots shared the kill, but the aircraft recognition problems common to air combat deceived them. Lieutenant Jeram's error of five days previous was well within acceptable limits. But 893 had shot down an RAF Lockheed Hudson patrolling out of Gibraltar.

With RAF and American fighters now ashore, the carriers pulled off. So ended 1942, the year in which Martlets were engaged against German, Italian, Vichy and Japanese aircraft, claiming sixteen Axis planes shot down for the loss of two.

During 1943 Martlets didn't engage in combat until July, supporting the invasion of Sicily from the *Formidable* and patrolling the North Sea in the *Furious*. Numbers 881 and 890 Squadrons splashed three Blom and Voss 138 seaplanes in northern waters. Then in September the scene switched back to the Med, where Operation Avalanche saw the majority of FAA fighter squadrons flying Seafires. But 888 off the *Formidable* bagged a big Cant Z.506B floatplane on 9 September, probably the last Italian aircraft shot down before Mussolini's regime was overthrown.

A unique situation existed in the South Pàcific during May through July, as a British and American carrier worked together. The *Victorious* embarked some three dozen Martlet IVs, providing Task Group 36.3 fighter protection while the *Saratoga* functioned as the strike carrier with Dauntless and Avenger squadrons in addition to twelve F4F-4s. The Martlet IVs were F4F-4Bs, not wholly compatible with their American counterparts (owing to different engines), hence the division of labor between each ship. But the sweep of the Solomons area added an intriguing, if uneventful, page to Wildcat history.

The year ended in familiar style. The escort carrier *Fencer* in the Atlantic flew 842 Squadron, a composite unit of Martlets and

Swordfish. On 1 December an FW-200 approached a Gibraltar convoy and two Martlet IVs dealt with it. In Grumman trivia, this was the last shootdown credited to Martlets. For in early 1944 the Royal Navy decided to standardize aircraft names, and Martlets finally became Wildcats. About this time, the first of 311 FM-1s began arriving in the Fleet Air Arm, and they were designated Wildcat Vs.

One of the old-line squadrons by now was 881, teamed with 896 aboard the *Pursuer* on the Gibraltar run. This was the first all-fighter carrier on the route to The Rock since the *Audacity*, but business was brisk. On 12 February 1944 German heavy bombers attempted a strange new tactic, launching glider-bombs. Four Wildcat Vs intercepted the mixed formation of FW-200s and Heinkel 177s at dusk, shooting down one each of the four-engine giants. On the 16th another composite squadron, 811 in the *Biter*, had a similar opportunity when two Wildcat IVs chased down a four-engine Junkers 290. The rare bomber, looking like a twin-tailed FW-200, was the only one of its type destroyed by Royal Navy Grummans.

One of the more intense convoy battles of 1944 occurred during the Arctic passage of JW-58. The *Activity* and *Tracker* embarked 819 and 846 Squadrons respectively, both experienced convoy-protection units. JW-58 was persistently harried by German bombers from 30 March to 1 April, and in those three days the Wildcats splashed six hostiles, including three FW-200s and the 31st. They were the last Kondors hacked down by the little Grummans, ending a three-and-a-half-year feud.

The departure of JW-58 served as cover for another northern operation. Tungsten, the largest Royal Navy air strike yet, involved two fleet carriers and four CVEs with some 160 aircraft. Their target was the battleship *Tirpitz*, a continuing threat to Arctic convoys though nestled deep in her Norwegian fjord. Tungsten was sprung on 3 April, including forty Wildcat Vs from the *Pursuer* and *Searcher* as flak suppression. The *Tirpitz* wasn't sunk, but damage inflicted by Barracuda dive-bombers kept her idle for several months.

In August, the *Pursuer* and *Searcher* supported "the other D-Day" with twenty-four new Wildcat VIs of 881 Squadron and twenty-eight Marks Vs of 882. They were part of a Royal Navy task force involving six carriers in the invasion of southern France. The carrier planes saw very little air combat, and Wildcats devoted their attention to strike and ground support. From September to November the British Wildcats added additional names to their world travels, participating in missions against German bases in the Aegean.

The year closed out with more activity in Norwegian waters when

Campania and *Nairana* Wildcats splashed three BV-138s during November and December. January and February 1945 brought more Arctic convoys. The *Tracker*, *Vindex*, and *Nairana* squadrons dumped three more shadowers during this period, but things were winding down.

By March the *Searcher* was back with the Home Fleet, now flying Wildcat VIs of 882 Squadron. On the 26th, in company with the *Fencer* and *Queen*, she patrolled the Norwegian coast with a flight of 882 fighters up and waiting. Though the end in Europe was plainly in sight, the Luftwaffe chose to contest the matter. Messerschmitt 109Gs of III Gruppe, JG-5 bounced the Wildcats, badly damaging one in their first pass. But the FM-2's maneuverability allowed the Britishers to reverse the situation, and they claimed four kills. Though Martlets had briefly tangled with 109s in North Africa, this was the first conclusive engagement between the two types. It was also the last combat fought by Royal Navy Wildcats. Six week later the long war with Germany was over.

By V-J Day over thirty Royal Navy squadrons had flown Martlets or Wildcats operationally, from a similar number of carriers. These units were credited with fifty-three enemy aircraft shot down: thirty-eight German, eight Italian, six Vichy and one Japanese. Only the Fulmar claimed more aerial victories in the Fleet Air Arm.

Losses in aerial combat were exceedingly light—evidently under ten—owing largely to the nature of the Martlet's opponents. Eighty-eight percent of the shootdowns were maritime reconnaissance or other multi-engine types; usually meat on the table for a Wildcat.

Such was the erratic nature of the Martlet's career that very few pilots experienced more than one or two combats. Only seven were credited with more than one victory (whether by fractions or whole) and of those, Lieutenant C. C. Tomkins of 881 Squadron and Sub-Lieutenant Eric Brown of 802 were the most successful, with two-and-a-half and two respectively.

Among Martlet squadrons, 881's tally of eight was tops for the Royal Navy: five Vichy and three German planes. Another three squadrons gained five kills each, of which the *Formidable*'s 888 Squadron became the most cosmopolitan. The globe-trotting "Triple Eight" was perhaps the only Allied squadron of the war to confirm victories over German, Italian, Vichy *and* Japanese aircraft.

Thus ended the success story which was the Wildcat in British service. A good many former Fleet Air Arm pilots share Winkle Brown's recollection that, "It was love at first sight."[19]

10. THE WILDER WILDCAT

"I have fought a good fight, I have finished my course, I have kept the faith."

II Timothy 4:7

GRUMMAN WAS OUT OF THE Wildcat business by June of 1943. For that matter, Bethpage also divested itself of the Avenger. The reasons were two-fold: the Navy's crying need for additional aircraft early in the war, and the advent of the Hell-cat. Eventually the Navy wanted nearly as many F6Fs as Grum-man could produce, and in order to concentrate on the new carrier fighter, the two older designs were to be built by another contractor.

In a whirlwind of negotiating activity which even now seems incredible for wartime urgency, the decision had been made by February 1942. General Motors was to convert its five idle east-coast automobile plants to aircraft production. Or, more precisely, the newly established Eastern Aircraft Division of GM would do so. But it wasn't an entirely amicable arrangement at first. The deal was more imposed than negotiated—"a sort of shotgun marriage with the War Production Board as father of the bride."[1]

Despite the all-too-obvious urgency, elements on both sides harbored reservations. Said a Grumman historian, "GM started out with the idea that it would show the aeronautical industry how to mass-produce airplanes."[2] On the other hand, experienced aviation people openly doubted whether the automotive industry could meet and

233

maintain the precise tolerance necessary in aircraft. Production and even management techniques were vastly different.

First priority was given to the Wildcat project, and Eastern built a large shed at Bethpage so its people could learn the ropes of manufacturing F4F-4s. A General Motors report characterized this undistinguished building as "perhaps the fastest built, least ostentatious office in GM's history."[3]

Wildcat production would be moved to GM's Linden, New Jersey complex, only about 40 air miles west of Bethpage. The Eastern Avenger would be built at Trenton. But before General Motors could start building Wildcats, considerable remodeling was necessary. The Linden facilities lacked adequate engineering space, so GM subcontracted for demolition of some buildings to make room for the future. Much of the demolished equipment was declared unsalvagable, but clean up crews dismantled other gear for long-term storage in a new warehouse.

Following completion of the demolition phase at the end of April, construction of the Wildcat factory proceeded rapidly. But the residue of the automotive business remained. Five miles of monorail and conveyor equipment was torn down. Some 14,000 square feet of boiler plate was dismantled, with enough industrial piping to reach halfway from New York to Philadelphia. Hundreds of jigs, ovens, heaters, and motors had to be removed, and completed 1942 model cars were hauled away on trailers. Electricians installed new lighting and heating systems while bulldozers cleared the surrounding area, improving drainage and leveling the clay soil for parking lots, hangars and runways.

Grummanites told Eastern engineers that an F4F-4 contained 10,963 parts, and the GM folks would have to know each one by heart. Linden received Grumman-built parts for the first two fighters (FM-1s, identical to the F4F-4 except most had four guns instead of six) and assembled the Wildcats under Grumman supervision. The next six contained only one-eighth prefabricated parts, and after that Eastern was largely on its own.

Despite the corporate rivalries, each side discovered it could learn something from the other, and things smoothed out considerably. And the automotive people learned fast. Their first Wildcat was accepted by the Navy in September 1942, followed by three the next month and five in November. By year-end Linden had delivered twenty-one FM-1s. That figure was matched in January 1943 alone, as Grumman wound down its Wildcat program by building the last 100 F4F-4s between January and the end of May.

But Grumman influence wasn't entirely lacking in the Eastern program. Back in November 1942 the first XF4F-8 had jumped off the ground for the first time. It was a lightened Wildcat, powered by the Wright R-1820-56. The second dash eight featured an eight-and-a-half-inch taller vertical stabilizer and rudder to handle the Cyclone's 1,350 horsepower. And the results were remarkable. With an overall weight saving of some 530 pounds, the experimental dash eights outclimbed the F4F-4 by almost 1,000 feet per minute, and service ceiling rose to over 36,000 feet.

In early 1943 the "Wilder Wildcat" was ordered into production by Eastern as the FM-2. The first was accepted by the Navy in September, and FM-1 production ended in December. Total GM fighter deliveries for that year amounted to 1,120 Wildcats as production moved steadily, if erratically, upward.

By the spring of 1944 the production schedule was running with amazing consistency. There were 214 acceptances in January, 258 in February, and then came the peak of 276 in March. After that, FM-2 acceptances ran at a constant 280 per month through September. The monthly average for all of 1944 was 240, compared to about 400 Corsairs (F4Us, FGs and F3As) and 500 Hellcats. But the new Wildcat wasn't needed in the quantity of other naval fighters, and its peak month was just half those of the Corsair and Hellcat.

During 1944 the Linden plant turned out 2,890 of the tubby little rascals—41 percent of all Wildcat production. From November 1944 to April 1945 acceptances ran regularly at 150 to 175 per month, and even hard-core Grummanites expressed admiration for the quality of GM aircraft.

So did pilots. In October 1944 Army, Navy, and various company test pilots participated in one of the fighter evaluation boards held periodically throughout the war. Their overall summary affords a balanced view of the FM-2 as seen by experienced aviators.

Twelve categories were appraised in each fighter, ranging from cockpit layout and comfort to ground handling to a variety of flight characteristics. The cockpit was rated "small, compact, but comfortable," though rearward vision was "bad" and several pilots thought the FM-2's cockpit was hotter and noisier than the F4F-4's.

Like the dash four, the FM was marginal for taxiing, especially in a crosswind. The increased torque induced a tendency to swing on takeoff, but approach and landing qualities received praise. In fact, one pilot considered the FM-2 the best in this category of all fighters evaluated. However, there was one inevitable complaint about "the job of cranking the wheels up."[4]

The overall consensus of flight regimes was almost entirely favorable. The board found good stall warning and recovery, and good stability in all axes and flight conditions. The controls were deemed responsive and effective, though a few pilots thought the forces somewhat high. As for combat qualities, the only drawback was seen in top speed—about 320 mph. Most fliers wanted more speed, but acceleration was good, and there were "a number of favorable comments on the high rates of climb."[5]

Inevitable equipment additions (including rocket rails) cut into the FM-2's superiority over the F4F-4, but not by much. In squadron service the Eastern bird was about 80 pounds heavier at normal load, and its service ceiling fell below the dash four. But the bread-and-butter categories all favored the FM; it was 12 to 22 knots (14 to 25 mph) faster depending upon altitude, had more range, much better climb, and superior maneuverability. In short, the Wildcat was a contender again, and a match for the Zero.

As long as FM pilots kept their airspeed above 160 knots (200 was better) they could generally handle even late-model Zekes. And the record proved it. Operating solely from escort carriers during 1944 and 1945, FM-2s were credited with shooting down 422 Japanese aircraft. By way of comparison, carrier-based F4Fs claimed 270 victories in the Pacific throughout 1942 and into early 1943. Land-based F4Fs reported another 603 shootdowns during the same period.

While these numbers may seem small in comparison to Hellcat and Corsair claims from flattops (4,947 and 578 respectively), the operating environments need to be kept in mind. By the very nature of their work, the CVE-based Wildcats had limited opportunity for air combat. Their primary missions were ground support and its affiliated duties, anti-sub patrol, and CAP. But when they did engage airborne hostiles, the FM-2s got results. Composite squadrons—CVE units flying FM-2s and TBM-3s—produced at least five aces in the Wilder Wildcat.

The Battle of Leyte Gulf was the first naval-air operation involving substantial numbers of FM-2s. And that was almost as much by misfortune as by design. Eighteen escort carriers participated, deployed in three task groups of the Seventh Fleet. Officially, the CVE Group was Task Force 77.4, and the three tactical units were known by their code names: Taffy One, Two, and Three. Taffy One's commander was Rear Admiral Thomas L. Sprague, who also ran the whole Escort Carrier Group. Two of his baby flattops embarked CVE air groups, which flew Hellcats instead of FMs for fighters. In all, Sprague's jeep carriers had some 228 Wildcats, 40 Hellcats and 170

Avengers to support General Douglas MacArthur's return to the Philippines.

The Leyte landings on 20 October sparked the Japanese fleet response which turned into the sprawling three-day naval battle that same week. One Taffy Three FM pilot hit the aerial jackpot on the 24th as a division of *Kalinin Bay* Wildcats was directed to a lone bogey over the Leyte Gulf. Lieutenant Kenneth G. Hippe of VC-3 identified the twin-engine stranger as a Kawasaki Type 99 bomber—the Japanese Army's Lilly—and promptly shot it down. Shortly thereafter Hippe's division received an urgent radar vector to a much larger contact—twenty-one Lillys in all. The Wildcats attacked, and in a ten-minute running battle Hippe himself splashed four more. The other three *Kalinin Bay* pilots, reinforced by additional Taffy Three fighters, left just one Lilly survivor.

Though it hardly seemed possible, this same day saw another FM pilot top Hippe's score. Lieutenant Commander Harold N. Funk, skipper of VF-26 off the *Santee* in Taffy One, splashed five bandits in one mission and added another in his second sortie. But the Taffy Two Wildcats were also heard from. Lieutenant Ralph Elliott of VC-27 opened the string which would make him the most successful of all FM-2 pilots. He knocked down three bombers unassisted and shared a fourth with his wingman. And next day the 24-year-old Illinois pilot splashed three more. Six and a half kills in two days was a fast pace, and Elliot finished with a total of nine and a half in early 1945. Four other *Savo Island* aviators tallied four and a half kills each, boosting VC-27 to first place among CVE units with a total of sixty-two shootdowns, including four by TBMs.

But the morning of 25 October began poorly for the CVEs, and that is an understatement. Taffy Three commenced flight ops at 0530 as Rear Admiral Clifton Sprague (no relation to Taffy One's commander) sent twelve fighters over Leyte Gulf to cover the invasion transports while TBMs took up anti-sub patrols. It was known that Third Fleet fast carriers had pummeled a heavy Japanese force on the westward side of the Philippines the day before, and the hostiles were thought retiring.

That illusion was dispelled shortly before 0700. A patrolling Avenger reported battleships with pagoda masts approaching from the north. Vice Admiral Takeo Kurita had transited San Bernardino Strait during the night, arriving in Leyte Gulf with four battlewagons, eight cruisers, and eleven destroyers. Taffy Three was the only American force between this astonishing armada and the nearly defenseless transports. Halsey's fast carriers and battleships were pounding north to engage the Japanese decoy carriers, and could offer no timely help. Clifton Sprague had six CVEs, three destroyers and four destroyer-escorts. Period.

As the escorts dropped astern to make smoke, the Kaiser-built carriers churned eastward at a maximum 19 knots. Steaming in a 2,500-yard circle, they had the wind off the port bow and commenced launch immediately with whatever was spotted on deck: Avengers with depth charges or 500-pound bombs, Wildcats with rockets if they were lucky. Sprague hollered for help from Taffy One and Two. The former was about 130 nautical miles to the south, off Mindanao, and could provide little help in the limited time available. But Rear Admiral Felix Stump's Taffy Two, operating fewer than 30 miles away, was in a far better position to lend a hand.

Between them, Sprague and Stump had over 180 FM-2s and about 170 TBM-3s. But only a portion would be available at any one time. Apart from those flying scheduled missions for MacArthur's troops, many were still on their hangar decks being armed or fueled. Torpedo-packing Avengers were the most urgently needed, but it took time to check out each "fish" and load the 1,900-pound weapons into a TBM's belly.

And time was not on Taffy Three's side. The *Gambier Bay* was one of the rearmost carriers in the task group, now beginning to receive cruiser gunfire. She'd lauched eight VC-10 Wildcats for the dawn CAP and currently had ten FMs and seven TBMs spotted on deck. With the wind quartering from port the takeoff was a little tricky, made no easier by the concussion of 8-inch shells exploding nearby. But they all made it off.

The first four belonged to Lieutenant Dick Roby's fighter division. Ensign Chuck Dugan had barely started to crank up his wheels when he got his first good look at the Japanese force closing in from astern. His reaction was profanely concise. Almost from the beginning the CVE fliers knew they were in big trouble, and few expected their baby flattops to survive. But they could try.

Slim, blue-eyed Dick Roby decided to harass two destroyers cutting in from the starboard quarter. Each pilot made at least three passes, pushing his runs to the limit, recovering in sudden high-G pullups. Dugan pulled out so abruptly that he blacked out in each of his four passes. Fearful of diving into the water, he trimmed his Wildcat nose-up and regained consciousness each time heading into the 1,500-foot overcast.

The combined firepower of sixteen .50-calibers was formidable. The stubby FM-2s bored in low and close, the dark gray forms of the destroyers looming larger in their gunsights as tracers lanced out in both directions. Little white motes of light played over the superstructure as the heavy bullets hammered against steel plates.

Roby lost contact with his three pilots after the second pass, but it was enough. Both DDs heeled hard over, temporarily veering away from Taffy Three. After that, individual Wildcats from all the carriers did what they could to fashion impromptu co-ordinated attacks. Commander R. L. Fowler of VC-5 off the *Kitkun Bay* was the senior aviator in the task group, and he did what he could to organize things from his TBM. But the situation was too far gone for effective control on even a squadron basis, let alone for the whole group.

Usually it was one or two FMs, often from different ships, joining a handy Avenger and diving ahead to help suppress flak. In a few minutes most of the fighters were out of ammuniition. They kept buzzing the lethal, looming warships anyway. Some Wildcat pilots made twenty passes, often with expended ammo in half the runs.

Having cleared his decks, Sprague turned his outnumbered, outgunned force southward, hoping to open the distance a bit. But Japanese gunnery began to tell as the range steadily diminished. The *White Plains* took a hit, temporarily losing steering control, but was covered by a providential rainsquall. The *Kalinin Bay* sustained the first serious damage at 0750 from battleship and cruiser shells, and the flagship *Fanshaw Bay* counted four 8-inch hits. But the *Gambier Bay* had the worst of it. As four cruisers closed in she was raked repeatedly and dropped behind. Abandoned at 0850, she sank about ten minutes later.

There was no chance of getting aboard any Taffy Three carrier, and Taffy Two's ships were engaged in heavy flight ops of their own, trying to help Sprague. The best option for airborne planes was to head for newly won Tacloban airstrip on Leyte. It was a 100-mile flight to the rough field at the water's edge, but it was a case of any old port in a storm.

However, it wasn't a very friendly port. Trigger-happy Army AA gunners shot at U.S. and Japanese planes with almost total impartiality. An Avenger crashed in flames on the beach while trying to land. Furthermore, the runway was a bomb-pitted obstacle course of soft dirt and the field was rapidly becoming choked with homeless CVE planes. Bulldozers filled holes and leveled earth even as aircraft landed. An Army radio jeep, called sign Halifax, vainly attempted to coordinate the aerial rat-race, advising "Don't land unless you have less than ten minutes of gas."[6] But no fuel gauge was that accurate. Planes queued up in the pattern, alternately making procedure turns and dodging American flak.

Even those planes which did land were far from safe. Several were wrecked when they ran into shell holes; others turned over in the soft dirt. And with growing congestion there were several collisions. Chuck Dugan of VC-10 was almost involved in one. He had parked his FM and was unsnapping his seatpack parachute when a TBM careened out of control directly towards his Wildcat. Dugan scrambled onto the wing, intending to jump and run for it, when he was pulled up short. His chute, still attached to his harness by one snap, had caught on the canopy rail. The curly-haired ensign found himself dangling over the side, watching the errant TBM finally straighten out. But Dugan remained ignominiously suspended until a pilot from another squadron came by and helped him down. "It was really quite embarrassing," he recalled.[7]

The Tacloban madhouse continued the rest of the day. Many carrier planes flew local missions while others tried to get back to the task group. A division led by Lieutenant John Stewart, VC-10's senior fighter pilot, tangled with Zekes and shot down at least one. Nearing the strip, the Wildcats ran afoul of zealous Army gunners who succeeded when the Japanese had failed. Lieutenant (jg) C. F. Hunting had his wheels and flaps down when he was boresighted by a big 90-mm battery. His stricken Wildcat crashed 100 yards offshore and his squadronmates landed to report another pilot MIA.

Two Filipinos in an outrigger canoe saw the aviator in the water and cautiously approached. They knew American guns had shot the plane down and logically assumed it was hostile. But drawing closer, they saw Hunting's blond hair and pulled him aboard. Paddling back to shore, the front oarsman turned around and grinned at Hunting. "Mistake, mistake," the Filipino said over and over.

Hunting wasn't mollified. "You're goddam right it was a mistake," he growled.[8]

A few *Gambier Bay* pilots did get back aboard a flattop. Three VC-10 Wildcats accompanied VC-80 planes to Taffy Two and flew from the *Manila Bay* for awhile. But the big story was the near-miraculous survival of Taffy Three. Between the persistent, determined air attacks and a magnificent performance by the destroyers, Kurita was convinced he'd attacked a fast carrier task group. He abandoned the chase just as his victory was nearly complete. As it was, Sprague lost two CVEs and three escorts, but with help from Stump he'd prevented the massacre of MacArthur's transports.

By January 1945, twenty-one escort carriers were deployed in the

Western Pacific with a total of 375 FM-2s. A noteworthy example was VC-91 in the *Kitkun Bay*, with sixteen conventional Wildcats and the only FM-2P in the Pacific. Avengers ordinarily handled CVE photo chores, but this field mod became the last recon Wildcat, following the contrails of the F4F-3Ps and dash sevens.

The biggest collection of Wilder Wildcats aboard a single ship were the twenty-eight fighters of VOC-1, embarked in the *Wake Island*. This globe-trotting squadron established records in both main theaters of war, and its unique career is worth examination.

Commissioned as Observation-Fighter Squadron One (VOF-1) in December 1943, the unit was only the third Navy outfit—after VF-17 and VF-12—to receive F4U-1s. Combat experience gained during the North African and Sicilian invasions showed the vulnerability of conventional VOS aircraft to light flak and enemy aircraft. Curtiss SOCs, cruiser-launched float biplanes, were the most widely employed in observation chores at the time, and they simply couldn't survive in hostile airspace. Therefore, VOF-1 was formed with Corsairs as a means of providing naval gunfire spotters which could defend themselves.

The CO from start to finish was Lieutenant Commander William F. Bringle, an uncommonly handsome trade-school professional from Tennessee. Bush Bringle's troops thought the world of him: "a skipper who has repeatedly shown himself to be one of the finest flyers we've met and who has always been an indefatigable fighter and leader of men."[9]

Bringle took his squadron to the Army's artillery school at Fort Sill, Oklahoma in early 1944 to learn the basics of gunfire spotting. But hardly had VOF-1 completed the course when its Corsairs were taken away. "Somebody in AirLant had heard that you couldn't fly F4Us off carriers," Bringle explains, "despite the fact that we'd cured the landing gear oleo problem while qualifying aboard *Charger*." Re-equipped with Hellcats, the VOF pilots were little mollified; as far as they were concerned, after F4Us "it was downhill from there."[10]

Consequently, VOF-1 flew F6F-5s from *Tulagi* during the invasion of southern France in August 1944. Its team-mate was VF-74 in the *Kasaan Bay*, which eventually became VOC-2.

Following a breathtaking turnaround, VOF-1 rode the *Tulagi* to Hawaii, arriving in early November. But more surprises were in store. While based at Barbers Point, Bringle and company received word from ComAirPac that Hellcats couldn't be spared for CVE duty, and on the 24th VOF-1 became VOC-1, trading in its F6F-5s for twenty-eight FM-2s and a half-dozen TBM-3s.

Another change also occurred. The squadron was transferred to

Kanului on Maui, where further checkouts were completed in gunnery, field carrier landings, and some night flying. Car-quals followed a week later aboard the *Wake Island*, and they clicked off without difficulty. By now almost all the pilots had flown the Corsair, Hellcat, and Wildcat aboard ship. Most of Bringle's pilots had accumulated 500 or more hours, and most were combat-experienced; six already had whole credits or shares in shooting down German aircraft over France. So VOC-1 fielded a strong team upon entry into the new league.

On 15 December, first anniversary of the squadron's commissioning, VOC-1 sailed from Pearl Harbor, WestPac-bound aboard the *Wake Island*. The thirty-three day stay in Hawaii had been hectic: transition to new aircraft, a change of base and a three-day shakedown cruise. But the squadron was confident and ready when the *Wake Island* joined Rear Admiral Cal Durgin's Task Group 77.4 in the Palaus and proceeded to the Philippines.

There, on 6 January (barely four months after flying its last mission over France) VOC-1 broke into the Pacific War. In the following two weeks Bringle's squadron flew only one spotting mission, being mainly concerned with direct ground support. But reminiscent of its missions up the Rhone Valley were armed recons the length of Luzon, seeking targets of opportunity. The cost was one pilot killed while strafing a Japanese truck convoy. But the Wildcats saw far more airborne hostiles than they had during Operation Anvil-Dragoon, and eleven shootdowns were recorded. Then it was back to Ulithi for briefing on Operation Detachment, the occupation of Iwo Jima.

Iwo, in the vivid description of one Marine, was "a bad-smelling pork chop, burned black, five miles long and two-and-a-half miles wide."[11] D-Day for the ashstrewn pile of sulphur was 19 February and the *Wake Island*, now in TG-52.2, began operations on D-minus-three and continued to D-plus-twenty. In that period the squadron flew nearly 900 sorties totaling 2,375 hours. It was a long, gruelling campaign calling for two flights a day for most pilots; sometimes three. Normal ordnance load was six rockets—occasionally two bombs—with a four-hour cycle time. This usually amounted to three hours of calling gunfire for battleships, cruisers, or destroyers and one hour of freelance work, just to break the monotony.

Roaming alone over the triangular-shaped island, VOC-1 pilots experienced "our first big spotting adventure."[12] Typically, a cruiser or battleship's six-gun salvo had a dispersion of 100 yards. With good shooting, a competent spotter could call for ten-yard corrections to walk the shells smack on target. Usually the FM-2 pilot had a close-up view, as most days the low ceiling required flying at 800 to 900 feet.

In fact, the weather was frequently so poor that VOC-1 had the only aircraft over the island because lowering clouds and visibility prevented ordinary air strikes. One pilot failed to return from a spotting mission for the battleship *Idaho*, perhaps due to the worsening weather. But there were a few compensations, as on 23 February when VOC-1 pilots saw the 28th Marines raise the American flag on Mount Suribachi.

Hardly had the CVEs departed Iwo on 11 March for a brief refit at Ulithi when Operation Iceburg began with occupation of Kerama Retto as an anchorage for the Okinawa invasion. VOC-1 flew a few strikes in addition to more spotting missions for the Kerama occupation in late March, but immediately turned its attention to the main event. The landings occurred on 1 April, with the *Wake Island* FM-2s and TBM-3s spotting and observing naval gunfire, but it was a short-lived business. On the evening of the third two Zekes dived on the CVE, intent on suicide.

One barely undershot and smashed into the sea "about an arm's length away from the port bow."[13] The other kamikaze had slightly better aim and exploded just below the waterline. There were no personnel casualties, but the *Wake Island* put into Kerama Retto where damage appraisers said she'd have to be repaired at Guam.

Bringle's pilots figured they'd earned a ticket home. But a half-hour before getting underway on the fifth, VOC-1 was ordered to the *Marcus Island*. The specialized skills of artillery spotters couldn't be spared at Okinawa, even with the presence of Lieutenant Commander R. M. Allison's VOC-2 in the *Fanshaw Bay*. Shortly before dark VC-87 traded places with the *Wake Island*'s aviators. Bringle's people simply moved in where VC-87 left off, and began flying at dawn on the sixth with the *Marcus Island*'s aircraft.

Okinawa had already cost VOC-1 two pilots, and three more were lost while flying from the *Marcus Island*. As the tempo increased, with more and more spotting missions, so did local and target CAPs, with ground support thrown in for variety. The fast carriers handled most fleet defense work, with their expanded seventy-three-plane fighter squadrons, but the CVEs also got their share. On one such mission Bush Bringle and his wingman caught two kamikaze Vals, closing near enough to see the Japanese pilots flying in ceremonial robes but "looking scared to death."[14] The suiciders took no evasive action; the Wildcats simply flew formation and executed them.

The eighteen CVEs working around Okinawa kept busy elsewhere in the Ryukyus, supporting neutralization or occupation of smaller outlying islands. One such strike hit Minami-Daito, "those little dots on the map between Okinawa and Iwo."[15] They featured airdromes well-defended with intense, accurate AA fire, and Bringle discovered just how accurate it was first-hand.

Leading a strafing mission, the CO took a hit in the engine on his second pass. The Cyclone stopped cold and Bringle prepared for a water landing, tightening his shoulder straps and jettisoning the canopy. But unaccountably the Wright restarted at about 50 feet, showing 1,200 rpm and 35 inches on the gauges. It wasn't much, but the skipper happily took it. He pulled up and turned away, nursing the abused R-1820 without throttle or prop control. In high pitch, low RPM and "full" manifold pressure (about 37 inches) Bringle followed his wingman back to the ship at 170 knots.

It was nearly an hour's flight, and the CO had ample time to ponder the upcoming landing. He had wheels, of course, but no flaps and no throttle control. So he'd have to make a fast, flat approach using his magneto switch for rough power adjustments. Once settled into the groove, watching the LSO's paddles, Bush Bringle knew he was committed. No waveoff was possible.

Alternately turning his mag switch off and on to add or reduce power, the skipper managed a Roger pass and plunked his shot-up Wildcat onto the wooden deck. It was a superior feat of airmanship, though Bringle attributed much of the credit to the oft-maligned Wright Cyclone engine.

At the end of April the *Marcus Island* returned to Guam for a two-week rest. But VOC-1, now accustomed to shifts of fortune, found itself reassigned to the patched-up *Wake Island*. She sortied 21 May with some new Wildcats and resumed the familiar chores off Okinawa where VOC-1 concentrated on spotting destroyer gunfire in the southern half of the island. But there was no rest for the observation pilots, even while their carrier refueled and replenished well out to sea. For seven of the last thirty days of Iceburg, over half Bringle's pilots flew ashore to Yontan airfield. The rain and mud which characterized life at Yontan did little to improve morale, nor did the loss of yet another flier. But at least the *Wake Island*'s pilots never had to worry about job security. If anything, the Navy should have had another VOC squadron to ease the workload for VOC-1 and -2.

The *Wake Island* departed Okinawa waters on 19 June. By that time, most organized resistance had collapsed and "the big guns of the Navy stopped firing for the first time in over three months."[16]

During its short, intense career VOC-1 may have logged more

combat hours per pilot than any squadron in the U.S. Navy. Its total of 26,000 flight hours included 12,994 hours in combat, with the large majority accumulated during the Philippines, Iwo Jima and Okinawa operations.

With twenty victories, VOC-1 was tied for third (with VC-84) among all FM squadrons; a rare achievement for a unit devoted to gunfire spotting. But the records came at a price. Eight pilots—a quarter of the authorized strength—were killed in the Pacific.

Through it all the maintenance department kept the FM-2s at an exceptional level of availability. Certainly the Wildcat's simple, easily-repaired systems contributed to this success. It was a big factor in the average pilot time of 800 hours during the eighteen months from commissioning in December 1943 to arrival at Guam in late June 1945.

Wildcats finished the war, appropriately, flying over Japan's home islands, where CVE fighters were active almost till the end. The FM-2's final shootdowns were recorded on 5 August while Task Group 95.3 plied the East China Sea southwest of Kyushu. A VC-41 division off the *Makin Island* was on ForceCap at 5,000 feet when vectored out to investigate a bogey at 7,000 feet to the northeast at 1430. Two Frances bombers were eyeballed above the Wildcats, and both Japanese immediately jettisoned their loads, slanting into a 15-degree dive. The FM leader, Lieutenant H. L. Hokanson, ordered his pilots to drop their wing tanks but only Ensign Frank Yates got rid of both externals. Leaving the others astern, Yates chased the second Fran down to sea level, indicating 230 knots at 51 inches and 2,600 rpm. The lead Fran got away but Yates clung to the second 1,000 feet back, even as it bobbed up and down.

Yates began shooting at zero deflection and boresight range. His first burst flamed the port engine, his second chopped pieces out of the fuselage and the next two wrecked the starboard engine. Yates then shifted aim to the cockpit and continued firing as the Fran dopped into a diving turn into the sea, 40 miles from the ship.

A Marine F4U off the *Cape Gloucester* splashed another Fran in almost the same place later that afternoon. The pilot was Lieutenant Colonel Don Yost, a Guadalcanal F4F veteran of VMF-121. But at 1710 another single was plotted, bearing 070, headed southwest at 180 knots. Lieutenant E. R. Beckwith's VC-98 division off the *Lunga Point* made contact, and this time all four FMs shucked their drop tanks. They slowly overhauled the speedy Fran in a 100-mile tail-chase, and one eager ensign got so close that he tried to saw off the Jap's rudder with his prop. But Beckwith employed more conventional methods. His four .50-calibers burned the Yokosuka and it smashed into the water 55 miles west-southwest of the task group. Beckwith's victim was the last in the Wildcat's long string. Ten days later Imperial Japan agreed to surrender.

The Navy had accepted the last sixty FM-2s in May, but that was the end of the line. There was no post-war career for the Wildcat, which was already obsolete in the dawn of the jet age. The final FM-2s were reported in squadron service in September, and the Wildcat's five-year war was finally over.

From 1940 to 1945 the F4F and its relations had fought a truly global war; from the South Pacific to the Arctic, in locales as diverse as the tropical Solomons to the desert wastes of North Africa. In the service of three air arms (the U.S. Navy, Marine Corps, and Royal Navy) various Wildcats had successfully engaged four Axis powers. With the benefit of forty years' hindsight, it seems apparent now that the F4F's contribution peaked in November 1942, with passage of the crisis at Guadalcanal. Secretary of the Navy James Forrestal went so far as to say that Grumman saved Guadalcanal—something of an exaggeration, but an understandable one in view of the fact that the Wildcat was the only effective fighter available at The Canal during most of the period the Cactus Air Force plied its trade.

But history is ill-served by ignoring the F4F's very real short-comings, which were happily overcome in the main with advent of the FM-2. It's an important distinction, for the two Wildcats were in many respects different airplanes. Aviators who flew both types are careful to distinguish between the two, and the commonest description of the F4F seems to be "clunker."

Nevertheless, it was vastly preferable to the only alternative in that crucial year after Pearl Harbor, and if the Wildcat wasn't a war-winning design, we should remember to ask ourselves the tough question, "What would we have done without it?" And remember too that fighter pilots with the stature of Joe Foss and Eric Brown still retain highly favorable opinions of the scrappy little fighter from Long Island.

The comments of another aviator of stature are worth recording as the final word on the subject. Bill Leonard of VF-42 and VF-11, with combat in F4F-3s at Coral Sea and in -4s at Midway and Guadalcanal, has figured prominently in these pages. His summation four decades later: "I always loved the Wildcat, even when it was outclassed by sparkier performers. Its durability, reliability (and a few other 'ilit-ies') were mighty endearing."[17]

Appendices

A. SURVIVING WILDCATS

IN 1982 FEWER THAN TWENTY INTACT WILDCATS WERE known remaining in the world. Only two of these were Grumman-built aircraft: the sole surviving Martlet I at the Fleet Air Arm Museum in Yeovilton, Oxfordshire and an F4F-4 in the Marine Corps Museum at Quantico, Virginia. The National Air and Space Museum's FM-1 in Washington, D.C. is the only other "short-tailed" Wildcat. An FM-2 resides in the Naval Aviation Museum at NAS Pensacola, Florida.

At the end of 1981 the Federal Aviation Administration carried fourteen "Grumman FM-2s" on its aircraft registry. Not all were airworthy, and perhaps only six or eight were regularly flown. The majority were owned by individuals associated with the Warbirds of America organization, though a few are displayed in private collections such as the Champlin Fighter Museum at Mesa, Arizona.

One of the fourteen FM-2s on the 1981 FAA register has since left the United States. Mr. Steven Gray, a British citizen residing in Switzerland, already owned an F8F-2 Bearcat. In 1982 he purchased a flyable but unrestored FM-2 and had it flown across the North Atlantic with the aid of external fuel tanks.

Another Wildcat will be found in another distant, but more appropriate, locale. Propped up in a clearing near Honiara on Guadalcanal is the airframe of an F4F-4. Stripped to bare metal, missing most of its innards, the Gruman serves as a reminder of what happened in the skies above that contested island four decades ago.

B. WILDCAT VARIANTS

XF4F-1   Successor to the F3F series, a biplane design never produced.

XF4F-2   Mid-wing monoplane, the original prototype Wildcat. Pratt-Whitney R-1830-66 with single-stage supercharger. First flew September 1937.

XF4F-3   Redesigned XF4F-2 with new empennage and wings. XR-1830-76 with two-stage supercharger. First flew February 1939.

F4F-3   First production model Wildcat, with R-1830-76 or -86. Four .50-caliber machine guns in non-folding wings.

F4F-3A   Production model XF4F-6. R-1830-90 with single-stage, two-speed supercharger.

XF4F-4   A single F4F-3 with hydraulically-folding wings. First flew April 1941.

F4F-4   Production aircraft with folding wings and six .50-caliber guns.

F4F-4A   Intended to use the R-1830-90 engine but no aircraft built.

F4F-4B   See Martlet IV.

XF4F-5   F4F-3 with Wright R-1820-40. Two delivered in 1940, further modified for supercharger tests on other 1820-series engines.

XF4F-6   F4F-3 with R-1830-90. Delivered late 1940. Prototype for F4F-3A.

F4F-7   Photo version of F4F-3; highly modified with 555 gallons of fuel in non-folding wing. Armor and armament deleted, camera installation in aft fuselage. 21 delivered in 1942.

XF4F-8   F4F-4 with Wright R-1820-56. Two aircraft; first was delivered late 1942. Prototype for Eastern FM-2.

FM-1   F4F-4 built by Eastern Aircraft of General Motors Corporation. Four .50-calibers in most production models.

FM-2   Production model of XF4F-8, built by Eastern. R-1820-56 or -56A. Four .50-calibers plus three rocket rails under each wing.

G-36A   Export F4F-3 originally ordered by French. Wright R-1820-G205A-2. Reverted to British with fall of France in 1940. See Martlet I.

G-36B   See Martlet II.

Martlet I   81 G-36As delivered to Royal Navy July-October 1940. Retro-fitted for British use with standard throttle, instrument and armament.

Martlet II   G-36B with Pratt-Whitney Twin Wasp S3C4. Single-stage, two-speed supercharger similar to R-1830-90 in XF4F-6 and F4F-3A. First ten aircraft with fixed wings and four .50-calibers. Remainder had six guns in folding wings.

Martlet III First thirty F4F-3As intended for Greece, taken by British at Gibraltar, April 1941.

Martlet IV F4F-4B with Wright R-1820-G-205A-3. Six British M-53A Browning .50-caliber.

Martlet V Eastern FM-1.

Martlet VI Eastern FM-2.

C. WILDCAT PRODUCTION

From Bureau of Aeronautics monthly acceptance records

Type	Dates	U.S. Navy	Royal Navy	Total
G-36A	July-October 1940	—	81 (Mark I)	81
G-36B	Feb. 1941-April 1942	—	100 (Mark II)	100
F4F-3	July 1940-October 1941	285	—	285
F4F-3A	March-May 1941	65	30 (Mark III)	95
F4F-4	Nov. 1941-May 1943	1,169	—	1,169
F4F-4B	February-November 1942	—	220 (Mark IV)	220
F4F-7	January-December 1942	21	—	21
	Grumman total	1,540	431	1,971
FM-1	Sept. 1942-Dec. 1943	909	311 (Mark V)	1,220
FM-2	Sept. 1943-May 1945	3,720	340 (Mark VI)	4,060
	Eastern total	4,629	651	5,280
	GRAND TOTALS	6,169	1,082	7,251

D. WILDCAT ACES

NAVY WILDCAT ACES

Name		Squadrons	Credited Victories	Comments
Lt.	Ralph E. Elliott	VC-27*	9	
Ens.	Donald E. Runyon	VF-6	8	Plus 3 in F6Fs
Lt.	Stanley W. Vejtasa	VF-10	7¼	7 on 10-26-42
LCdr.	John S. Thach	VF-3	6½	
LtJG	Arthur J. Brassfield	VF-42, VF-3	6⅓	
LtJG	E. Scott McCuskey	VF-42, VF-3	6⅓	Plus 7 in F6Fs
LCdr.	James H. Flatley	VF-42, VF-10	6	
LCdr.	Harold N. Funk	VF-26*	6	All on 10-24-44
Lt.	William N. Leonard	VF-42, VF-3, VF-11	6	2 with VF-11
Lt.	Carlton B. Starkes	VF-5	6	
LtJG	Charles R. Stimpson	VF-11	6	Plus 10 in F6Fs
Lt.	Ross E. Torkelson	VGF-11, VF-21	6	5 with VF-21; KIA 7-43
LtJG	George H. Davidson	VF-21, VC-27*	5½	4½ with VC-27
LtJG	Thomas D. Roach	VF-21	5½	
Lt.	John C. C. Symmes	VF-21	5½	
Lt.	Albert O. Vorse	VF-3, VF-2, VF-6	5½	Plus 6 in F6Fs
Ens.	George L. Wrenn	VF-72	5¼	5 on 10-26-42
Lt.	Mark K. Bright	VF-5	5	Plus 4 in F6Fs; KIA 2-45
Lt.	Noel A. M. Gayler	VF-3, VF-2	5	3 with VF-3
LtJG	Vernon E. Graham	VF-11	5	All on 6-12-43
Lt.	Kenneth G. Hippe	VC-13*	5	All on 10-24-44
LtJG	Lee P. Mankin	VF-6	5	
Ens.	James D. McGraw	VC-10*	5	Last 2 with VC-80 when the *Gambier Bay* sank.
Lt.	Edward H. O'Hare	VF-3	5	Plus 2 in F6Fs; KIA 11-43
Lt.	John F. Sutherland	VF-8, VF-72, VF-10	5	3 with VF-72
LtJG	Walter A. Haas	VF-42, VF-3	4⅚	
LtJG	James S. Swope	VF-11	4⅔	Plus 5 in F6Fs

An asterisk indicates a squadron equipped with FM-2s. Others are F4F-3 and F4F-4.

Haas and Swope are listed as Wildcat aces because of the peculiarity of their totals relating to fractional credits. Several other pilots were credited with 4½ victories in Wildcats.

MARINE CORPS WILDCAT ACES

Name	Squadrons	Credited Victories	Comments
Maj. Joseph J. Foss	VMF-121	26	5 on 10-25-42
Maj. John L. Smith	VMF-223	19	
Capt. Marion E. Carl	VMF-221, 223	16½	Plus 2 in F4Us
Maj. Robert E. Galer	VMF-224	14	
1/Lt William P. Marontate	VMF-121	13	KIA January '43
2/Lt Kenneth D. Frazier	VMF-223	12½	Plus 1 in F4Us
2/Lt Eugene A. Trowbridge	VMF-223	11	KIA October '42
LCol Harold W. Bauer	(VMF-223, 224), 212	10	5 with 212; KIA November '42
1/Lt Jack E. Conger	(VMF-223) 212	10	8 with 212
2/Lt Thomas H. Mann	(VMF-224) 121	9½	5½ with 121
Capt. Gregory K. Loesch	VMF-121	8½	
1/Lt Jefferson J. DeBlanc	VMF-112	8	5 on 1-31-43; plus 1 in F4Us
Capt. Loren D. Everton	(VMF-223) 212	8	5 with 212
Maj. John F. Dobbin	VMF-224	7½	
M.G. Henry B. Hamilton	(VMF-223) 212	7	3 with 212
2/Lt George L. Hollowell	VMF-224	7	
2/Lt Joseph L. Narr	VMF-121	7	
1/Lt James E. Swett	VMF-221	7	All on 4-17-43; plus 8½ in F4Us
2/Lt Roger A. Haberman	VMF-121	6½	
2/Lt William B. Freeman	VMF-121	6	
2/Lt Charles M. Kunz	VMF-224	6	
2/Lt Zenneth A. Pond	VMF-223	6	
1/Lt Robert F. Stout	(VMF-224) 212	6	5 with 212
Capt. Donald K. Yost	VMF-121	6	Plus 2 in F4Us
Maj. Frederick R. Payne	(VMF-223) 212	5½	4 with 212
Maj. Leonard K. Davis	VMF-121	5	
2/Lt Cecil J. Doyle	VMF-121	5	
1/Lt Frank C. Drury	(VMF-223) 212	5	3 with 212; plus 1 in F4Us
Maj. Paul J. Fontana	VMF-112	5	
2/Lt Charles Kendrick	VMF-223	5	KIA October '42
2/Lt Hyde Phillips	VMF-223	5	
Capt. Francis E. Pierce	VMF-121	5	
1/Lt James G. Percy	VMF-112	5	Plus 1 in F4Us
2/Lt Orvin H. Ramlo	VMF-223	5	

() indicates pilot scored at least one victory on detached service with that squadron.

NOTES

CHAPTER ONE

1. Lt. J. B. Pearson to Roy Grumman, 30 June 1936.
2. Roy Grumman to Bureau of Aeronautics, 1 July 1936.
3. Horikoshi, p. 43.
4. Ibid., p. 50.

CHAPTER TWO

1. Greene, *History of the Grumman Wildcat*.
2. William N. Leonard to author, 16 February 1982.
3. Semmes.
4. Leonard, op. cit.
5. Interview with Wallace F. Madden. La Jolla, California, 20 January 1981.
6. Grumman shop memo for October 1941.
7. U.S. Navy monthly location of aircraft report.
8. Horikoshi, p. 101.

CHAPTER THREE

1. James S. Gray in Naval Institute *Proceedings*, December 1981.
2. Sherrod, p. 1.
3. Kenneth A. Walsh to author, undated.
4. John F. Kinney to author, 18 April 1981.
5. Ibid.
6. Ibid.
7. Dull, p. 25.
8. Kinney and another Marine escaped from POW camp in China near the war's end. They returned to the U.S. in June 1945.
9. Sherrod, p. 43.
10. Van Vleet, Clarke. "The First Carrier Raids." *The Hook*, Winter 1978. P. 15.
11. Stafford, p. 52.
12. Frank and Harrington, p. 43.
13. William N. Leonard to author, 25 February 1982.
14. Most details of the 20 February action from contemporary accounts and data from John B. Lundstrom.

CHAPTER FOUR

1. Interview with William N. Leonard. Virginia Beach, Virginia, April 1981.
2. Ibid.

3. Frank and Harrington, p. 76.
4. Ibid., p. 84.
5. Johnston, p. 194.
6. John P. Adams to author, 1 August 1980.
7. William N. Leonard to author, 20 July 1981.
8. Leonard interview, April 1981.
9. Interview with Marion E. Carl. La Pine, Oregon, March 1979.
10. Heinl, p. 27.
11. Carl interview, March 1979.
12. Ibid.
13. Ibid.
14. Translation of Japanese after-action reports, 4 June 1942.
15. Ibid.
16. Stafford, p. 92.
17. Transcript of Task Force 16 radio log, 4 June 1942.
18. *Yorktown* Air Group action report, 4 June 1942.
19. Conversation with John S. Thach, San Diego, California, June 1970.
20. Interview with Henry A. Carey. Portland, Oregon, April 1981.
21. Ibid.
22. Task Force 16 radio log, op. cit.
23. Ibid.
24. Frank and Harrington, p. 135.
25. Radio log, op. cit.
26. Ibid.
27. Frank and Harrington, p. 149.
28. James S. Gray to author, 4 March 1982.
29. BuAer interview with Lt. Cdr. John S. Thach, 26 August 1942.
30. Gray, op. cit.
31. Leonard interview, April 1981.

CHAPTER FIVE

1. Sherrod, p. 83.
2. *Fortitudine*, Fall-Winter 1981.
3. Polmar, p. 249. American documentation is contradictory on the matter of Bettys, but Polmar's data came from General Minoru Genda.
4. Griffith, p. 119.
5. Robert E. Galer to author, 24 February 1981.
6. BuAer interview with Thach, op. cit.
7. Interview with Marion E. Carl. Roseburg, Oregon, March 1981.
8. Entry from Marion Carl's diary, 14 September 1942.
9. Galer, op. cit.
10. Wendell P. Garton to author, 27 January 1982.
11. Ibid.
12. Ibid.
13. Entry from Marion Carl's diary, 28 September 1942.
14. Miller, p. 105.
15. Wilcox, Richard. "Captain Smith and His Fighting 223." *Life*, 7 December 1942. p. 130.
16. Interview with Joe Foss. Champlin Fighter Museum, 21 October 1981.
17. Ibid.
18. Foss and Simmons, p. 34.
19. Ibid., p. 81.
20. Foss interview.
21. Foss and Simmons, p. 122.
22. Interview with Henry A. Carey. Portland, Oregon, 28 March 1981.
23. Miller, p. 203.

CHAPTER SIX

1. Morison, Volume V. P. 91–92.
2. Henry Rowe to author, 17 April 1982.
3. Stafford, p. 135.
4. VF-6 action report, 24 August 1942.
5. Interview with Richard E. Harmer. Seattle, Washington, 3 March 1981.
6. VF-6 action report.
7. VF-5 action report, 24 August 1942.
8. Ibid.
9. Harmer interview.
10. VF-10 action report, 26 October 1942.
11. Telephone interview with George L. Wrenn, 18 July 1982.
12. Ibid.
13. Ibid.
14. VF-10 report.
15. Ibid.
16. Ibid.
17. Wrenn interview.
18. VF-72 action report, 26 October 1942.
19. Ibid.
20. VF-10 report.
21. Ibid.

CHAPTER SEVEN

1. Miller, p. 209.
2. Griffith, p. 260.
3. James E. Swett to author, 18 March 1981.
4. Interview with Joe Foss. Champlin Fighter Museum, 21 October 1981.
5. Ibid.
6. Phone interview with Carl Anderson. 15 April 1981.
7. Lord, Walter. *Coastwatchers of the Solomons.* P. 140.
8. Herman Hansen to author. 21 March 1981.
9. Ibid.
10. Sherrod, p. 138.
11. Swett, op. cit.
12. Ibid.
13. William N. Leonard to author. 2 May 1982.
14. Unofficial VF-11 history. August 1943.
15. Information based on interviews by Henry Sakaida with former Zero pilots in Japan during 1981.
16. Interview with Charles R. Stimpson. Rancho Sante Fe, California, March 1981.
17. VF-21 action report, 30 June 1943.
18. Ibid.
19. Ibid.
20. Ibid.
21. Sherrod, p. 148.

CHAPTER EIGHT

1. Interview with Armistead B. Smith. La Jolla, California, 20 January 1981.
2. VF-29 history.
3. Wordell, p. 17.
4. Ibid., p. 36.
5. Smith interview.
6. Wordell, p. 55.
7. Wordell, p. 60.

8. C. F. Shores to author, 16 April 1982.
9. Shores et al, p. 34.
10. Ibid., p. 35.
11. Interview with Wallace F. Madden. La Jolla, California, 20 January 1981.
12. Shores et al, p. 36.
13. Ibid., p. 38.
14. Ibid., p. 38.
15. VF-29 history.

CHAPTER NINE

1. Most of the known details are from 804 Squadron's diary.
2. Grumman contract, 26 September 1940.
3. Grumman notice, February 1941. It should also be noted that the British were responsible for the six-gun armament which led to controversy in the F4F-4.
4. Brown, Eric. *Wings of the Navy*, p. 40.
5. Interview with Eric M. Brown. Copthorne, Sussex, 8 May 1981.
6. Thruelsen, p. 131.
7. Rutter, p. 212.
8. Interview with Kenneth J. Dowell. London, 1 May 1981.
9. Actually, the FW-200 had no pilot-operated guns. One ventral-mounted machine gun could fire forward from amidships.
10. Brown, Eric. *Wings On My Sleeve*, p. 17.
11. Rutter, p. 3.
12. Ibid.
13. Eric Brown to author, 31 March 1982.
14. Brown, *Wings On My Sleeve*, p. 21.
15. C. F. Shores to author, 18 November 1981.
16. Shores et al, p. 1.
17. Rutter, p. 234.
18. Shores et al, p. 46.
19. Brown interview.

CHAPTER TEN

1. Thruelsen, p. 154.
2. Ibid., p. 155.
3. *History of Eastern Aircraft Division*, p. 31.
4. Fighter evaluation report, October 1944.
5. Ibid.
6. Interview with Richard W. Roby during *Gambier Bay* reunion. Philippines, September 1977.
7. Interview with Charles Dugan during *Gambier Bay* reunion. Philippines, 1977.
8. Ibid.
9. VOC-1 history.
10. Interview with William F. Bringle. Rancho Sante Fe, California, 22 September 1981.
11. Simmons, p. 156.
12. VOC-1 history.
13. Ibid.
14. Bringle interview.
15. VOC-1 history.
16. Ibid.
17. William N. Leonard to author, 1 April 1982.

SOURCES

In 1981, nearly forty years after the Battle of Midway, one of the Wildcat pilots who flew in that engagement provided a small glimpse of how climactic events can affect the participants decades later. Leaning back in the chair of his paneled study, the former naval aviator said, almost to himself, "You know, it takes a long time for a burning airplane to fall 14,000 feet." He almost visibly shook himself out of his recollection of the first aircraft he shot down. Then he looked at me and asked, "Do any of the others ever mention it? I mean, do they still have dreams about it?"

The fact is, different events affect people in different ways. But it is well to remember that behind the dates and places and narratives—the basic framework of history—are flesh-and-blood human beings. During World War II, men sustained a wild variety of experiences and emotions; some good, some bad, many tragic. The large majority of these men adjusted and got on with their lives, but most were changed to one degree or another. A few grew stronger beause of it. A former Marine Corps pilot and Guadalcanal veteran is an example. He says flatly of his military career, "I've seen so many dead bodies, so many mutilated corpses, that death has no effect on me anymore. I've been close enough to it enough times to know there's no sense worrying. I know I can do whatever I have to do to survive."

This, then, is largely the story of the survivors; Wildcat pilots who beat the not-inconsiderable odds against them during a watershed period in history. And history is fortunate that the contributors to this volume possessed the skill and luck to come through the biggest crapshoot of all time. The Wildcat story could not be told properly without them.

First, foremost and always is Rear Admiral Bill Leonard. This book is dedicated to him for the simple reason that it would be unthinkable to do otherwise. A superior airman who flew F4Fs when the going was roughest, he has either critiqued or provided first-hand information for each volume I've written. Bill's exceptional memory and lucid comments are, to use an overworked word, invaluable. And I fear he was overworked himself, reading the entire manuscript as each chapter was finished. Bill, I couldn't have done it without you.

Standing tall among the other contributors is Marion Carl—and not just because he's six-feet-four. Besides writing the foreword, he took time to read the Midway and Guadalcanal chapters in addition to sitting through two separate sessions at his home on the North Bank of the Umpquah. Edna, still a good Marine herself, was sweet enough to keep me fed the whole time.

The Carls' former Patuxent River colleagues, Eric and Lynn Brown, provided similar hospitality in the U.K. Eric kindly read the Fleet Air Arm chapter, making helpful comments, as did another Martlet pilot, Ken Dowell. I'm obliged to my friend and colleague Chris Shores for arranging the latter meeting, and also for reading the Royal Navy chapter and providing photos.

Other aviators who read portions of the text or contributed especially detailed information include Henry Carey, Hank Rowe (fighter direction), Bob Galer, Dick Mangrum, and Jim Swett. Special thanks go to my boss, Doug Champlin of the Champlin Fighter Museum, for providing access to his FM-2 and for arranging an interview with Joe Foss.

Extra help was provided by Charlie Stimpson, top gun of VF-11, who not only told of his F4F experience at Guadalcanal, but as host of The Inn at Rancho Sante Fe has been a continuing source of support in every project since *Hellcat*. The warmth and generosity displayed by Charlie and Dorothy with Danny Royce have afforded a comfortably, easy-going means of conducting interviews in the San Diego area.

Much the same can be said of Bob and Betty Dose of La Jolla. Such is their friendliness that a phone call one evening during the Crusader research turned into a three-day stay—the first of several. And in the Bay area, Alex and Kay Vraciu have practically adopted me over the past several years.

Archival and photo assistance came from individuals and agencies I've relied upon repeatedly. These range from Dean Allard's Operational Archives office in the Washington Navy Yard to quasi-official contacts with the Tailhook Association. Bob Lawson, editor of

The Hook, lent the benefit of his numerous contacts and access to Richard M. Hill's donated photo library.

John Lundstrom of the Milwaukee Public Museum very generously made available material from his lengthy research into the aerial phase of the Pearl Harbor to Midway period, and I trust our trading leads and information was also useful to him. For greater detail than space allows here, the reader is unhesitatingly recommended to John's forthcoming book, *The First Team*. I make no exaggeration by saying it is in a class by itself.

Another diligent individual researcher is Frank Olynyk of Aurora, Ohio. His magnificent compilation of all U.S. Marine Corps aerial victory claims is already a standard reference work, and he kindly provided a sneak preview of the companion volume on Navy fighter credits.

Then of course there's Grumman. Schony Schonenberg and Lois Lavisolo lent time, resources and enthusiasm, along with Ralph Clark, for "our" third book. Grumman's history office is rare in the industry since it is genuinely devoted to history, and not merely an adjunct of pubic relations. Other aircraft manufacturers would do well to emulate the professional, extremely helpful setup at Bethpage.

Following is a list of all individuals directly connected with the Wildcat who provided first-hand information on either the F4F, the FM series, or both. Some may be surprised to find themselves listed, considering the long-ago and sometimes impromptu nature of interviews, but they all helped just the same.

Mr. Carl Anderson	Grumman Aircraft
Capt. John P. Adams, USN (Ret)	VF-42, VF-3
Adm. William F. Bringle, USN (Ret)	VOC-1
Capt. Eric M. Brown, RN (Ret)	802 Squadron
LCdr. Henry A. Carey, USN (Ret)	VF-8, VF-72, VF-10
MGen. Marion E. Carl, USMC (Ret)	VMF-221, VMF-223
LCdr. Kenneth J. Dowell, RN (Ret)	805 Squadron
Lt. Charles E. Dugan, USNR (Ret)	VC-10
RAdm. Edward L. Feightner, USN (Ret)	VF-10
BGen. Joseph J. Foss, USMC (Ret)	VMF-121
BGen. Robert E. Galer, USMC (Ret)	VMF-224
LCol. Wendell P. Garton, USMC (Ret)	VMO-251
Capt. James S. Gray, USN (Ret)	VF-6
Col. Herman Hansen, USMC (Ret)	1st Marine Air Wing

Capt. Richard E. Harmer, USN (Ret)   VF-5
BGen. John F. Kinney, USMC (Ret)   VMF-211
RAdm. William N. Leonard, USN (Ret)   VF-42, VF-3, VF-11
Capt. Wallace F. Madden, USN (Ret)   VF-4, VF-41
Cdr. Richard H. May, USN (Ret)   VF-10
Col. Robert Bruce Porter, USMC (Ret)   VMF-121
Capt. Richard W. Roby, USN (Ret)   VC-10
Capt. Henry A. Rowe, USN (Ret)   Fighter Director
Capt. Armistead B. Smith, USN (Ret)   VF-9
Cdr. Charles R. Stimpson, USN (Ret)   VF-11
Col. James E. Swett, USMC (Ret)   VMF-221
Capt. Harold E. Vita, USN (Ret)   VF-9
LCol. Kenneth A. Walsh, USMC (Ret)   VMF-121
Capt. Malcolm W. Wordell, USN (Ret)   VF-41
Cdr. George L. Wrenn, USN (Ret)   VF-72

BIBLIOGRAPHY

BOOKS

Belote, J.H. and W.M. *Titans of the Seas*. New York: Harper and Row, 1975.
Brown, David. *Carrier Operations in WW II. Volume I: The Royal Navy*. Annapolis: Naval Institute Press, 1974.
Brown, Eric M. *Wings On My Sleeve*. U.K.: Airlife Publications, 1978.
────── *Wings of the Navy*. London: Jaynes, 1980.
DeChant, John. *Devilbirds*. New York: Harper Brothers, 1947.
Dull, Paul S. *A Battle History of the Imperial Japanese Navy, 1941–1945*. Annapolis: Naval Institute Press, 1978.
Foss, Joseph J. and Simmons, Walter. *Flying Marine*. Washington D.C.: Zenger, 1979.
Frank, P. and Harrington, J. *Rendezvous at Midway*. New York: Warner, 1968.
General Motors Corporation. *History of Eastern Aircraft Division*. 1945.
Green, William, *Famous Fighters of the Second World War. Volume II*. London: Macdonald, 1962.
Green, Frank L. *The Grumman F4F-3 Wildcat*. Profile Number 53. U.K.: Profile Publications.
────── *History of the Grumman Wildcat*. Distributed by Grumman Aircraft, 1962.
Griffith, Samuel B. *The Battle for Guadalcanal*. New York: Bantam, 1980.
Heinl, Robert D. *Marines at Midway*. Washington D.C.: U.S. Marine Corps, 1948.
Horikoshi, Jiro. *Eagles of Mitsubishi*. Seattle: University of Washington Press, 1981.
Johnston, Stanley. *Queen of the Flattops*. New York: Ballantine, 1970.
Lord, Walter. *Incredible Victory*. New York: Harper and Row, 1967.
────── *Lonely Vigil: Coastwatchers of the Solomons*. New York: Viking, 1977.
Mikesh, Robert C. *Zero Fighter*. New York: Crown Publishers, 1980.
Miller, Thomas G. *The Cactus Air Force*. New York: Harper and Row, 1969.
Morison, Samuel Eliot. *History of U.S. Naval Operations in WW II. Volume V: The Struggle for Guadalcanal*. Boston: Little, Brown, 1969.
Okumiya, Masatake, et al. *Zero!* New York: Ballantine, 1971.
O'Leary Michael. *U.S. Naval Fighters of WW II*. U.K.: Blandford Press, 1980.
Olynyk, Frank J. *U.S.M.C. Credits for the Destruction of Enemy Aircraft in Air-to-Air Combat, World War 2*. Aurora, Ohio: privately published, 1981.
Polmar, Norman. *Aircraft Carriers*. Garden City: Doubleday, 1969.
Rutter, Owen. *The British Navy's Air Arm*. New York: Penguin Books, 1944.
Sherrod, Robert. *History of Marine Corps Aviation in WW II*. Washington D.C.: Armed Forces Press, 1952.
Shores, C.; Ring, H. and Hess, W. *Fighters Over Tunisia*. London: Neville Spearman, 1975.

Simmons, Edwin H. *The United States Marines: The First Two Hundred Years*. New York: Viking, 1976.
Stafford, Edward P. *The Big E*. New York: Dell, 1964.
Thruelsen, Richard. *The Grumman Story*. New York: Praeger, 1976.
Tillman, Barrett. *The Dauntless Dive Bomber of WW II*. Annapolis: Naval Institute Press, 1976.
Wordell, Malcolm T., and Seiler, Edward N., with Ayling, Keith. *Wildcats Over Casablanca*. Boston: Little, Brown, 1943.

ARTICLES

Cressman, Robert J. "Who Said a Wasp Couldn't Sting Twice?" *The Hook*, Spring 1979.
——— "That Gallant Ship." *The Hook*, Spring 1981.
Gates, Thomas F. "Fight as a Team—Felix the Cat, Part 2." *The Hook*, Fall 1980.
Semmes, Raphael. "The First Navy Cat." *Aerospace Historian*, March 1981.
Tillman, Barrett. "Operation Leader." *Aviation News* (U.K.), November-December 1976.
——— "Three Wars and Thirty Years. The Story of VF-111" American Aviation Historical Society *Journal*, Winter 1976.
Van Vleet, Clarke. "The First Carrier Raids." *The Hook*, Winter 1978.
Wilcox, Richard. "Captain Smith and His Fighting 223." *Life*, 7 December 1942.

INDEX